# Translation Studies

# Translation Studies

## Contemporary Perspectives on Postcolonial and Subaltern Translations

*Edited by*

**Piyush Raval**

Viva Books

New Delhi | Mumbai | Chennai | Kolkata | Bengaluru | Hyderabad | Kochi | Guwahati

**Publishers note**

Every possible effort has been made to ensure that the information contained in this book is accurate at the time of going to press, and the publisher and author cannot accept responsibility for any errors or omissions, however caused. No responsibility for loss or damage occasioned to any person acting, or refraining from action, as a result of the material in this publication can be accepted by the editor, the publisher or the author.

Every effort has been made to trace the owners of copyright material used in this book. The author and the publisher will be grateful for any omission brought to their notice for acknowledgement in the future editions of the book.



First Published 2012
Reprinted 2016, 2017, 2018, 2019, 2020, 2024

Viva Books Private Limited

- 4737/23, Ansari Road, Daryaganj, New Delhi 110 002
  Tel. 42242200, 23258325, 23283121, Email: vivadelhi@vivagroupindia.net
- 76, Service Industries, Shirvane, Sector 1, Nerul, Navi Mumbai 400 706
  Tel. 27721273, 27721274, Email: vivamumbai@vivagroupindia.net
- Megh Tower, Old No. 307, New No.165, Poonamallee High Road, Maduravoyal
  Chennai 600 095, Tel. 23780991, Email: vivachennai@vivagroupindia.net
- B-103, Jindal Towers, 21/1A/3 Darga Road, Kolkata 700 017
  Tel. 22816713, Email: vivakolkata@vivagroupindia.net
- 194, First Floor, Subbarama Chetty Road, Basavanagudi, Bangalore 560 004
  Tel. 26607409, 26607410, Email: vivabangalore@vivagroupindia.net
- 101-102, Moghal Marc Apartments, 3-4-637 to 641, Narayanguda, Hyderabad 500 029
  Tel. 27564481, Email: vivahyderabad@vivagroupindia.net
- First Floor, Beevi Towers, SRM Road, Kaloor, Kochi 682 018
  Tel. 0484-2403055, 2403056, Email: vivakochi@vivagroupindia.net
- 232, GNB Road, Beside UCO Bank, Silpukhuri, Guwahati 781 003
  Tel. 0361-2666386, Email: vivaguwahati@vivagroupindia.net

www.vivagroupindia.com

ISBN: 978-81-309-2052-8

Published by Vinod Vasishtha for Viva Books Private Limited, 4737/23 Ansari Road, Daryaganj, New Delhi 110 002.

Printed & bound at Replika Press Pvt. Ltd.

L0000

# Contents

## PROBLEMS OF PRAXIS: TRANSLATING INDIAN LITERATURES

# Acknowledgements

I express foremost gratitude to my teacher and the Director of the Centre for Contemporary Theory, Baroda, Prof. Praffula C. Kar, for always encouraging me to make higher academic pursuits. I thank Viva Books and their Publishing General Manager S. Sreetilak for furnishing information about the publishing process and subsequently agreeing to publish the book. I also thank the contributors for submitting and giving consent to publish their articles. Many thanks to my colleagues at the Department of English, Sardar Patel University, and my friend Hemant Dave, for helping me in whatever way they could in preparation of the book. Last but not the least, I am deeply grateful to my family, without whose constant support and cooperation this work would not have been possible.

Piyush Raval

# Introduction

## Postcolonial and Subaltern Translations: A Vindication of Cultural Translation

The modern discipline of Translation Studies, since its inception in 1980s by valiant efforts of translators and translation scholars like James Holmes, André Lefevere, Itamar Even-Zohar, Anton Popovic and Susan Bassnett, has passed through different contours and its "metadiscussion" has now arrived at the significant phase of postcolonial and cultural translations, though even today the discipline remains marginal as Lawrence Venuti complains. As a pioneer and strong proponent of the discipline, James Holmes (1924–1986) presented the manifesto of the discipline in the crucial 1972 Copenhagen conference paper "The Name and Nature of Translation Studies", pointing out two major hurdles to what he calls the "disciplinary utopia": (a) the employment of sophisticated terminology, or invention of neologisms for Translation Studies and (b) the lack of general consensus on the scope and structure of the discipline. What is crucial to Holmes' endeavours towards the establishment and progress of the discipline, and also crucial for us to understand the contemporary marginal status of the discipline is that, Holmes advocated interdisciplinary model for Translation Studies and personally sought cooperation between ideologically and geographically diverse scholars and schools. In terms of interdisciplinary orientation of the discipline, 1990s have been regarded as a milestone when Translation Studies joined hands with Postcolonialism (which operated under the wide umbrella of Cultural Studies in the Western metropolis) applauded within Translation Studies as the "Cultural Turn". André Lefevere's *Translation, History, Culture: A Sourcebook* (1990), Eric Cheyfitz's *The Poetics of Imperialism: Translation and Colonization from The Tempest to Tarzan* (1991), Tejaswini Niranjana's *Siting Translation: History, Post-Structuralism and the Colonial Context* (1992), Gayatri Spivak's "The Politics of Translation" (1992), Samia Mehrez's "Translation and the Colonial Experience: The Francophone North African Text" (1992), Robert Schwartz's *Misplaced Ideas* (1992), Anthony Kwame Appiah's "Thick Translation" (1993), Homi Bhabha's *The Location of Culture* (1994), Anuradha Dingwaney and Carol Maier's *Between Languages and Cultures: Translation and Cross-Cultural Texts* (1995), Susan Bassnett and Harish Trivedi's *Post-colonial Translation: Theory and Practice* (1999), etc. are important deliberations, admitting all their differences of opinion, produced by this postcolonial or "cultural turn" in Translation Studies.

As José María Rodrígues García in "Introduction" to the special issue of *Diacritics* on "Literary into Cultural Translation" argues, "The cumulative work carried out between 1965 and 1980 by such thinkers as Barthes, Derrida, and Foucault, who treated the concepts of 'origin', 'author', 'reality', and 'truth' as functions of a discourse rather than as prelinguistic entelechies, created the conditions for the appearance of a more sophisticated thinking about translation in the years to follow" (Garcia, 2004: 9). Certainly the tenets of poststructuralism had a strong bearing on postcolonialism; its seminal figure Derrida occupies a reverential intellectual position within Cultural Studies. Under the impact of Derrida's views on translation in works such as *The Ends of Man* (1981) and "What Is a 'Relevant' Translation?" (1998), in addition to his interrogations of questions of power and imperialism in more than a dozen books, the phenomenon of "Cultural Translation" was espoused by postcolonial theorists like Homi Bhabha and Gayatri Spivak who underpinned both poststructuralist and Marxist ideologies in their theoretical writings on colonialism, and importantly, who read postcolonial writings by "Third World" writers like Salman Rushdie, J.M. Coetzee, Toni Morrison, Wilson Harris, Derek Walcott, V.S. Naipaul, Hanif Kureishi, Jhumpa Lahiri, etc., as "cultural translations". A basic understanding of their theoretical assumptions regarding cultural translation is necessary, which will not only illuminate the subject better but also assist in defending it against the heavy critical guns loaded against it by some Translation Studies scholars in the postcolonial world who understand translation in the narrow sense.

To begin with Homi Bhabha, who, envisaging the potentiality of the Third Space in *The Location of Culture* expresses: "...we should remember that it is the 'inter' – the cutting edge of translation and renegotiation, the *in-between* space – that carries the burden of the meaning of culture. It makes it possible to begin envisaging national anti-nationalist histories of the 'people'. And by exploring this Third Space, we may elude the politics of polarity and emerge as the others of ourselves" (Bhabha, 1994: 38–39). In the sixth chapter "Signs Taken for Wonders: Questions of ambivalence and authority under a tree outside Delhi, May 1817" of *The Location of Culture*, Bhabha explores the relationship between translation and colonial authority through the discovery of the English book in three diverse examples, a discovery which leads to the degree of the English book "being repeated, translated, misread, displaced" (Bhabha, 1994: 102). Bhabha names this displacement of the natives by the colonial authority as hybridity which he explains: "Hybridity is the sign of the productivity of colonial power, its shifting forces and fixities; it is the name for the strategic reversal of the process of domination through disavowal…" (Bhabha, 1994: 112) but it is also "a problematic of colonial representation and individuation that reverses the effects of the colonialist disavowal, so that other 'denied' knowledge enter upon the dominant discourse and estrange the basis of its authority – its rules of cognition" (Bhabha, 1994: 114). Such an exposition of the notion of hybridity in the context of the colony leads Bhabha to develop the idea of cultural translation in the much celebrated eleventh chapter "How Newness Enters the World: Postmodern Space, Postcolonial Times and the Trials of Cultural Translation." Transnational migrations and diasporic settlements have led to living double-lives – both here and there – in the postcolonial world. The transnational phase of late capitalism, as Fredric Jameson views, has also led to the emergence of new historical subjects who inhabit interstitial disjunctive spaces. This impels Bhabha to examine the narratives of borderline cultural experience like Salman Rushdie's *Satanic Verses* (1988) and Derek Walcott's poem "Names" as borderline negotiations of cultural translation.

Saladin Chamcha, a narrative spokesperson for author Salman Rushdie, who has transformed himself into a borderline figure, living in-between two border conditions – homeland and the new imperial land of migration – "in the midst of incomprehensible" like Conrad's Marlow, which for Bhabha is not only a "transnational" phenomenon but also a "translational" one. For the metropolitan counterpart of Chamcha, Sufyan, the problem of postcolonial migrants, conceived in contrast between Lucretius and Ovid, consists in "whether the crossing of cultural frontiers permits freedom from the essence of the self (Lucretius), or whether, like wax, migration only changes the surface of the soul, preserving identity under its protean forms (Ovid)" (Quoted in Bhabha, 1994: 224). Living in-between these two conditions described by Bhabha as "liminality of migrant experience" and by Benjamin in *Illuminations* (1968) as "that element in a translation which does not lend itself to translation," (Quoted in Bhabha, 1994: 224) is the phenomenon of translation, or translationalism. The experience of migrant/minority culture, as marked by hybridity, is untranslatable. The conflictual debates over *The Satanic Verses* are presented in spatial and binary terms such as Islamic fundamentalism vs. Western literary modernism, ancient migrants vs. modern metropolitans, as a consequence, Bhabha argues, it obscures "the anxiety of the irresolvable, borderline culture of hybridity that articulates its problems of identification and its diasporic aesthetic in an uncanny, disjunctive temporality that is, at once, the *time* of cultural displacement, and the *space* of the 'untranslatable'" (Bhabha, 1994: 225). Rushdie's secular blasphemy in *The Satanic Verses* is a transgressive act of cultural translation, a subversion of authenticity of Koranic readings through the act of cultural translation. This brings us to the strong defense of migrant experience and migrant's task of cultural translation from no other than Bhabha himself: "If hybridity is heresy, then to blaspheme is to dream. To dream not of the past or present, nor the continuous; it is not the nostalgic dream of tradition present not the Utopian dream of modern progress; it is the dream of translation as "survival" as Derrida translated the "time" of Benjamin's concept of the after-life of translation, as *sur-vivre*, the act of living on border-lines. Rushdie translates this into the migrant's dream of survival: an initiatory *interstices*; an empowering condition of hybridity; an emergence that turns 'return' into reinscription or redescription; an iteration that is not belated, but ironic and insurgent. For the migrant's survival depends, as Rushdie put it, on discovering 'how newness enters the world'. The focus is on making the linkages through the unstable elements of literature and life – the dangerous tryst with the 'untranslatable' – rather than arriving at ready-made names" (Bhabha, 1994: 226–227). Comparing the newness of cultural translation with Benjamin's description "foreignness of languages", Bhabha insists upon "foreignness" (as the performance of cultural difference) of cultural translation because the foreign element in translation not only reveals the interstitial space through which newness can enter the world, but also destroys the original's structures of reference and sense communication through negation and negotiation of cultural disjunction. In this way, translation becomes a performative act of cultural communication. The task of cultural translation, finally for Bhabha, "desacralizes the transparent assumptions of cultural supremacy, and.... demands a historical differentiation within minority positions" as can be witnessed in productive engagements of feminists, minority artists and others with Rushdie's cultural translation in *The Satanic Verses.* The idea of cultural translation seeks such intellectual embrace and if possible, its extension, but unfortunately it is derided at the present in the postcolonial world.

The intersection of Cultural Studies with Translation Studies has also inspired Gayatri Spivak to offer postcolonial and subaltern understanding of translation specifically in her two important essays: "The Politics of Translation" (1992) and "Translation as Culture" (2000). Working within the tradition of bhakti/devotional poetry and the Derridean deconstructive idea of translation as under erasure, Spivak in "The Politics of Translation" considers translation as the most intimate act of reading, assigning more premium and responsibility to the reader, and identifies the task of the feminist translator in the Third World as to surrender herself to the linguistic rhetoricity of the original text and to consider language as a clue to the workings of gendered agency. The Third World women translators are supposed to be more cautious about this sort of politics of gendered translation. A translator from the Third World language should also be in sufficient touch with "what is going on in literary production in that language to be capable of distinguishing between good and bad writing by women, resistant and conformist writing by women" (Spivak, 2000: 404). Elaborating on the differences between translation of Derrida's *De la grammatologie* and of Mahasweta Devi's "Standãyini", Spivak as a woman and a feminist translator feels intimacy with Devi and has no fear of being judged most accurately by the readers of what she has translated and what she thinks as a woman. As a postcolonial thinker, Spivak also endorses translation as the process and condition of human migrancy and, as a lesson to the translator in the narrow sense (interlingual translator), reads J.M. Coetzee's *Foe* (white creole translating *Robinson Crusoe* by representing Friday as the agent of withholding), Toni Morrison's *Beloved* (the change of the mother-tongue from mother to daughter) and Wilson

Harris's *Guyana Quartet* (the (re)birth of the native imagination as the translation and the transubstantiation of the species) as cultural translations.

The idea of translation as love and surrender in Spivak's translations of non-European texts like Farhad Mazhar's *Ashoumoyer Noteboi* ("Untimely Notebook") calls upon the ethical responsibility to preserve the trace of the other, the cultural and epistemological otherness more pressingly at work in language. Like her essay "Can the Subaltern Speak?" (1988) that, J. Maggio (Maggio, 2007: 419–443) argues, makes a plea for translation of the everyday culture of the subaltern, Spivak's "Translation as Culture" understands translation as catachresis, "the making of the subject in reparation" (Spivak, 2007: 271), and urges to translate the idiom of the subaltern into standard language: "No speech is speech if it is not heard. It is this act of hearing-to-respond that may be called the imperative to translate" (Spivak, 2007: 274). As a member in Subaltern Studies group, Spivak has been carrying out the task of attending to the idiom of the subaltern in translation: "These Sabars, women and men, constantly translate for me, consciously, between their speech, their Creole, my Bangla" (Spivak, 2007: 276).

In addition to cultural theorists, creative writers such as Rushdie and Lahiri have thought of themselves as cultural translators and promoted their diasporic writings as cultural translations. Considering the Latin etymological meaning of translation as "bearing across" and migration as metaphor for migrant narratives, Rushdie, in *Imaginary Homelands*, expresses: "Having been borne across the world, we are translated men. It is normally supposed that something always gets lost in translation; I cling obstinately, to the notion that something can also be gained" (Rushdie, 2010: 17). Lahiri thinks of translation as an ongoing cultural act and outlines the significance of activity of cultural translation for her immigrant self in "My Intimate Alien". She writes, "Unlike my parents, I translate not so much to survive in the world around me as to create and illuminate a nonexistent one. Fiction is the foreign land of my choosing, the place where I strive to convey and preserve the meaningful. And whether I write as an American or an Indian, about things American or Indian or otherwise, one thing remains constant: I translate, therefore I am" (Lahiri, 2000). The creative writers' views though should not be taken at their face value but when examined in the context of their respective personal careers, their expressions hold significance for all those who pass through similar experiences of cultural and geographical displacements.

Further, in the era of globalization, terrorism and US imperialism, Tomislav Z. Longinovic has offered a twelve-part Manifesto for cultural translation as an interdisciplinary field of study, identifying the aim of cultural translation as initiation of a dialogue between specific cultural localities and a variety of transnational projects instrumental in furthering rival political agendas. Paradoxically, André Lefevere and Susan Bassnett who welcomed the "cultural turn" in Translational Studies in their "Introduction" to *Translation, History, Culture: A Sourcebook* (1999) by understanding translation broadly as an activity essentially made with "the intention of influencing the development of a Literature" (Lefevere, 1992: 8) and who pleaded for integration of "different Universes of Discourses" (Lefevere, 1992: 10) into the discipline, wrote in 1998 an essay "The Translational Turn in Cultural Studies" lamenting their efforts towards the "cultural turn" and asking now to reverse the trend. Harish Trivedi, the trenchant opponent of the phenomenon of cultural translation, gives a reason for such a decisive and disturbing move: "...the Cultural Turn in translation studies had proved to be an act of transformative redefinition, the Translation Turn in cultural studies still remains an unfulfilled desideratum, a consummation yet only wished for" (in Peirre and Kar, 2007: 82). Despite several commonalities between Cultural Studies and Translation Studies, Cultural Studies operate in one language only, English, while Translation Studies deal with two languages, one of which can be English. In addition to this, Trivedi carries a massive assault on cultural translation, as understood and celebrated by postcolonial theorists and writers, for following reasons:

1. The collocation "cultural translation" does not indicate translation of culture and does not find any entry in encyclopedias and anthologies mentioned by him.
2. Cultural translation has emerged without any such awareness of it within Translation Studies and its emergence marks an extinction and erasure of empirical translation.
3. Its major theoretical proponent, Homi Bhabha, deploys Derrida's deconstruction of Benjamin's concept of translation as an after-life or survival in a completely new context of Rushdiean migrancy and hybridity without any such intention by Derrida or Benjamin. The idea of cultural translation shrouded in his opaque theoretical formulation means only the process and condition of human migrancy and not literary translation.

4. This non-textual and non-linguistic idea of cultural translation has its several adherents in contemporary critical and creative thinking like Tejaswini Niranjana, Salman Rushdie, Hanif Kureishi and Jhumpa Lahiri, while the term is an accurate description only for the diasporic writer Kureishi.
5. The use of the term "translation" in "cultural translation" is usurpation, an abuse, and therefore it should be patented by all scholars of Translation Studies. They should demand for the omission of the term "translation" from the collocation and for its replacement by different terms like migrancy, exile, diaspora.
6. The pursuit of cultural translation would not only bring about a wholly translated, monolingual, monocultural and monolithic world but also the demise of literary translation.

Cultural studies and translation are not so antithetical towards each other, as Trivedi makes them out to be by following a rigid interpretation of translation as only literary translation involving two languages. The translation scholarship and practice of Lawrence Venuti which draws on both the disciplines illustrates this. The double marginality of disciplines in the institutional space is a cause of this controversy: "The theoretical orientation of cultural studies has marginalized research into specific translations and translation practices, whereas the empirical orientation of translation studies has marginalized research into issues of philosophy and cultural politics" (Venuti, 2003: 241). The subject of colonialism draws cultural theorists to translation, even the very practice of translation in the case of Gayatri Spivak, but the large theoretical and speculative turn of Cultural Studies since 1980s thwarts textual analysis and empirical research of the kind carried out in the discipline of Translation Studies. On the other hand, the dominance of empirical orientation of Translation Studies since 1960s has made the participants in the discipline concentrate on discursive strategies in their textual analysis, neglecting philosophical, cultural and political issues raised by the practice of translation. Translation, thus, is not only limited by theoreticism and speculative nature of Cultural Studies, but also by empiricism of linguistic approaches to it. As Venuti says, he translated Jacques Derrida's "What is a 'Relevant' Translation?" (Derrida, 2000) in order to show how the two discourses of Cultural Studies and Translation Studies have (self)imposed limitations on translation, and in order to transform them by demonstrating, in a more satisfactory manner than as Bassnett and Lefevere have done, how their diverse disciplinary orientations can be conjoined and directed into rejuvenation through cross-fertilization of both disciplines. Venuti's materialistic approach to translation in translation of Derrida's lecture contributes to theoretical speculation in Cultural Studies, and his philosophical and socially conscious approach contributes to empirical research in Translation Studies. Gayatri Spivak, who is aware of criticism of her translations of Derrida and Devi with political and ideological imperatives, has been making some efforts towards understanding and elucidating the empirical mode of translation. We hope more interdisciplinary endeavours of the kind Venuti has exemplifed occurs in future to bridge the much divided disciplinary gulfs. In that spirit, the task of cultural translation would prove fruitful for the discipline of Translation Studies.

*****

The present anthology on Postcolonial and Subaltern Translations brings exploration of both perspectives discussed above, though it aims to explore largely cultural translation and the role of a translator as intercultural interlocutor in the contemporary world of socioeconomic and political crises. This concept of translation is widely popular in postcolonial studies, yet, as we have seen, there is an undermining of this idea by confining translation to the familiar practice of translating from one language to the other. The book endorses cultural translation carried out by postcolonial writers as a significant task in resolving cultural tensions. It is divided into three sections: (i) Theoretical Perspectives, (ii) Questions of Cultural Identity, and (iii) Problems of Praxis: Translating Indian Literatures.

The first section on "Theoretical Perspectives" explores theoretical and philosophical arguments in translation and suggests postcolonial and subaltern understandings of cultural translation as an important contemporary phenomenon in the age of globalization and migration. The tradition of translation, task of the translator and development of Translation Studies till the advent of Postcolonial and Subaltern Studies is understood historically and the defence of the idea of cultural translation is made in these articles.

Stephanos Stephanides in his article "Stories and Myths in Translation Theory and the Rethinking of Cultural Tradition" makes an argument for translation as a useful model for elucidating intercultural relations in the present world characterized by profound economic, social and political upheavals. He begins with the idea that since translation has an inextricable relationship with transformation and shaping of tradition which is embedded in its stories and myths, translation should be studied in relation to its ontology, cosmogony and eschatology. Myths and stories reveal the turns in translation which affect the tradition, just as the legend of the Septuagint revealed the central problem of translation as mediation in the Western tradition, and influence the perception of translation as travesty or tradition. Observing that the exploration of relationship between translation and tradition has a long history in Europe which conceived the origins of its languages and cultures as languages and cultures of translation, Stephanos proceeds to explore the relationship between the practice of translation and the concepts of tradition/heritage within broad socio-political transformations, like rise of humanism and postcolonialism and globalization, occurring in Europe and the world. He first presents the theoretical background of the development of Translation Studies by discussing the major writings of Walter Benjamin, Fernando Ortiz and Jorge Luís Borges. The concepts like "afterlife" and "foreignness" in Benjamin provide him with the conceptual framework for explaining the relationships between the reception of literary texts and the ideas of heritage. He then analyzes the ideas of translation as cultural mediations in anthropology and ethnography, disciplines founded upon the notions of other's "translatability", by making references to Claude Lévi-Strauss, Clifford Geertz and James Clifford, and shows through Oswald de Andrade's "Manifesto" how such ideas about translation led to the appropriation and celebration of *antropophagia*/cannibalism in Brazilian modernist movement. Later on Haroldo de Campos' postmodern version of creative *antropophagia* "fed" upon European heritage, resisted monocultural vision of the future and attempted to recover the Brazilian cultural heritage suppressed by European colonizers. This theoretical context helps Stephanos explore the concepts of literary heritage in contemporary Europe where there is a reversal in the process of emigration and where the idea of "heritage" cannot be thought as a stable, monocultural institution. The reading of the Moroccan immigrant Tahar Ben Jelloun's and the Antillean Edouard Glissant's writings demonstrates that the simple binary of self (home) and other (foreign) is not a proper description of the migrant translator who is caught in-between two cultures. Likewise, Stephanos argues, Rushdie's writings are fraught with the question of multicultural heritage which extend the idea of migration to translation by reversing the binary logic. In losing his language and home, the migrant is not only transformed but also transforms the new world. Construction and reconstruction are acts of translation through which a migrant like Rushdie tries to accommodate the heritage of the dominant culture. Finally, after exploring linkages between translation and metamorphosis of the subject after violent displacement, and understanding heritage as 'an unfinished genesis of imagination' in Wilson Harris' novel *Jonestown* (1996), Stephanos considers cultural translation in the age of globalization and migration as a pertinent insight. The article thus concludes with the reclamation of cultural translation: "Recent scholarship often claims the distinction between globality and worldliness (as implied in Heidegger's idea of the worlding), reclaiming for the latter the world making function in human experience and intentionality, historical contingency, and the relentless sensuality of nature. In contrast to the inexorable movement of capital, it is worth returning to the attempts of artists and intellectuals to achieve autonomy through transculturation. If the term is often appropriated by the globalization process, we must reclaim it for the world and the worldly text, and here translation both as metaphor and practice plays a central role."

In the next article, Sachin Ketkar argues that the notion of translation is inseparable from the metaphysical worldview which underpins several cultural discourses and the philosophers have, in their thinking, deployed it as an important philosophical trope/metaphor for the act of human communication and understanding. Therefore, contemporary Translation Studies should explore further the complex configuration of translation and philosophical discourses together. As Jacques Derrida expresses in his *Ear of the Other* (1985), "The origin of philosophy is translation or the thesis of translatability, so that whenever translation in this sense has failed, it is nothing less than philosophy that finds itself defeated" (120). Derrida's epistemological and ontological questioning about the empirical practice of translation in his deconstructive philosophy cannot be thought in conventional manner and accommodated in areas of Translation Studies suggested by Susan Bassnett. This absence creates the need for interdisciplinary fields of study like translation and philosophy. With such conviction, the article offers a discussion of philosophical statements on translation by prominent Western thinkers like George Steiner, Walter Benjamin, Octavio Paz, José Ortega y Gasset and Jacques Derrida, and concludes by examining the idea of translation as rebirth perceived with a difference in two contesting Indian philosophical traditions of Brahmanism and Buddhism. The study of translation in philosophical schemas, Ketkar argues, will produce important insights into epistemological and ontological considerations of human language and the relation of language to reality.

Perceiving the pivotal significance of Derrida's lecture "What is a 'Relevant' Translation?" (1998) in channelizing contemporary postcolonial discourse on cultural translation, and addressing the relevance of pursuing translation in the Third World, Piyush Raval in his article "The Task of the Postcolonial (-Subaltern) Translator" presents ground-breaking theoretical definitions of translation and enunciations of the task of the translator both within the Judaeo-Christian tradition from Walter Benjamin to Jean-Luc Nancy and within the postcolonial world, particularly India. These definitions, the article argues, elucidate the theorization, understanding and the practice of translation in the postcolonial world and help map the future trajectory of translation and Translation Studies. The contemporary fusion of Cultural Studies and Translation Studies in controversial phenomenon like cultural translation by postcolonial theorists and creative writers like Bhabha, Spivak, Rushdie, Coetzee, Harris, Kureishi, Lahiri, etc., is thought as enormously significant. Towards conclusion, a caution is expressed towards the nativist formulation of Indian theory of translation and a plea is made to expand the borders of the discipline by carrying the task of translation of critical and cultural theory in Indian vernaculars "so as to make their users aware of the social hierarchies in which languages and cultures are positioned... and respond to the cultural and social effects that follow upon the global dominance of English" (Venuti, 2003: 259).

The second section on "Questions of Cultural Identity" deals with the crucial issue of postcolonial and subaltern identity through concentrating upon cultural translations made by postcolonial and subaltern writers like Salman Rushdie, J.M. Coetzee, Akhtaruzzaman Elias, and Sindhi writers like Mahesh Nenvani. The articulation of marginal/subaltern cultural identities built on the axis of race, gender, class, community, nation and region is explored through the readings of postcolonial and subaltern narratives of these authors.

Keeping with the thrust of the anthology, the article by Manish Solanki on "Salman Rushdie and Cultural Translation: A Bhabhaian Reading of *Midnight's Children*" examines Rushdie's political (politicized?) aesthetics in the light of postcolonial discourse by Homi Bhabha and Gayatri Spivak on migrancy and cultural hybridity. It first locates Rushdie's fiction amidst postcolonial theoretical debates on geographical displacement and cultural dislocation in contemporary postnational globalized world, and then proceeds to address how these factors influence, and subsequently question the Western humanist conception of the stable "self". Rushdie has become an emblematic figure for such deconstructive literary practices in the field of postcolonial writings and theorization. The article focuses on his cult-novel *Midnight's Children*, specifically the trajectories of careers provided by two of its major characters, Saleem Sinai and Jamila Singer (or Brass Monkey). It shows how Rushdie, by offering a parallel treatment to their respective careers, brings to light the inherent ambiguity of apparently stable identity as defined by homogenizing and monolithic cultural ambience. Rushdie places these two characters, first in India with its pluralistic culture respecting cultural-linguistic-religious-geographical polysemy and then in Pakistan with its religiously fanatic desire for cultural "purity", and demonstrates the respective acculturation of Saleem and Jamila as they pass through this experience of migrancy and cultural translation. Towards the end, the article analyses Rushdie's theoretical position on migrancy, as not an *act* but as a *condition* of human life in the contemporary world, and on hybrid identities. The Rushdiean assertion of new, plural and eclectic identities, of which Saleem is exemplary in *Midnight's Children*, can offer a way out of racisms, xenophobic religious fundamentalisms and jingoistic nationalisms besetting our contemporary global order.

In her article "We, the Castaways of History: Translating the Passion for South Africa of the 'Interregnum'", Aroma Kharsiing takes up the South African author J.M. Coetzee's novel *In the Heart of the Country* to theorize, metaphorically, Coetzee as a cultural translator, who involves actively in the process of negotiation across cultural divides and attempts to break free from the "unfreedom" of White Writing in South Africa characterized by a lack of love for the people and polity of the country. The article invokes Bhabha's use of translation as a metaphor for postcolonial literature and enunciates implications of writing from within the politically subversive liminal, hybrid "Third space". It also invokes Spivak's emphasis on a critical self-awareness of the investigating subject, her concept of "ethical singularity" to discuss Coetzee's scrupulous ethical position on the condition of writing in a country like South Africa. The phenomenon of "cultural translation" has a social and political impact which acquires its special significance in the historic process of nation-building. In the multi-lingual, multi-ethnic mosaic of South African society, Aroma thinks, it is relevant to consider postcolonial literature as cultural translation, carried out in a highly complex contact zone. Transculturalisation is tainted by the history of racism and apartheid in the "Rainbow" nation of South Africa. In such a situation, a white writer like Coetzee finds himself in a liminal position, suspended between the claims of complicity in the history of racism on one hand, and his allegiance to the multicultural "Rainbow" nation of South Africa on the other. The uncertainty of narrative authority, instead of vitiating articulation, opens a new perspective of "narrative in-betweenness". Coetzee adopts the narrative mode of the "middle voice" for articulating the "narrative in-betweenness" and responds to the accusation of complicity by self-reflexively examining the specific form of marginality that he represents and thereby highlights the crisis of authority in writing in South Africa. He is critically aware of his "writing self" by writing in the "middle voice", constantly under suspicion and interrogation. Therefore, Coetzee posits a wary, marginal narrative subject who, as David Attwell says, "deftly negotiates the interstices of power, maintaining its ethical integrity but avoiding not only appeals for inclusion but also any overstatement of its own legitimacy and authority." The article then discusses elaborately how Coetzee's novel *In the Heart of the Country* displays a wary marginal narrative subject, Magda, who attempts to intervene and subvert the dominant narrative of colonialism through the vector of gender. The female protagonist throws into sharp relief not only the inherent problems and eventual breakdown of colonial patriarchy, but also constitutes a strategic position of weakness from which Coetzee can dismantle colonial authority. As a displaced subject poised on the verge of unreason, Magda not only dramatizes Coetzee's own crisis of authority and representation in writing, but also provides him with a model of marginality that necessarily disrupts the attempts of the hegemonic power to frame and signify him, which itself is a historical act. Referring to Coetzee's 1986 essay, "Into the Dark Chamber: the Writer and the South African State", Aroma concludes, in the manner of David Attwell, by drawing attention to how the ethical vision in Gordimer's *Burger's Daughter* informs Coetzee's works, he, who brings up his ethical reconstruction at some "as-yet-unimagined historical moment", with a movement that begins with abnegation. Coetzee acknowledges the unbridgeable historical constraints of colonialism and apartheid, as well as the constraints of the postmodern decentered and dispersed self in the ethical mission of reconstruction and integration of the races.

The following article by Nazia Sultana on "Translating the Culture of the Subaltern in Elias's Novels" understands the idea of representation as translation and engages with translation of the subaltern culture in Bangladeshi novelist Akhtaruzzaman Elias's two novels, *Chilekothur Sepai* and *Khoabnama*. The idea of the subaltern is a complex one and both Antonio Gramsci and Gayatri Chakravorty Spivak have foregrounded and adequated the theory of the subaltern. However, in her essay "Can the Subaltern Speak?" Spivak asks if a proper representation of the subaltern is possible because the mainstream representation of the subaltern often eclipses the voice of the subaltern. The dominant history has failed to narrativize the resistance of the subaltern. For Spivak, it is rather narrative itself which succeeds in representing as translating the dynamics of the subaltern life. The article uses insights produced on Spivak's essay "Can the Subaltern Speak?" by J. Maggio who argues that the essay pleads for translation rather than representation of the everyday culture of the subaltern by understanding the political logic of the culture of the subaltern and "unsilencing" the unique muteness of the subaltern. Translation, which is a desire to understand or respect the subaltern, is an appropriate mode than "representation" to understand the subaltern.

Using Spivak's idea of the subaltern in this way, Nazia argues that, among Bangladeshi novelists, Akhtaruzzaman Elias has successfully translated the dynamics of life as well as the resistance of the subaltern. In his novel *Chilekothar Sepai* Elias illustrates how Khijir and Chengtu have contributed to *Unosotturer Gonoovuuthan*/mass insurgency of 1969 and what their lives are about. Besides representing the Khijir and Chengtu, the novelist also has taken into account the lives of ticket blacker Bazlu, a house maid *Jummoner Maa*, Khijir's mother, etc. who are the urban proletariat or the subaltern. In his last novel

*Khoabnama*, Elias translates the life of an *adhiar*, Tamij who is involved in peasant uprising or *Tevaaga* movement in 1940s. But Khijir, Chengtu and Tamij do not fight in these insurgencies with a clear idea about their own political aim; rather, they do it out of material necessity and commonsensical idea about equality and freedom. The article demonstrates how Elias tries to translate this in *Chilekothar Sepai* and *Khoabnama* and deals with the subalterns' life and culture. Moreover, it makes an attempt to show how the historical shift from feudalism to capitalism in Bangladesh may offer a historical account but does not account for the lives and struggles of other disempowered groups, including peasants, women and indigenous groups. Finally, thinking that the subaltern's employment of various codes of communication should be understood by the translator of subaltern culture, the article concludes by demonstrating how Elias considered language as a part of identity and culture of the subaltern, at times expressed strong views on it and actually dealt with the subaltern's language in his two novels – *Chilekothar Sepai* and *Khoabnama*. These contain colloquial Bangla language, the language of the subaltern. Thus, the dominant mode of communication is not imposed upon the subalterns like Khijir and *Jummoner Maa* and the task of subaltern translation is performed metaphorically.

Soni Wadhwa in her article "Acts of Refuge, Acts of Naming: On Translating Sindhi Identity as 'Minor'", examines selected voices in Sindhi writing to explore how different Sindhi writers have reflected upon the past of the community as a whole. Accepting that their voices are not in any way representative of the Sindhi experience, she attempts to listen to their articulations, to identify their positions vis-a-vis the community and then to theorize their positions along the lines of the political implications of their arguments. The recurring patterns identified in some of the poems and stories in thinking about their present are: nostalgia for Sindh, feeling of alienation caused by displacement, the articulation of feeling marginalized because of being deterritorialized and further, locating the self and the other against such a deterritorialization. The article focuses on the recognition of the self vis-a-vis displacement and the gaze of the other, and thereby teases out ways in which the changes in their lived behaviour are reflected upon. One important insight into the aftermath of migration is the translation from being a "major" community in Pakistan (undivided India, before Partition) to a "minor" community in India. She does not make a claim that the Sindhi community as a whole is a marginalized community, instead discusses possible issues in Sindhi writing that are linked to the minority status of the language. Her argument borrows largely from this concept of "minority" and attempts to extend it to the "minor" as a metaphor and a literary-political term as used by Gilles Deleuze and Félix Guattari. The "minor" is a sensibility and a tradition that is revolutionary in the sense that it refuses to speak on the lines of the "major" which is the norm.

The article then attempts first to relate this notion of "minor" to the notion of the "subaltern", suggesting that the voice of the refugee is deprived and marginalized, an outsider in the rhetoric of the nation, without being offered any space in the hierarchy of the nation. In the case of the Sindhi refugee and her voice in literature, it is this deprivation that makes a case for her to be understood in terms of the subaltern. The idea of the nation becomes important here because the coming in of the refugee does not fit into the political definition of migration/ exile from one country to another. Though Wadhwa recognizes that an immediate reaction to the suggestion of the subaltern perspective being used to understand the voice of the Sindhi refugee would be that Sindhis are not perceived as marginalized people and they do not consider themselves to be marginalized, she thinks it is not in any case an important criterion for them to be studied in the light of the concept of the subaltern. Secondly, the Sindhi community in the contemporary set-up is also not subaltern, but it is the refugee in selected (translated) Sindhi writing that can be understood to be subaltern. Thirdly, she is also a subaltern because the Partition has caused a rupture in the cultural sensibility – the loss of the influences of Persian, Arabic and Sufi syncretic traditions – that the Sindhi refugee could have inherited, had she not been displaced. As a member of Sindhi community, Wadhwa also recognizes that Sindhis who came to India are primarily Hindus and are therefore a majority, "major", the norm which would turn them into the dominant, elite people who from the mainstream marginalize the others, below in the hierarchy. Even if the argument of seeing the community as the "major" holds to be true, it does not in any way disqualify it from being understood as "subaltern". On the theoretical basis of arguments by Gayatri Spivak, Dipesh Chakravorty, Abdul JanMohamed, David Lloyd, Bijay Danta, Fred Dallmyr, etc. the article then generally tries to see the overlaps across history and identity along the agency of space, and examines post-Partition Sindhi experience and concerns of Sindhi community through important voices in Sindhi literature. Regarding the subaltern, the minor, the refugee and the migrant as important strands to study marginalization, Wadhwa finally refers to views on immigration and multiculturalism by Suárez-Orozco and Austin Sarat in *Engaging Cultural Differences* to theorize ideas of identity and difference, and views on diaspora by Amitav Ghosh to understand how the constitution of difference in Indian culture has led to the (mis)recognition of Sindhi refugees as "'parasitic' aliens inviting doubts about their ethics and business practices."

The third and final section of the book, "Problems of Praxis: Translating Indian Literatures", addresses, in line with the earlier section, the questions of marginal/subaltern identity in translation in the era of globalization, but largely moves onto the direction of offering a minute examination of the contextual problems of translating marginalized/subculture text, issues of meaning and translatability/untranslatability of cultural nuances in cultural translation and in widely known empirical practice of translation with reference to regional Indian literatures like Gujarati. The cultural nuances of Indian culture expressed in regional or "Bhasa" literatures (as G.N. Devy says) of India pose a challenge to the postcolonial translator who wants to offer these translations specifically to the Western reader. The problems of praxis in translation are highlighted in this section through the discussions of Gujarati short-stories by Jayant Khatri and Nazir Mansuri and Gujarati poetry by Harish Meenashru.

As a mode of intercultural communication, the practice of translation is highly political in terms of the translocation of "meaning" as a cultural artifact that it boldly undertakes. The article by Hemang Desai on "Mediation of 'Meaning' beyond Consumption and Production: Translating Identity in Marginalized Texts" interrogates the strategies a translator of "rooted" literary texts employ in post-colonial and post-global milieu. The primary contention here is that witting or unwitting subscription to either aesthetic or consumerist assumptions as to the production/control of the meaning of a marginalized/subculture literary text seriously undermines the cultural identity and values of a given community. The most urgent obligation of a translator negotiating such texts is to protect and preserve the quintessential cultural superstructure underpinning the text against the sweeping tide of global, capitalist and consumerist hegemony. Against the backdrop of the experience of translating Nazir Mansuri's Gujarati short stories (*Dhal Kachbo*, "Shielded Tortoise", 2002) which are set in a typical rustic locale, around straggly villages on the sea shore of Diu and Daman and which give an unprecedented insight into the primitivistic and dark life as lived by the subaltern fishermen community, the article also touches upon the issues of knowledge, motivation and skills required of a translator approaching such a text.

The next article by Manoj Chhaya "Translating Culture and 'Cultural Translation' in Jayant Khatri's Gujarati Short Stories" analyzes selected short-stories of Jayant Khatri, the pioneer of modernism in Gujarati short-fiction, with a view to evolving the poetics of translation for Gujarati literature which has been misunderstood due to lack of its translations in other languages. In his three collections of short-stories *Foran* ("Droplets", 1944), *Vehtaan Zarnaan* ("Flowing Streams", 1952) and *Kharaa Bapor* ("High Noon", 1968), Jayant Khatri, a Marxist with a great empathy for marginalized and subaltern classes of society, chose Gujarati over Kachchhi as the medium of his writing despite his Kachchhi roots. But this choice creates the possibility of translating Kachchhi culture into Gujarati. The fact that Kachchhi and Gujarati as languages share dialectical relationship with each other and that Kachchh as a cultural region could/did not assimilate itself into the mainstream Gujarati culture, might have inculcated feelings within Khatri as a writer to narrate the culture of his region through the mainstream medium of Gujarati. Thus, Khatri becomes, for Chhaya, the postcolonial cultural translator before Rushdie, Lahiri and Kureishi evolve the idea in a transnational/translational context of migration. The postcolonial view on cultural translation also finds relevance in translation of Khatri into English. Khatri offers a rich narrative and linguistic experience to those lamenting the turn towards cultural translation. The article then discusses the challenges posed in translation of Khatri's short-stories, like kinship terms, grammatical categories of tense and time and cultural nuances which require a translator's cultural familiarization. Finally, arguing that the short-story was a European genre domesticated in Gujarati literature, translation of Khatri's short-stories into English would be transformation of the genre and would stamp distinct identity on them by making hybrid.

The final article in the anthology by Asha Makhecha on "Problems of (Cultural) Translation: Translating Gujarati Poetry" presents a broad historical survey of translation of poetry in Western tradition and in Indian tradition. Viewing briefly translation activities carried out into the region of Gujarat with a lament for lack of translations of Gujarati literature into English, the article engages with the translation of a poem by the contemporary Gujarati poet Harish Meenashru from his anthology *Pankhipadarath* and on its basis, articulates socio-cultural problems of translating Gujarati poetry. In addition, it also addresses lexical, musical, semantic and grammatical features in translation of a poem. Meenashru's Gujarati poetry is culturally loaded and full of Sanskrit and Urdu terminologies. The qualities in his poetry like the subtleties of tone, rhyme, rhythm, word-play, conversational phrases, allusions and new coinages are likely to be lost in their translations into English, but much is gained than what is lost in translating his poetry. Inverting the phrase "No text can be completely original" from Octavio Paz's famous statement on translation by Jacques Derrida's view that since every original work is translation, every translation is an original work, the article concludes by understanding the process of translation (like translating poetry) as "re-creation".

Thus, the book maps the trajectory of Translation Studies in its new compounding with Cultural Studies by relocating the idea of cultural translation in different geographical and cultural contexts, lays open the achievements and significance of this contemporary approach of understanding translation, assimilates the empirical practice of translation by examining cultural problems in translation and charts overall the future of translation and Translation Studies.

## Works Cited

Bassnett, Susan and Harish Trivedi. *Post-colonial Translation: Theory and Practice*. London and New York: Routledge, 2000.

Bassnett, Susan. *Translation Studies*. London: Routledge, 1980.

Bhabha, Homi K. *The Location of Culture*. London and New York: Routledge, 1994.

García, José María Rodrígues. "Introduction: Literary into Cultural Translation." *Diacritics* 34.3/4 (Autumn – Winter, 2004):2–30.

Holmes, James. "The Name and Nature of Translation Studies." *The Translation Studies Reader*. Ed. Lawrence Venuti. London and New York: Routledge, 2000. 172–185.

Lahiri, Jhumpa. "My Intimate Alien". *Outlook* (New Delhi), Special annual issue on "Stree" (Woman), (2000):116–20.

Lefevere, André. *Translation, History, Culture: A Sourcebook*. London and New York: Routledge, 1992.

Longovic, Tomislav Z. "Fearful Asymmetries: A Manifesto of Cultural Translation." *The Journal of the Midwest Modern Language Association* 35.2 (Autumn, 2002):5–12.

Maggio, J. "'Can the Subaltern Be Head': Political Theory, Translation, Representation and Gayatri Chakravorty Spivak". *Alternatives* 32.4 (Oct. – Dec. 2007):419–443.

Rushdie, Salman. *Imaginary Homelands*. India: Random House, 2010.

Spivak, Gayatri. "The Politics of Translation." *The Translation Studies Reader*. Ed. Lawrence Venuti. London and New York: Routledge, 2000. 369–388.

———. "Translation as Culture." *In Translation: Reflections, Refractions, Transformations*. Ed. Paul St. Pierre and Prafulla C. Kar. Amsterdam and Philadelphia: John Benjamin's Publishing Company, 2007. 263–276.

Snell-Hornby, Mary. *The Turns of Translation Studies*. Amsterdam and Philadephia: John Benjamin Publishing Company, 2006.

Trivedi, Harish. "Translating culture vs. cultural translation." *In Translation: Reflections, Refractions, Transformations*. Ed. Paul St. Pierre and Prafulla C. Kar. Amsterdam and Philadelphia: John Benjamins Publishing Company, 2007. 277–287.

Venuti, Lawrence. "Translating Derrida on Translation: Relevance and Disciplinary Resistance." *The Yale Journal of Criticism* 16.2 (2003):237–262.

# Theoretical Perspectives

# 1

# Stories and Myths in Translation Theory and the Rethinking of Cultural Tradition[1]

*Stephanos Stephanides*

Tradition is normally embedded in myths and stories. As I will argue that translation is inextricably linked with the continual transformation and shaping of tradition, it is important to begin by examining translation in relation to its ontology, cosmogony and eschatology. One of the first stories and myths of translation in the Western tradition is the legend of the Septuagint, which tells of the translation of the Old Testament from Hebrew to Greek and dates to the third century before Christ in Alexandria. It tells of the work of the seventy-two translators (six from each of the twelve tribes of Israel) in seventy-two days who worked in seclusion on the island of Pharos where they ritually washed their hands every morning before they embarked onto the task of translation in isolation from each other. The translations were miraculously the same as it was said they communicated directly with God without other interference. This highlights the central problem of translation as one of mediation, and also embeds the narrative in the Western mythology and metaphysics of the Fall. Translation is exile and fall from the unmediated language of Eden. The need for mediation arises in the post-Babel crisis. The story provides for the guilt of translation for coming into being

1. The Greek translation of this article was published in *Spaces of Theory: History and Geography of Critical Narratives* (eds. Apostolos Lampropoulos and Antonis Balasopoulos, Athens, Metaihmio, 2010: 377–405 (in Greek, translated by Vangelis Roumeliotis).

after the original. It might be argued that Western translation tradition is overly preoccupied with its own metaphysics of the Fall and of exile from Eden. The concern is to exclude the impurities of mediation. Walter Benjamin also suggests an Edenic language when he uses the idea of *reine Sprache* or "pure language". If pure language is unmediated, it is impossible in the human realm. Nonetheless, despite this impossibility, it is the translator's quest to follow the promise of pure language. The promise is in the process of translation, which follows a Utopian impulse to wholeness, which is neither in the original or source text nor in the target, neither of which are whole, but in their relationship.

Our perception of the problem of mediation varies according to the alternative mythologies in which translation may take place, and which gods and goddesses affect or manipulate the agents of translation, and what vision they incorporate of an originary unity. The Greco-Roman and Hindu mythologies of the four ages or *yugs:* golden, silver, bronze, and iron perceived as a cyclical process of diminution and recovery provide such an alternative perspective on translatability. It is noteworthy that the last decade of the second millennium witnessed a plethora of translations of Ovid's *Metamorphoses.* I quote the beginning of Ted Hughes' award winning translation as an example of how the process of metamorphoses may invest the notion of translatability and its relation to entropy:

### Metamorphoses

Now I am ready to tell how bodies are changed
Into different bodies

I summon the supernatural beings
Who first contrived
The transmogrification
In the stuff of life.
You did it for your own amusement.
Descend again, be pleased to reanimate
This revival of those marvels
Reveal, now, exactly
How they were performed
From the beginning
Up to this moment.

Before sea or land, before even sky
Which contains all,
Nature wore only one mask –
Since called Chaos.
A huge agglomeration of upset.
A bolus of everything – but
As if aborted.
And the total arsenal of entropy
Already at war within it.

In his introduction to his translation, Hughes tells us that Ovid's stories "establish a rough register of what it feels like to live in the psychological gulf that opens at the end of an era." (Hughes, 1997: xi) The instability of the human subject links Ovid's theme of metamorphoses to contemporary obsessions and its opening lines read like a statement on translatability, which we may trope in the Benjaminian sense as the claim of a text to be translated. If in the story of the Septuagint, this claim is located in God and takes place without the intervention of the desire of the subject, in the *Metamorphoses* subject, body and desire are interlinked, and perceived in the dis-membered and re-membered bodies in translation. These translative bodies could be said to be like the bodies of the Bacchantes who dismember Pentheus, caught between the demise of the old religion and birth of the new:

All as if naked anonymous, free
Into the ecstasy,
The dementia and the delirium
Of the new god. (Hughes, 1997: 185)

The tension in Hughes seems to be in the gap between a culture's rational or skeptical impulses and its erotic and spiritual nature as we find in the stories of Pentheus (the rational ruler of Thebes) who challenges the divinity of Bacchus, or Niobe who scorns the gods and tells the people about the folly of their worship:

Isn't this insane?
Aren't you all out of your minds
To offer tributes to these gods in the sky
Who exist only by hearsay? (Hughes, 1997: 213)

The acts of metamorphoses, Hughes says, seem to arrive when the unendurable emotional intensity of their emotions lifts the episodes onto the mythic or divine plane. If translatability is in metamorphoses, it finds its articulation in the human victims of metamorphoses who are transformed and remain in cultural memory in the forms they have attained.

Like Derrida in a lecture entitled "What Is a 'Relevant' Translation," (Derrida, 2001: 177) one could say that in Ovid's tales, bodies endure and exhibit translation as the memory or stigmata of suffering [*passion*] or, hovering above it, as an aura or halo. As in the final story of Hughes' translation, Pyramus and Thisbe are remembered by the colour of the mulberry fruit, which was transformed by their blood. About to die, This be exclaims: "Remember how we died. Remember us/By the colour of our blood in your fruit... The gods were listening and were touched...Ever after Mulberries, as they ripen, darken purple" (Hughes, 1997: 254). Speaking of translatability, Walter Benjamin says that when we speak of an unforgettable life or moment, we imply a claim not fulfilled by men; and thus refers to a realm in which it is fulfilled: "God's remembrance" (Benjamin, 1973: 70). The *poesis* of the mode of translation is therefore in the promise of fulfillment that lies in translatability even when it is beyond the ability of men to translate. In which god or gods this promise is found depends on the history and culture where memory is embedded. The life of stories, myth and translation is not in the transfer of information, but in cultural memory. In a dialogue such as that of translation there is a reversible process where the source becomes the target or reception and the reception source. It is the lagging effect between emission of the signal and its reception that opens up the space where the interferences may enter. Myths and stories are often revealing of the forces behind the exclusions or inclusions in the interferences and the turns in translation, which affect tradition. It is the affective space evoked by the myths and stories with which the mediation and transformation are invested, and which influence the perception of translation as travesty or tradition. In times of cultural change, these are perceived as struggling against each other.

## TRANSLATION: TRAVESTY OR TRADITION

There is a well-known Italian maxim, *traduttore tradittore*, which is a play on words linking the practice of translation to notions of betrayal. More often than not, the pun has been interpreted as a comment on the difficulty of fidelity in translation and the related problem of equivalence. Translation, in other words, always involves traducing the original. Thus, critics concerned exclusively with issues of precision and fidelity have frequently evoked the idea of translation as an untrustworthy, albeit necessary, activity. With the cultural turn in translation studies over the last 30 years, however, the maxim can be read in a new light. Perhaps what is more telling about the Italian pun is the way it underscores a link between *traduzione* (traducement) and *tradizione* (tradition). Translation might be infidelity but as such it is also an agent for reshaping tradition. Read in this context, the maxim suggests that the site of translation is tradition itself.

The relationship between translation and tradition has long preoccupied European scholars, especially since many European languages and cultures have originated as languages and cultures of translation. The modern European consciousness of what it means to "translate" dates from the rise of Humanism. It is worth noting Gianfranco Folena's observation (Folena, 1973) that in Florentine humanism there was a semantic shift in which *traducere* prevailed over other contending terms such as *transladare* (indicating a leading across rather than moving across), or terms such as "interpret" and "transfer". This shift has remained embedded in the word for translation in modern Romance languages: French *traduire*, Spanish *traducir*, and Portuguese *traduzir*. According to Folena, Leonardo Bruni introduced the use of the word *traducere* in 1400 with reference to a passage from Aulus Gellio, where there is mention of a "vocabulum graecum traductum in lingua romana".

What is at stake in this shift is the emphasis on the agency of the translator in literary and cultural innovation. Folena quotes an anti-humanist response to Bruni by Domenico da Prato (c. 1420), who states that the old translators were content to be anonymous, and that they were not motivated by vanity. He disputes the authorship of the translator and declares that whereas the original authors are still alive, their dry *traduttori*, be they bilingual or trilingual, are always dead. This deliberation about translation, authorship, accessibility and authenticity anticipates many of the debates during the Reformation, when the dissolution of a unified religious community in Europe coincided with the spread of "national" vernaculars and the rise of new printing technologies that facilitated their dissemination.

It is no coincidence that the historical relations between translation and tradition and the authority of the translator have gained renewed impetus in translation and cultural theory during the last two decades. Post-colonialism and globalization, it could be argued, mark a period of momentous change for the idea of European heritage and culture not dissimilar to the period of European expansion that followed in the wake of the rise of humanism. My aim in this article is to explore the relations between the practice of translation and the concepts of tradition or heritage within these broad socio-political transformations taking place in Europe and the world. In an increasingly multicultural and polyglot Europe and globalized world, the issue of translation has come to the fore, and my interest is in the way in which "minority" and "peripheral" groups translate the dominant culture and are reciprocally incorporated into that culture through a process of translation. As Homi Bhabha has stated: "Where once we could believe in the comforts and continuities of Tradition, today we must face the responsibilities of cultural Translation". (Quoted and discussed in Robins, 1999)

While the focus of this article is primarily on literary texts, the questions it raises extend well beyond the scope of literary criticism to suggest how cultural formation is inseparable from questions of translatability. Thus, I endeavour to adumbrate a general theoretical approach to translation, drawing on insights yielded from literary studies and anthropology, within which particular case studies might then be considered. Before turning to look in more detail at a range of postcolonial literary texts, my aim is to survey the theoretical ground of translation studies as this has developed over recent years. I begin with a particular emphasis on the writings of Walter Benjamin, who has much to say on the question of translation. Subsequent sections examine ideas of translation within the context of anthropology and ethnography – disciplines which are founded upon notions of the other's "translatability". This process of ethnographic translation often involves the violent incorporation of difference, which is frequently figured as a cannibalistic ritual of ingestion. As we shall see in our discussion of twentieth-century Brazilian *antropofagia*, however, "cannibalism" can function as an important trope within postcolonial strategies. Be that as it may, the act of translation involves a familiarization and hence a domestication of the "foreign" (Venuti, 1993: 209). This is true of ethnographic fieldwork, which as James Clifford suggests: "obliges its practitioners to experience, at a bodily as well as an intellectual level, the vicissitudes of translation"[2] (Clifford, 1988: 23–24). Clifford suggests that there is a close relationship in ethnographic and historical writing between spatial and temporal dimensions. The past is viewed as a "foreign country" in which, to borrow L.P. Hartley's famous phrase, "they do things differently" (Hartley, 1953). In summary, then, my aim is to draw upon a range of critical writings in order to show how the theoretical and practical issues raised by translation provide a useful point of departure for exploring the reformulation of "heritage" in a "new", multicultural Europe. As the past is renegotiated and institutionalized in new ways, questions about what past is being preserved, and for whom, begin to take on a greater significance. Indeed, as I have already indicated, it may well be that translation and heritage have conjoined histories; that in investigating one we are necessarily confronted with the problem of the other. Far from remaining a peripheral activity, translation emerges as a key concept for elucidating heritage debates in contemporary Europe.

## WALTER BENJAMIN'S AFTERLIFE

The importance of the ideological and culturally competitive aspects of translation has been analyzed by the so-called "polysystems" theory of translation introduced by Itamar Even-Zohar and Gideon Toury in the 1970s and 1980s. This explored how translation acts not only on the languages involved, but also on the various semiotic systems that contribute to the construction of cultures and how these relationships are affected by the power relations among unequal cultures. Translation was redefined not as a purely text-bound practice but as a wider socio-political process central to the constitution of culture (Even-Zohar and Toury, 1981; Toury, 1987).

More recently, the work of the cultural critic Walter Benjamin has been rediscovered as an occasion to meditate on the relationship between story/history and "translatability", both within the context of specific texts and of culture as a whole. Benjamin's discussion wrests on the concept of translation from the classical paradigm of mimesis and moves towards a concept of kinship between "self" (target language and culture) and "other" (source language and culture). According to

2. For an account of the violence involved in the "Translation of the Third World", see Talal Asad and John Dixon, "Translating Europe's Others" *Europe and Its Others*, eds F. Barker et al.

Benjamin's philosophy of history, the past lays "claim" to the present, just as the present struggles to accommodate the past. Rendering a "foreign" language into a "native" language finds its equivalence in our "translation" of the past – which is always inalienably unfamiliar – into the present. Thus, in his "Theses on the Philosophy of History", Benjamin remarks: "Like every generation that preceded us, we have been endowed with a weak Messianic power, a power to which the past has a claim. That claim cannot be settled cheaply" (Benjamin, 1973: 254). At the same time, Benjamin suggests that translation "claims" the source text for present generations and becomes an allegory of the past's resurrection, not its decay.

Likewise, for Jacques Derrida, who draws on Benjamin, translation is a moment of growth, in as much as the original requires supplementation "because at the origin it was not there without fault, full, complete, total, identical to itself" (Derrida, 1985: 188). Perhaps Derrida's most significant contribution to the present discussion of translation and tradition is in questioning the stability and unity of an "origin". There is never an unsullied "original" text, but rather, an endless chain of reinterpretations or former translations. If heritage is most effectively approached as a semiotic system whose claims and meanings are set in motion by cultural and social processes, then it is not merely a way of preserving tradition, but of translating it. The role of memory and forgetting are important here.

In "The Storyteller", an essay on the Russian writer Nikolai Leskov, Benjamin reflects on the meaning of "storytelling" and, in particular, on the role of the "storyteller". He describes how a story is perpetuated as a memory in the minds of its listeners, who become storytellers in their turn, reshaping earlier versions according to what they have remembered or forgotten. The transmission, or translation, of a story becomes analogous with tradition, which is shaped and reshaped by its inheritors. While heritage is backward-looking, in that it articulates a desire to preserve tradition, it also gestures toward the future and the community's desire to live on. Benjamin draws a distinction in "The Storyteller" between what he calls the verifiable, functional "information" contained within the story, and the poetic, cyclical "art of storytelling" itself. This distinction helps us to think about heritage as an equivalent of storytelling. In heritage, we may distinguish between the factual "information" that historical artefacts communicate from the past and the kinds of stories that we make them tell in the present.

Benjamin elaborates this idea in more detail in his seminal essay "The Task of the Translator", in which he introduces the concept of the 'afterlife' and observes: "a translation issues from the life of the original – not so much from its life as from its afterlife" (Benjamin, 1973: 71). The impulse to salvage the life of the original lies at the heart of the process of translation. This is not simply nostalgia for some lost original, but also an attempt to "salvage a future from the ruins of the past". As such, it is a gesture toward the "afterlife". Benjamin depicts this process in his graphic description of the "angel of history", which he evokes with reference to Paul Klee's painting "Angelus Novus". This is how one pictures the angel of history. His face is turned toward the past. Where we perceive a chain of events, he sees one single catastrophe which keeps piling wreckage upon wreckage and hurls it in front of his feet. The angel would like to stay, awaken the dead, and make whole what has been smashed. But a storm is blowing from Paradise; it has got caught in his wings with such violence that the angel can no longer close them. This storm irresistibly propels him into the future to which his back is turned, while the pile of debris before him grows skyward. This storm is what we call progress (Benjamin, 1973: 257–58). The "angel of history" shares a similar mode of being with the translator. Whereas the angel moves towards paradise, the translator attempts to capture the "pure language" *reine Sprache*) of an immaculate original. In this biblical vision, however, "pure language" has been corrupted, and an original purity can never be retrieved (Benjamin, 1973: 70). In short, the translator is forever torn between a desire to look back at an original, "to make whole what has been smashed", and to acknowledge the exigencies of the present. Translation, as a practice, like heritage, is marked by this tension between an acceptance of loss and a desire for retrieval, between forgetfulness and memory.

In Benjamin's translation theory, translation is a provisional way of coming to terms with what he calls "the foreignness of languages" in much the same way as heritage seeks to accommodate the unfamiliarity of the past in the present. This idea is articulated in Benjamin's metaphoric description of the language of translation as a garment, which envelopes "its content like a royal robe with ample folds. For it specifies a more exalted language than its own and thus remains unsuited to its content, overpowering and alien" (Benjamin, 1973: 75). Here the language of translation is an imperfect fit of an original. The capacious robe self-consciously draws attention to the insuperable differences and foreignness of the "other" language, with which it can never be identical. Significantly, Homi Bhabha singles out Benjamin's image in his discussion of hybridity and cultural difference. As Bhabha suggests, Benjamin's metaphor helps us to consider how acts of cultural translation are only possible if the language of translation recognizes its own ambivalence on the "borderline" of different systems (Bhabha, 1990: 314). For example, as we have noted in the myth of the Fall, the fall of language implies a breakdown of immediacy, and language is mediated in a gesture toward the recovery of the whole. The remembering that goes on in the storytelling situation creates a future in the process of re-creating the past. The story itself is an example of a palpable object promising wholeness. In *The Origin of German Tragic Drama*, Benjamin states that the object is incapable of emanating any meaning of its own, but gains its significance from the allegorist. Through the object, the allegorist speaks of something different, thus making the object a key to the realm of hidden knowledge and revering it as the emblem of this (2003: 184). The object or spoken past seeks shape in the written (fallen) present and in a future in which the whole story may be told. This scheme of allegory has the same temporal dimension as the scheme we have discussed in translation. The movement from oral story to writing furnishes an analogy between writing and allegory.[21] This should not be glossed simply as a decline from orality to *écriture*, but as a beginning afresh, as in writing as a response to writing (i.e. *in* translation) (Stephanides and Singh, 2000: 100–101). Thus translatability in Benjamin is glossed as resistance to decay, erosion or death, and marks the possibility of historical and cultural change. The translation *claims* the text of the past for future generations, thus becoming an allegory of its resurrection.

The promise is in the movement of translation itself which is perceived as foundational rather than derivative. Given that language cannot strive to be adequate to an original presence, it may give new life to the text through translation as counterpoint, irreverence or sacrilege. The irreverent and the sacrilegious have characterized the translation traditions of the modern cultures of the Americas, and which are characterized by processes of syncretism and creolization. We could argue the transformation or travesty of translation is privileged in the formation of culture no doubt in an effort to assert autonomy and differentiation from a colonial culture that came from elsewhere. The precarious relationship modern American cultures have with their pre-Columbian indigenous pasts has meant that identity in the American cultures usually emerges through difference with the cultures brought or left behind from other continents. It is not often remembered that the terms counterpoint and transculturation discussed in relation to translation were coined by the Cuban anthropologist Fernando Ortiz in postcolonial Cuba and bring translation sensibility to the centre of the formation of the cultures of the Americas (Ortiz, 1995). More well-known are the essays of Borges who brings translation to the centre of literary practice. No doubt this is due to his impact on North American and European post-modern writing, but it is worth remembering that he also wrote within the cultural processes that shaped the twentieth century cultures of the Americas.[3] Borges' phrase "translation against", therefore, implies texts, cultures, places and spaces in contest, thus highlighting the role of translation in the creation of literariness and in emerging and changing cultures and identity. Thus, in his classic essay, "The Translators of *The Thousand and One Nights*" (*Los traductores de Las 1001 noches)* he states "Lane translated against Galland, Burton against Lane; to understand Burton, we must understand this hostile dynasty" (Borges, 1996–97: Vol. 1: 109; Borges, 1999: 92). Borges extends this idea to include writing, the task of which is, like translation, to appropriate and change or, as he irreverently states, to distort or falsify. This irreverence is reaffirmed in another well-known essay, "Some Versions of Homer", ("*Las versiones homéricas*") where he states that all modification is an inevitable sacrilege since there is no definitive text except in religion or exhaustion. Texts (translation or writing) are only versions or drafts that create transformations and a repertoire of possibilities, and the idea that translations are inferior is our superstition. "The original is unfaithful to the translation," (Borges, Vol. 2: 109; Borges, 1999: 239) he says with reference to Henley's English translation of Beckford's "Vathek" written in French. His debunking of the notion of fidelity places the emphasis on the reception of the text rather than on an essential meaning of the original. This is articulated in his famous fiction on rewriting "Pierre Menard, Author of the Quixote", a text George Steiner has called a summa of all translation theory (Steiner, 1975: 70).

3. For a fuller discussion of Borges' irreverent syncretist aesthetics see Eleni Kefala.

## *ANTROPOFAGIA*: ETHNOGRAPHY, POSTMODERNISM AND CULTURAL TRANSLATABILITY

So far I have sought to highlight the critical perspectives on the politics of difference involved in the process of translation. Benjamin's concepts of the "afterlife" and of "foreignness", I have suggested, provide useful conceptual frameworks for elucidating the linkages between the reception of literary works and ideas of inheritance or heritage as they extend from the literary text to culture as a whole. In the remaining pages of this article, I want to explore in more detail how translation relates to ethnographic practice, before returning to a focused discussion of literary works which deal explicitly with issues of translation, displacement, and heritage.

As Wolfgang Iser has observed in his discussion of tradition and translation, any resuscitation of the past takes place within a context of present needs. Accordingly, the past "is not just an available entity waiting to be channeled into the present, but is variously invoked according to present exigencies. In other words, current necessities are projected onto the past in order to make it translatable in the present. This mutuality ultimately decides the nature of the past invoked." Moreover, it follows that just as "memory crosses boundaries to a past", so "otherness crosses boundaries to an outside" (Iser, 1998: 296–97). Clearly, this idea of translation, conceptualized as a crossing of borders, is closely connected to the interpretative procedures of anthropology and of ethnography as a practice, which, like literary translation, is predicated upon the representation of a fundamental "otherness".

Claude Levi-Strauss, for example, was concerned with the issue of translatability when he stated: 'When we consider some system of belief [...] the question which we ask ourselves is indeed, "what does all this mean or signify?" and to answer it, we force ourselves to translate into our language rules originally stated in a different code (Lévi-Strauss, 1960: 80). Ideas of authorship and translation, as these relate to ethnographic fieldwork, have been explored by, among others, Clifford Geertz and James Clifford. Indeed, Clifford speaks of his writings as provisional paths rather than a final fixed and authoritative map, remarking that "given the historical contingency of translations, there is no single location from which a full comparative account could be produced" (Clifford, 1997: 11). Just as translation has been used as a metaphor within ethnography, the figurative language literary translators use to describe the source text is similar to that used by ethnographers to describe their relationship to the "field", providing insights into the nature of the cross-cultural relationship. Susan Bassnett, for example, explores the figurative language that translators use to describe their relationship to the source text. Her observations include references to garments, reflecting light, property and class relations, being faithful or unfaithful. While some translators "capture" and "penetrate" the source text, others attempt, like mothers and midwives, to nurture and give new life to the text. Likewise, ethnographers frequently envisage cultures as bodies to explore, map, consume or penetrate. In recent years, anthropologists and literary translators alike have been interrogating the basis of their own authority and asking: "Who writes? Who speaks?" (Barthes, 1993) and "What is an author?" (Foucault, 1979)

Through their figurative language, translators and ethnographers make their roles as cultural mediators visible. As Lawrence Venuti has suggested, there is now an imperative for translators to make their presence felt and "demystify", as he puts it, the illusion of invisibility. Venuti argues that the translator's invisibility can be seen as a "concealment of the multiple hierarchies and exclusions", in which translation, as a practice, is implicated (Venuti, 1995: 16). In much the same way, post-colonial ethnography, in its anxiety to give a voice to the "other" and shatter the illusion of its documentary objectivity, has sought to scrutinize its own reductive procedures and reveal the ideological contexts which have shaped its development. As Clifford reminds us, the process of translation is not one-way (Clifford, 1994). On the contrary, translation should be seen as a reciprocal process. Clifford illustrates the collusions in the complex relationship of this reciprocity when he discusses how French ethnographic practice in Africa provided a perceptual leap that fed into the artistic avant-garde of Paris in the 1920s, and had an influence on European surrealism (Clifford, 1988).

This idea of mutual translation also underlies the appropriation of cannibalism *(antropofagia)* in Brazilian *modernismo* in the 1920s and 1930s. Indeed, one of the most significant documents of the movement was the so-called "Antropophagic Manifesto", published by Oswald de Andrade in the *Revista de Antropofagia.* In this text, Andrade endeavours, as he puts it in the "Manifesto", to transform "the taboo into a totem" (Bellei, 1998). The celebration of cannibalism and of the Tupi tribesman as the original Brazilian, (Morse, 1995) *Antropofagia* functioned as an important postcolonial strategy in the creation of a Brazilian national culture; it suggested how Brazil could simultaneously look to its own cannibal past and satisfy its "primitive" appetite by ingesting the heritage of the colonizers. To that extent, at least, *antropofagia* marked both a break with the past and an engagement with European modernist forms. In short, Brazilian cannibalism was a regenerative process, and not merely mimicry of a "foreign" culture – a feeble Brazilian homegrown version of Parisian anthropophagy, expressed in Francis Picabia's *Cannibale Dada*. (Bellei, 1998: 95)

Andrade's ideas were to move into the mainstream, displacing ideas of "purity" in a dynamic model of postmodern carnival and multicultural hybridization. As the Brazilian translator and critic Haroldo de Campos – undoubtedly the most important theorist of this postmodernist version of *antropofagia* – has remarked: "In Latin America as well as in Europe, writing will increasingly mean rewriting, digesting, masticating" (Bellei, 1998: 100). In de Campos's conception of the cannibalistic banquet, culture is a process of constant translation (Vieira, 1999). The cannibal-translator devours the source text in a ritual act that results in the incorporation of the "other" and engenders the hybrid. De Campos's metaphor of a creative cannibalism extends to his own literary output, which has consciously and playfully "fed" upon a European literary heritage. Thus, he entitles his translation of Goethe's *Faust*, *God and the Devil in Goethe's Faust*, echoing the title of the renowned Brazilian film by Glauber Rocha, *God and the Devil in the Land of the Sun* (Madureira, 1998). If the cannibal metaphor challenges both traditional hierarchies and the boundaries between source language and target language, it also has strong political implications, suggesting a resistance to any monocultural vision of the future. It represents an attempt to recover a heritage that has been suppressed by European colonizers as a "taboo". In effect, the "Manifesto" is a celebration of the Brazilian native character as it is expressed in traditional Brazilian folklore and a radical appropriation of the cannibal as the primitive "specimen" of European anthropology. As Richard Morse has observed, for Andrade "cannibalism recognized both the nutritive property of European culture and a transformative process of appropriation" (19).

## MIGRATION, TRANSLATION, TRANSCULTURATION

De Campos's vision of mutual ingestion as an emblem of "transculturation", a practice that aims at "thinking the national in its dialogical relationship with the universal", has implications for our understanding of a multicultural World. According to de Campos, for example, the ingestion of foreign discourses leads to a "playful and freely associative multiculturalism, an open, multilinguistic hybridization, a carnivalized transencyclopedia of the new barbarians where everything can coexist with everything else" (Bellei, 1998: 102). It is a vision not dissimilar to that articulated by Fredric Jameson when he writes in *Postmodernism, or, The Cultural Logic of Late Capitalism* of postmodernism as a force that "ceaselessly reshuffles the fragments of pre-existent texts, the building blocks of older cultural and social production, in some new and heightened bricolage: metabooks which cannibalize other books, metatexts which collate bits of other texts." (Jameson, 1991: 96)

This theoretical context provides a useful way of exploring concepts of a literary heritage in contemporary Europe, where the process of colonial emigration has been dramatically reversed and where it is no longer possible to consider "heritage" as a static and monolithic institution. Over the course of the last half-century, the writing of immigrants from former colonies to the European continent has had an increasingly powerful impact on European literature and culture. This is especially, though not exclusively, the situation of literatures written in English and French where many of the most-lauded writers are of Asian, African and Caribbean origin. In the binary of "strong" and "weak" cultures that polysystems theory proposes for translation, the situation of the migrant is ambivalent. While migrants may be a minority in the host culture, they are often perceived by the country of origin as holding a privileged position in the global literary system.

For example, the Moroccan immigrant Tahar Ben Jelloun is sometimes accused of catering to French audiences for writing in French; he contends, however (using translation metaphors of fidelity), that he is unfaithful to both his wife and mistress, Arabic and French. In *French Hospitality* he explores the French reception to foreigners by bringing together nostalgia for North African traditions of hospitality with philosophical concepts of hospitality borrowed from the works of Emmanuel Levinas and Derrida (Jelloun, 1999). If the insider – outsider division is problematic as "self"and "other" collude in the construction of culture, this is exacerbated in the case of the French Antilles, which are inside Europe politically but outside it geographically. The Antillean writer Edouard Glissant demonstrates how translation is not merely a theoretical issue in the Caribbean, but part of Caribbean language and cultural practices. In *Caribbean Discourse* he points out that in Martinique he has observed more than a dozen Creole translations of the French bumper sticker "ne roulez pas trop près", revealing a cultural instinct to constantly defer and differ through translation. He comments that the car owners exhibit an "inability to settle a common way of writing; subversion of the original meaning; opposition to an order originating elsewhere" (Glissant, 1989), if there is such a place. In the exploration of the inter-space between Creole and French there is no *retour*, only *detour*, and Creole identity is embedded in a "*poétique de relation*" (cross-cultural poetics) rather than in roots. For the migrant, the boundaries between the home and the foreign have always been blurred. If in translation theory the "self" is the target or home culture and the source is the "other" or foreign culture, this easy binary becomes problematic with the migrant translator caught in-between.

The writer Salman Rushdie, born in Bombay in 1947, explores many of these ideas in his writings, and particularly the fraught question of "heritage" in a world characterized by violent displacements. In the title essay of his volume *Imaginary Homelands* (1991), for example, Rushdie's point of departure is the opening sentence of L.P. Hartley's *The Go-Between*: "The past is a foreign country – they do things differently there". As he looks at a photograph of his family house in Bombay, taken in 1946, he suggests that Hartley's formulation might be inverted, since the present feels foreign and as he looks at the picture, the past is experienced as a reality. Rushdie elaborates this sensation in his description of an actual visit to the house after an absence of more than half his life and the mental effort involved in trying to piece together shards of memory, like the fragments of ancient pots out of which the past can sometimes, but always provisionally, be reconstructed.

Rushdie's metaphor, here, is strikingly similar to Walter Benjamin's image of the amphora as a metaphor for translation, and it was precisely at this moment, he maintains, that his novel *Midnight's Children* (1981) was really born. While conceding that the past is a country from which we have all migrated, Rushdie suggests that the experience of this uprooting or loss is intensified in the migrant who is distant in space as well as time, out-of-country and even out-of-language. From his inversion of the idea that the past is a foreign country to the idea that the past is home, Rushdie extends the notion of geographical migration to translation and thus reverses the usual paradigm of the English translation tradition where the target language is "self" (or the domestic tradition) and the source is the "other". What eventually becomes evident in Rushdie's writing is that though he may begin with notions of the home and the foreign, "self"and "other", the binary logic collapses and the diasporic self becomes a hybrid encoded in modes of translation. In his essay "Errata", Rushdie explains and justifies deliberate errors of fact in his personal redefinition of Indian history. His subject, he declares, is not some Proustian search for lost time, but rather his interest is in "the way in which we remake the past to suit our present purposes, using memory as our tool" (Rushdie, 1991: 24). This is a theme to which Rushdie constantly returns. In an interview with Una Chaudhuri he has remarked: "The texture of the narrative is such that it almost depends upon being an error about history; otherwise it wouldn't be an accurate piece of memory, because that's what narrative is, it's something remembered" (Rushdie, 1990).

Although the migrant loses language and home he is not simply transformed by his act, but he also transforms his new world. It is out of this hybridization that newness can emerge[4]. Migrant writers, Rushdie claims in a memorable phrase, are "translated men", who (as the etymology of the word "translated" suggests) have been "borne across". For Rushdie, the English language and the migrants' ambiguity towards it, reflect an internal struggle within each of us between the different cultures that make up our composite "multicultural" heritage and give us our identities. While calling himself a "translated man", Rushdie insists on his agency in the translation. He is not simply "lost in translation". In the novel *Shame* (1983), he names one of his characters Omar Khayyam, after the author of the *Rubaiyat* translated by Edward Fitzgerald in 1859 and states: "I cling to the notion – and use, in evidence, the success of [Fitzgerald Khayyam] – that (in translation) something can also be gained" (Rushdie, 1983: 29). Like Benjamin,

---

4. This phrase from Rushdie inspires the title of Homi K. Bhabha's chapter 'How Newness Enters the World: Postmodern Space, Post colonial Times and the Trials of Cultural Translations,' *The Location of Culture*. Ed., Homi K. Bhabha (London and New York, 1994), pp. 212–35.

Rushdie suggests that any translation is inevitably provisional, since it is an expression of the historian's subjective desires. And in this context, we may recall Benjamin's statement that "to articulate the past historically does not mean to recognize it the way it really was… it means to seize hold of a memory as it flashes up at a moment of danger" (Benjamin, 1973: 255). In *Shame* the Benjaminian concern with the historical grasp of the past is however specifically related to the condition of the migrant subject: "I too like all migrants am a fantasist, I build imaginary countries and try to impose them on the ones that exist. I too, face the problem of history, of what to retain, what to dump, how to hold on to what memory insists on relinquishing, how to deal with change" (Rushdie, 1983: 87–88). This is surely an eloquent exposition of the problems faced by the "migrant" who is caught on the borderline of different cultures and struggles to create an adaptive system to accommodate them. The migrant remembers the heritage of his lost homeland in an act of imaginative reconstruction, even while he struggles to accommodate the heritage of the "host" country to which he has been displaced.

As we have seen, for Rushdie the construction and reconstruction of heritage are always acts of translation. And because of his marginal position, the migrant is doubly suspect. He wears the foreign robe of translation – a *traditore* that has overwhelmed a tradition. A voice in *Shame* tells the narrator: "Outsider! Trespasser! You have no right to this subject! Poacher! Pirate! We reject your authority. We know you with your foreign language wrapped around you like a flag: speaking about us in your forked tongue, what can you tell us but lies?" To which he replies with more questions: "Is history to be considered the property of the participants solely? In what courts are such claims staked, what commissions map out the territories?" (Rushdie, 28)

The critic Sara Suleri has argued in her discussion of *The Satanic Verses* (1989) that the novel embodies a poetics of relocation for the deracinated subject and that cultural leave-taking and homecoming in the work are mutually inter-changeable. Though Rushdie has been accused of traducing Islam, his blasphemy is not literal. Rather, the novel strives to mediate between the questions "what historical kind am I?" and "what kind of idea is Islamic culture?" (Suleri, 1992: 192) As such, the book does not replicate a tired binary opposition between Europe and its "other", but attempts to bring differences together in a complex process of reciprocal translation. Indeed, the preoccupation with cultural diversity is a major concern in Rushdie's *The Moor's Last Sigh* (1995). In this work, the Moor's beliefs and cultural heritage – indeed, his linguistic identity – come into contact and open conflict with a host of other contending beliefs and heritages, reflected in the novel's different characters. The challenge, Rushdie suggests, lies in creating a cultural system flexible enough to accommodate multiple cultural values and heritages.

## CONCLUSION

I have argued in this article for translation as a useful model for elucidating intercultural relations during a period characterized by profound economic, social and political upheavals. The focus has been on the ways in which "traditional" conceptions of translation, construed as a one-way process wherein a "foreign" source language is domesticated by the target language, has given way to a realization of translation as a dynamic and ongoing reciprocal process. With developments in critical and cultural theory in the last two decades, ethnography has also become increasingly aware that it is a cross-cultural practice. In a "new", multicultural Europe, I have sought to show how writers have been creatively translating between heritages to create new and stimulating works of literature.

I would like to conclude with a brief discussion of Wilson Harris's novel *Jonestown*, a work that explores the linkages between translation and the metamorphoses of the subject after violent displacement. In *Jonestown*, the protagonist, Francisco, writes a dream-book after experiencing his own death in the Jonestown holocaust. Echoing Benjamin's notion of "pure language", the hero seeks release from his suffering in a disconcerting dream where "unspoken prayer matches hidden texts." But what are these elusive "texts" or rather subtexts, which Francisco attempts to uncover? Harris intimates that they are emblems of the hero's fractured self, the sign of difference inscribed within language, the ungraspable and irreducible "other". "Dream-books", he writes, "are translations of the untranslatable" (Harris, 1996: 100). Harris reminds us here that our condition is always in some sense "split" since, as Montaigne observes in his essay on cannibals, "there is as much difference between us and ourselves as between us and others (Budick, 20)." Translation always involves, to some extent at least, "a crisis of alterity" (Budick, 22). In his dream-book, on his return from the future (his own death), Francisco has a vision of a goddess, whose oracular voice tells him that the act of translation is a "necessity" and a "debt", "if the past is to yield a kinship with futurity". As she proclaims: "I speak as Carnival oracle, Francisco. Not Delphic oracle! Carnival oracle [...] Oracles are steeped in hidden texts that may scarcely be translated. But still translations in your own tongue (let me say), orchestrated fabrics imbued with music – are necessary. Again such translations are the price you must pay, Francisco, to see the Dead alive after knowing them Dead" (Harris, 1996: 100). Here, Harris reclaims the carnivalesque meaning for the oracle as if to suggest that the translation of many partial truths whose masks are spectres of emergent social faces. In translation we return to a past that is always a different place with different ruins that reveal and conceal eclipsed communities piled up in the residues and legacies of former experiences. Spectres are fragmented into multiple actors whose articulation as emergent subjects is specific to historical and cultural conditions. In short, Francisco's dream-book provides a form of agency for the initiation of a new life after death, which is nothing less than the dream of translation. For Harris, heritage would be, to use his own term, an unfinished genesis of the imagination.

And in the early twenty-first century, as questions of migration and globalization come to the fore, it is a particularly pertinent insight. Indeed, the movement of meaning that inheres in the performance of translation has intensified in an age of globalization. While transculturation may have been a thorn in the side of the nation state and nationalism, in an age of global and trans-national economy and politics, one has to ask of which State or state. Recent scholarship often claims the distinction between globality and worldliness (as implied in Heidegger's idea of the worlding), reclaiming for the latter the world making function in human experience and intentionality, historical contingency, and the relentless sensuality of nature. In contrast to the inexorable movement of capital, it is worth returning to the attempts of artists and intellectuals to achieve autonomy through transculturation. If the term is often appropriated by the globalization process, we must reclaim it for the world and the worldly text, and here translation both as metaphor and practice plays a central role.

## Works Cited

Barthes, Roland. "Authors and Writers." *A Barthes Reader*. Ed. Susan Sontag. Trans. R. Howard. London: Random House Group, 1993. 185–210.

Bassnett, Susan. *Translation Studies*. London: Routledge, 1991.

Bellei, Sérgio Luiz Prado. "Brazilian Anthropology Revisited." *Cannibalism and the Colonial World*. Ed. F. Barker, P. Hulme and M. Iversen. Cambridge: Cambridge University Press, 1998. 87–109.

Benjamin, Walter. "The Task of the Translator: An Introduction to Baudelaire's *Tableaux Parisiens*." *Illuminations*. Ed. Hannah Arendt. Trans. Harry Zohn. London: Fontana Press, 1973. 69–82.

———. "Theses on the Philosophy of History." *Illuminations*. Ed. Hannah Arendt. Trans. Harry Zohn. London: Fontana Press, 1973. 253–264.

———. *The Origin of German Tragic Drama*. Trans. John Osborne. London: Verso, 2003.

Bhabha, Homi K. "Dissemination: Time, Narrative, and the Margins of the Modern Nation." *Nation and Narration*. Ed. Homi K. Bhabha. London: Routledge, 1990. 291–322.

Borges, Jorge Luis. *Obras Completas I-IV*. Buenos Aires: Emecé Editores, 1996–97.

———. "The Translators of *The Thousand and One Nights*." *Selected Non-Fiction*. Ed. E. Weinberger. Trans. E. Allen, S.J. Levine and E. Weinberger. New York: Penguin Putnam, 1999. 92–109.

———. "On William Beckford's *Vathek*." *Selected Non-Fiction*. Ed. E. Weinberger. Trans. E. Allen, S.J. Levine and E. Weinberger. New York: Penguin Putnam, 1999. 236–239.

Budick, Sanford. "Crises of Alterity: Cultural Untranslatability and the Experience of Secondary Otherness." *The Translatability of Cultures: Figurations of Space Between*. Ed. Sanford Budick and Wolfgang Iser. Standford: Stanford University Press, 1996. 1–22.

Clifford, James. *The Predicament of Culture: Twentieth-Century Ethnography, Literature, and Art.* Cambridge, MA: Harvard University Press, 1988.

———. "The Translation of Cultures: Maurice Leenhardt's Evangelism, New Caledonia 1902–1926." *Contemporary Literary Criticism: Literary and Cultural Studies.* Ed. R.C. Davis and R. Schleifer. New York: Longman, 1994. 626–641.

———. *Routes: Travel and Translation in the Late Twentieth Century.* Cambridge, MA: Harvard University Press, 1997.

Derrida, Jacques. "Des Tours de Babel." *Difference in Translation.* Ed. and Trans. J.F. Graham. Ithaca, New York: Cornell University Press, 1985. 165–207.

———. "What is a "Relevant" Translation?" Trans. Lawrence Venuti. *Critical Inquiry* 27.2 (Winter 2001):174–200.

Even-Zohar, Itamar and Gideon Toury, ed. *Translation Theory and Intercultural Relations.* Tel Aviv: The Porter Institute of Poetics and Semiotics, Tel Aviv University, 1981.

Folena, Gianfranco. "Volgarizzare e Tradurre." *La Traduzione: Saggi e Studi.* Ed. G. Petronio. Trieste: Lint, 1973. 57–120.

Foucault, Michel. "What is an Author?" *Textual Strategies: Perspectives in Post-Structuralist Criticism.* Ed. Josué V. Harari. Ithaca: Cornell University Press, 1979. 141–160.

Glissant, Edouard. *Caribbean Discourse: Selected Essays.* Ed. and Trans. J.M. Dash. Charlotteseville: University Press of Virginia, 1989.

Harris, Wilson. *Jonestown.* London. Faber and Faber, 1996.

Hartley, L.P. *The Go-Between.* London: Hamish Hamilton, 1953.

Hughes, Ted. *Tales from Ovid: Twenty-Four Passages from the Metamorphoses.* London: Faber and Faber, 1997.

Iser, Wolfgang. "Coda to the Discussion." *The Translatability of Cultures: Figurations of the Space Between.* Ed. Sanford Budick and Wolfgang Iser. Standford: Stanford University Press, 1996. 294–303.

Jameson, Fredric. *Postmodernism, or, the Cultural Logic of Late Capitalism.* Durham: Duke University Press, 1991.

Jelloun, Tahar Ben. *French Hospitality: Racism and North African Immigrants.* Trans. B. Bray. New York: Columbia University Press, 1999.

Lévi-Strauss, Claude. *The Scope of Anthropology.* Trans. S.O. Paul and R.A. Paul. London: Jonathan Cape, 1967.

Lowenthal, David. *The Past is a Foreign Country.* Cambridge: Cambridge University Press, 1985.

Madureira, Luis. "Lapses in Taste: 'Cannibal-Tropicalist' Cinema and the Brazilian Aesthetic of Underdevelopment." *Cannibalism and the Colonial World.* Ed. F. Baker, P. Hulme and M. Iversen. Cambridge: Cambridge University Press, 1998. 110–125.

Morse, Richard M. "The Multiverse of Latin American Identity, c.1820 – c.1970." *The Cambridge History of Latin America: Volume X: Latin America Since 1930: Ideas, Culture and Society.* Ed. L. Bethell. Cambridge: Cambridge University Press, 1995. 1–128.

Ortiz, Fernando. *Cuban Counterpoint: Tobacco and Sugar.* Trans. Harriet de Onís. Durham: Duke University Press, 1995.

Robins, Kevin. "Tradition and Translation: National Culture in its Global Context." *Representing the Nation: A Reader – Histories, Heritage and Museums.* Ed. D. Boswell and J. Evans. London and New York: Routledge, 1999. 15–32.

Rushdie, Salman. *Shame.* London: Jonathan Cape, 1983.

———. "Imaginative Maps." *Interview with Una Chaudhuri. Turstile* 2.1 (1990):36–47.

———. *Imaginary Homelands: Essays and Criticism, 1981–1991.* London: Granta Books, 1991.

Steiner, George. *After Babel: Aspects of Language and Translation.* London and New York: Oxford University Press, 1975.

Stephanides, Stephanos and Karna Singh, ed. *Translating Kali's Feast: The Goddess in Indo-Caribbean Ritual and Fiction.* Amsterdam and Atlanta: Rodopi, 2000.

Suleri, Sara. *The Rhetoric of English India.* Chicago: University of Chicago Press, 1992.

Toury, Gideon, ed. *Translation across Cultures.* New Delhi: Bahri, 1987.

Venuti, Lawrence. "Translation as Cultural Politics: Regimes of Domestication in English." *Textual Practice* 7.2 (1993):208–223.

———. *The Translator's Invisibility: A History of Translation*. London and New York: Routledge, 1995.

Vieira, Else Ribeiro Pires. "Liberating Calibans: Readings of *Antropofagia* and Haroldo de Campos' Poetics of Transcreation." *Post-colonial Translation: Theory and Practice*. Ed. S. Bassnett and H. Trivedi. London and New York: Routledge, 1999. 95–113.

# 2

# Beyond Words: Translation as a Trope in Philosophical Discourse

*Sachin Ketkar*

> "What does philosophy say? What does the philosopher say when he is a philosopher? He says: What matters is truth or meaning, and since meaning is before or beyond language, it follows that it is translatable. Meaning has the commanding role, and consequently one must be able to fix its univocality or, in any case master its plurivocality. If this plurivocality can be mastered, then translation, understood as the transport of a semantic content into another signifying form, is possible. There is no philosophy unless translation in this latter sense is possible. Therefore the thesis of philosophy is translatability in this common sense, that is, as the transfer of a meaning or a truth from one language to another without any essential harm being done....The origin of philosophy is translation or the thesis of translatability, so that whenever translation in this sense has failed, it is nothing less than philosophy that finds itself defeated." (Derrida, 1985: 120)

## TRANSLATION AND PHILOSOPHY

When Derrida writes, "the theme of a transcendental signified was constituted within the horizon of an absolutely pure, transparent and unequivocal translatability" (Quoted in Bass, 1978: xvi–xvii), we realize that his notion of translation is no longer the one which is "commonly understood". In fact, Derrida's philosophy questions the very possibility of delimiting any notion or concept to the domain that traditionally claims it – philosophy, literary studies, or "popular belief". For Derrida, translation as a notion is tied up not only to the areas conventionally dealing with translation such as translation studies, translation theory, linguistics or literary studies but is inseparable from the very structure of the Western thought that produces the disciplines mentioned above as well as discourses like metaphysics, religion, politics and aesthetics. Translation no longer remains a notion. It rather becomes a trope that is at once central and marginal in philosophical discourses, a philosophical trope, a metaphor, for the very act of human communication and understanding. On the other hand, when one considers the ideational topography of the discipline of Translation Studies, such as the one given by Susan Bassnett (1980: 7–8), in which this wide field has been divided into four general overlapping areas of interest: history of translation, translation and TL culture, translation and linguistics and lastly translation and poetics, we find that the deliberations such as those offered by Derrida cannot be easily accommodated in these schemas. Thus, any similar deliberation that deals with epistemological and ontological questions raised by the activity of translation and operates at a level of generalization and abstractness of philosophy will have to be put, rather uneasily, into the category of translation and philosophy. Then it will be convenient to address the questions of hermeneutics, cognitive sciences, or metaphysics raised by translation. In this article, I intend to discuss very briefly some of the philosophical statements on translation by major Western thinkers and in addition, also consider the idea of translation in the context of major Indian philosophies like Brahmanism and Buddhism and propose that "translation" in the philosophical schemas ought to be studied separately in translation studies.

## WESTERN PHILOSOPHY OF TRANSLATION

The word "translation" has a Latin etymology which means, "Carrying from one place to another". The etymological meaning is almost the same as that of the term "metaphor". In medieval Christianity, the word translation implied transfer of relics or remains of a saint from one place to another (Asad, 1995: 325). Yet translation has always got bad press in the mainstream Western philosophy. Even a seminal thinker like Heidegger (1971: 23) complains that the rootlessness of the Western thought begins with the translation of Greek philosophical terms into Latin. He notes that the process of translating Greek terms into Latin was by no means innocent. He says, "beneath the seemingly literal and thus faithful translation there is concealed, rather a *trans*lation of Greek experience into a different way of thinking. Roman thought takes over the Greek words without a corresponding, equally authentic experience of what they say, without the Greek word. The rootlessness of Western thought begins with this translation" (23). The lament is commonplace. The translation is by nature inauthentic in the Western worldview. The term "translation" itself becomes a trope for something secondary, derivative and so almost derogatory. Robert Frost's much-quoted quotable quote that poetry is what is lost in translation has become a sort of truism. The ancient Italian pun *traduttore, traditore* ("translator, traitor") is the best evidence about the Western attitude to translation. However, many philosophers have given it the importance it deserves in the philosophical thinking.

George Steiner in his seminal treatise *After Babel* discusses the historiography of translation and notes that the period between the essay by Schleiermacher in 1813 and the essay by Valery Larbaud in 1946 is the period "of theory and hermeneutic inquiry. The question of the nature of translation is posed within the more general framework of theories of language and mind .... it gives the subject of translation a frankly philosophical aspect" (1975: 237). He remarks that the significant essay by Walter Benjamin in 1923 "caused a reversion to hermeneutic, almost metaphysical inquiries into translation and interpretation". In fact, Steiner himself believes that translation is involved whenever the act of understanding takes place and it does not just take place between two cultures or languages but between classes, genders, and age groups, in short, between any two human beings. Moreover, along with thinkers like Derrida and others discussed in this paper, Steiner's major contribution was in this category of thinking about translation.

Walter Benjamin's "The Task of the Translator" written in 1923 is one of the most significant statements in the philosophy of translation. It is the essential statement in the Universalist, liberal-humanist tradition. Considering the plurality and heterogeneity of human languages in the post-Babelian world, Benjamin believes that translation "ultimately serves the purpose of expressing the central reciprocal relationship between languages. It cannot possibly reveal or establish this relationship itself, but it can represent it by realizing it in embryonic or intensive form" (72). Benjamin is trying to hypothesize the notion of a "pure language" of humanity, which includes all exclusive and different languages. There is a distinct influence of the Kabbalistic mysticism on Benjamin's thought, Steiner notes as Benjamin believes, in the holy language in which all languages unite at some messianic moment (Steiner, 1975: 62–64). As all the languages for him are incomplete in themselves, translation "in a singularly impressive manner it at least points the way to this region: the predestined, hitherto inaccessible realm of reconciliation and fulfillment of languages" (1968: 75). He becomes more philosophical while distinguishing between the original work and the translation, quoted below is one of his more "lofty" passages:

> The intention of the poet is spontaneous, primary, graphic; that of the translator is derivative, ultimate, ideational. For the great motif of integrating many tongues into one true language is at work. The language is one in which the independent sentences, works of literature, critical judgements, will never communicate – for they remain dependent on translation; but in it the languages themselves, supplemented and reconciled in their mode of signification, harmonize. If there is such a thing as a language of truth, the tensionless and even silent depository of the ultimate truth which all thought strives for, then this language of truth—is the true language. And this very language whose divination and description is the only perfection a philosopher can hope for, is concealed in concentrated fashion in translations. (76–77)

For Benjamin the original work remains within the specificity of a single isolated language organically, while translation forays into the realm of the universal monolithic language of man, which is also the language of truth. He quotes Mallarmé who said that as "the supreme language is lacking" if one were to remove the plurality of idioms on earth, one would materialize the truth. Translation becomes a trope for the crossing of limitations of single languages, which in themselves are incomplete.

This perspective is characteristic of what Steiner has categorized as the Universalist-humanist stand. Commenting on this stand Steiner remarks,

> The one (perspective) declares that the underlying structure of language is universal and common to all men. Dissimilarities

> between human tongues are essentially of the surface: Translation is realizable precisely because of these deep-seated universals, genetic, historical, social, from which all grammars derive can be located and recognized as operative in every human idiom, however singular or bizarre its superficial forms... Here the universalist position touches closely on the mystical intuition of a lost primal or paradigmatic speech. (76–77)

The opposing view to the Universalist position would be the relativist position, which Steiner terms as the "monadist" view. "It holds that universal deep structures are either fathomless to logical and psychological investigation or of an order so abstract, so generalized as to be well-nigh trivial... The extreme monadist position – we shall find great poets holding it – leads logically to the belief that real translation is impossible" (77). The Sapir-Whorf hypothesis in language and cognitive sciences of course is a good example of this perspective. It holds that the "real world" is largely unconsciously built up on the language habits of the groups or the community speaking that language. The people belonging to various language communities live in a different world. Chomskyan view on the other hand puts emphasis on the universal deep structures underlying all languages and is distinctly Universalist. G.M. Hyde offers an insightful critique of the notorious Sapir-Whorf hypothesis by pointing out that one does not have to be "a Chomskyan to see that all languages have built into them devices for circumventing their own limitations. On one view, literature itself is made up of a massive body of these devices, designed to institutionalize just these processes of circumvention" (1993: 7). This debate is central to cognitivist approach to the phenomenon of translation.

Octavio Paz (1992) believes that poetry is universal and communicates to the whole humanity, but unlike Benjamin, he points out, "while translation overcomes the differences between one language and another, it also reveals them more fully. Thanks to translation, we become aware that our neighbors do not speak and think as we do" (154). Paz is not worried by the fact that there is no single monolithic language of humanity of Pre-Babelian times, he values differences and considers them enriching. Although a Universalist, he does not want to straightjacket the human being. Universalism, in Paz's thought, does not deny the richness of plurality.

In contrast, the famous philosopher José Ortega y Gasset believes that translation is a utopian act, but then all tasks which a human being undertakes are utopian for, "The destiny of Man – his privilege and honor – is never to achieve what he proposes, and to remain merely an intention, a living utopia" (94). He then makes a distinction between a good utopian and a bad utopian. While the former thinks that because it would be desirable to free men from the divisions imposed by language, there is little probability that it can be attained; therefore it can only be achieved to an approximate measure, while the bad utopian thinks that because it is desirable, it is possible. All utopian acts of a good utopian are toward betterment and progress. Gasset interestingly suggests that it would be a great anguish if one were condemned to do only those activities that are deemed possible of achievement. Translation for Gasset is impossible and necessary (1992: 92–112).

## TRANSLATION IN DERRIDEAN DECONSTRUCTIVE PHILOSOPHY

Going back to Derridean philosophy, as it seems to be a critique of both the positions, translation seems to assume a crucial role. Derrida's philosophy is the philosophy of language, which analyzes the language of philosophy in a strategic way. In one of his interviews he remarks, "We are all translators, mediators" (1995: 1). His philosophy offers a critique of the notion of sign as divided into the signifier and the signified. The signified is believed to be something outside of language or the system of signification but actually, it is a part of the system because what we call signified is yet another signifier. It is the metaphysical desire for a transcendental signified or the concept independent of language, present without the need of mediating signifier, that creates the division between the signifier and the signified in the history of Western thought. This metaphysics creates desire for transcendental signified which acts as a sort of anchor, centre or ground outside of system or structure supposedly giving it coherence and unity which cannot be coherence or unity if this centre is transcendental and outside of the structure. Translation is tied up to the very notion of sign, which is a product of Western metaphysics. Derrida comments, "In the limits to which it is possible, or at least appears possible, translation practices the difference between signified and signifier. But if this difference is never pure, no more so is translation, and for the notion of translation we would have to substitute a notion of transformation: a regulated transformation of one language by another, of one text by another. We will never have, and in fact have never had, to do with some "transport" of pure signifieds from one language to another, or within one and the same language, that the signifying instrument would leave virgin and untouched" (1981: 20). Translation is founded on a myth that one can separate word/s from their "meaning", or can substitute other word/s from the same or some other language, and yet keep the "meaning" intact. This belief that the "meaning" can remain intact and unchanged if the 'word/s' are changed gives rise not only to the notion of translation but also to the notion of "transcendental signified". It presupposes the notion of unproblematic "translation" within the language itself as if pure synonymy exists within the language itself. Derrida reads the story of Babel and it "does not merely figure the irreducible multiplicity of tongues; it exhibits an incompletion, the impossibility of finishing, of totalizing, of saturating, of completing something on the order of edification, architectural construction, system and architectonics. What the multiplicity of idioms actually limits is not only a "true" translation, a transparent and adequate interexpression, it is also a structural order, a coherence of construct. There is then (let us translate) something like an internal limit to formalization, an incompleteness of the constructure" (1992: 208). For Derrida, the structure of difference between languages and within the language actually limits not just the possibility of translation, it also resists a systematic and coherent fabrication of any philosophical construct or system. In Derridean philosophy, the allegory of Babel becomes an allegory of not just "necessity and impossibility" of translation, necessity as impossibility, but also an allegory of deconstruction of philosophical system in the process of edification due to "differences" within the language. It is necessary to translate because of differential plurality and heterogeneity of idioms and languages and it is impossible to translate because of the same reason. As in most cases, in the Derridean approach, the reading of an allegory becomes the allegory of reading and interpretation itself.

In Derrida's philosophy, the idea of "origin" also becomes problematic as no "word" or sign in order to be a word or sign can be used once and for all or for the "first time". Signification in order to be significant has to be iterated and can never be for the first time. Hence, the loss of "origin" is a condition for signification. Thus no text can be original and what is "original" cannot be significant or text. The text is already an *anuvad* in its etymological sense, a repetition with a difference. It is already a translation. Octavio Paz in his essay echoes this perspective when he says, "Each text is unique, yet at the same time it is the translation of another text. No text can be completely original because language itself, in its very essence, is already a translation – first from the nonverbal world, and then, because each sign and each phrase is a translation of another sign, another phrase. However, the inverse of this relationship is also entirely valid. All texts are originals because each translation has its own distinctive character. Up to a point, each translation is a creation and thus constitutes a unique text" (154). Hence, all writing has to be rewriting in order to be writing, in order to have significance. Hence Lefevere's category of "rewriting" reserved for translation, criticism and so on is already problematic as it is again functioning within the same metaphysical Platonic distinction between the "original" versus "imitation"/"copy" which it seeks to overcome (1988). The same can be said about his category of "refraction", which assumes the existence of "non-refracted", pure, non-deviant writing.

Besides, Derrida reads political significance behind the desire for a single language of man, unique, homogenous, and undifferentiated – the desire that led people to construct the tower of Babel. This for Derrida is a desire "to bring the world to reason, and this reason can signify simultaneously a colonial violence (since they would thus universalize their idiom) and a peaceful transparency of the human community. Inversely, when God imposes and opposes his name, he ruptures the rational transparency but interrupts also the colonial violence or the linguistic imperialism" (1992: 226). He seems to be responding to George Steiner's query regarding the reason behind the existence of an immense plurality and heterogeneity of languages and his question whether such a plurality has a function in Darwinian scheme of evolution (Steiner, 54–55).

Towards the "end" of his commentary on the Babel allegory, Derrida in his distinctive style defends translation by arguing that paradoxically even to understand that translation is impossible, one would have to use "understanding" which in itself is an act of translation.Whatever reasons one may have for disagreeing with Derrida, it is a fact that the metaphysical underpinnings of culture affect the way translation is conceived, produced, and received. The Christian Platonic metaphysics attributes a secondary status to translation as it is a "copy" and not "original" and that it is because of post-Babelian condition that the Babel is seen as the other Fall (59).

## INDIAN PHILOSOPHY OF TRANSLATION: BRAHMANISM AND BUDDHISM

This is quite similar to the Indian *brahmanical* metaphysics, which is about essentialist, monistic, transcendental, unchanging, original and absolute nature of reality. It sees all change as illusionary and superficial *Maya*. The concept of rebirth is pervasive and crucial to the Hindu worldview and many people who reflect on translation have used this notion as a metaphor for translation. However, the application of this metaphor for translation can again be viewed from two contrasting perspectives in the Indian metaphysical thought. The first dominant view, which is also the brahminical view, holds that there is an inner eternal and transcendental essence, which remains unchanged, and rebirth is merely a change of outward appearance. The famous *shloka* of the *Srimad Bhagvad Gita*, one of the most important religious Hindu texts says "Even as a man casts off worn-out clothes, and puts on others which are new, so the embodied casts off worn-out bodies, and enters into others which are new" (Swami Swarupananda, 1909: 2.22). This notion of eternal and transcendental essence is comparable to what Derrida terms as "transcendental signified" of Western metaphysics which remains the "same" in spite of the change in material signifiers. It sees all transformation, including translation as illusion and deception of senses. In contrast to the Brahminical ideology, the Buddhist metaphysics, which also believes in rebirth, sees reality as immanent and in a state of constant Heraclitian flux and devoid of all essences and origins. In the Buddhist philosophy, *Anaatma* or non-self is truth and the selfhood is not organic awareness, it is divisible and heterogeneous. Reality is constantly being transformed. Transformation and change is the fundamental nature of existence. Best example of this view is found in the famous Debate of the King Milinda (Bhikkhu Pesala, 2001). The Buddhist metaphysics holds that in spite of absence of eternal transcendental self there is the cycle of birth and rebirth. Many, including the famous King Meander, a Bactrian King who is also known as Milinda, have thought that this is actually contradictory. Nagsena, in the book Milinda Panho, clarifies this Buddhist notion of rebirth using another sparkling metaphor. The dialogue goes something like this:

The King asks, "He who is reborn, Nagasena, is he the same person or another?"

"Neither the same nor another." Nagasena replies.

"Give me an illustration."

"In the case of a pot of milk that turns first to curds, then to butter, then to ghee; it would not be right to say that the ghee, butter and curds were the same as the milk but they have come from that so neither would it be right to say that they are something else."

In short, transformation of one material ensemble into another is what takes place in the Buddhist thinking about rebirth. Thus from the Buddhist perspective, nothing is permanent and the world is constantly being transformed into something else. Hence, we are constantly being translated along with the whole world. No wonder the Buddhists could accept translated texts in far more positive spirit rather than *Brahmins* and their "language of the gods".

## CONCLUSION

The whole notion of translation thus is inseparable from the metaphysical worldview, which underpins various cultural discourses. The philosophers or the people who have reflected at more abstract and wide-ranging level of thinking, have often been fascinated by the idea of translation and have deployed it as a seminal trope in their rumination. We realize that translation can be fruitfully considered a subject of philosophical reflection. It can yield some invaluable insights into the epistemological and ontological consideration of human language and its relation to reality. It becomes a metaphor for very act of human communication and understanding. Translation is seen not just as an activity of "interpretation of verbal signs from one language by the verbal signs from another language" but being of the nature same as interpretation and enmeshed in the whole philosophical and metaphysical deliberations about interpretation and what Benjamin terms as the "afterlife" of the text. It is for these reasons; I believe that the contemporary translation studies should consider the complex relationship between translation and philosophical discourses more seriously and to relative extent, separately.

## WORKS CITED

Asad, Talal. "A Comment on Translation, Critique, and Subversion." *Between Languages and Cultures: Translation and Cross-Cultural Texts.* Ed. Anuradha Dingwaney and Carol Maier. Pittsburgh: University of Pittsburgh Press, 1995. 325–332.

Bassnett, Susan. *Translation Studies.* London and New York: Methuen, 1980.

Benjamin, Walter. "The Task of the Translator: An Introduction to the Translation of Baudelaire's *Tableaux Parisiens.*" *Illuminations: Essays and Reflections.* Ed. Hannah Arendt. Trans. H. Zohn. New York: Schocken Books, 1968. 69–82.

Derrida, Jacques. *Writing and Difference.* Trans. Alan Bass. London: Routledge and Kegan Paul, 1978.

______. *Positions.* Trans. Alan Bass. Chicago: The University of Chicago Press, 1981.

______. *The Ear of the Other: Otobiography, Transference, Translation.* Ed. Christie McDonald. Trans. Peggy Kamuf. New York: Schocken Books, 1985.

______. "*From* Des Tours de Babel." *Theories of Translation: An Anthology of Essays from Dryden to Derrida.* Ed. Rainer Schulte and John Biguenet. Chicago: The University of Chicago Press, 1992. 218–227.

______. *Points...: Interviews,* 1974–1994. Ed. Elizabeth Weber. Trans. Peggy Kamuf and Others. Stanford: Stanford University Press, 1995.

Dingwaney, Anuradha and Carol Maier, eds. *Between Languages and Cultures: Translation and Cross-Cultural Texts.* Delhi: Oxford University Press. 1996.

Gasset, José Ortega y. "The Misery and the Splendor of Translation." *Theories of Translation: An Anthology of Essays from Dryden to Derrida.* Ed. Rainer Schulte and John Biguenet. Chicago: The University of Chicago Press, 1992. 93–112.

Heidegger, Martin. *Poetry, Language, Thought.* Trans. Albert Hofstadter. San Francisco: Harper and Row Publishers, 1971.

Hiriyanna, M. *Outlines of Indian Philosophy.* London: George Allen and Unwin, 1951.

Hyde, G.M. "The Whorf-Sapir Hypothesis and the Translation Muddle." *Translation and Literature.* Vol. 2 (1993):3–16.

Lefevere, Andre. *Essays in Comparative Literature: A Systems Approach.* Calcutta: Papyrus, 1988.

Paz, Octavio. "Translation: Literature and Letters." *Theories of Translation: An Anthology of Essays from Dryden to Derrida.* Ed. Rainer Schulte and John Biguenet. Chicago: The University of Chicago Press, 1992. 152–162.

Pesala, Bhikkhu. Ed. *The Debate of King Milinda: An Abridgement of Milind Pañha.* Penang, Malasia: Inward Path, 2001.

Schulte, Rainer and John Biguenet, eds. *Theories of Translation: An Anthology of Essays from Dryden to Derrida.* Chicago: The University of Chicago Press, 1992.

Steiner, George. *After Babel: Aspects of Language and Translation.* London and New York: Oxford University Press, 1975.

Swarupananda, Swami. *Srimad Bhagvad Gita.* Almora: Swami Vireshwaranda Ashrama, 1909.

# 3

# The Task of the Postcolonial (-Subaltern) Translator

*Piyush Raval*

## "RELEVANCE" OF TRANSLATION

"How dare one speak of translation before you who, in your vigilant awareness of the immense stakes – and not only of the fate of literature – make this sublime and impossible task your desire, your anxiety, your travail, your knowledge and your knowing skill?" (Derrida, 2001: 174) Thus speaks Derrida in his essay "What is a 'Relevant' Translation?" (*Qu'este-ce qu-une traduction 'relevante'?*, 1998), inverting the term "relevant" to question how the single term "relevant" that can be witnessed simultaneously in German and English and in the process of Frenchification/enfranchisement, the term whose "use floats between several languages" (181) and whose source language is undecidable, can be ascribed to any one of the two languages and translated into the third. The word "relevant" that helps us look deeper into the essence of translation and find the task of the translator remains, like the term "translation", untranslatable, according to the law of nothing translatable, yet it is translatable, as per the law of everything translatable. The definition of the essence of translation is implicated in the definition of a "relevant" translation which makes us go back to the question of what translation is or what the best possible translation should be, and therefore, Derrida argues, the term "relevant" should be jettisoned. Derrida is critical here of the idea of relevance in translation (*traduction relevante*) because the most relevant translation is "that which presents itself as the transfer of an intact signified through the inconsequential vehicle of any signifier whatsoever..." (195) According to Lawrence Venuti (Venuti, 2003), Derrida demystifies this "mystification" involved in the idea of relevant translation, an inevitable mystification in translation that positions itself between "absolute relevance, the most appropriate, adequate, univocal transparency, and the most aberrant and opaque irrelevance" (Derrida, 2001:179). In addition to demystification, Derrida through his interpretation of Shakespeare's *Merchant of Venice* also points out the "enthnocentric violence" and the mystification of "enthnocentric violence" through language. The process of translation (or translation as conversion) as both Cicero and Derrida think it – in case of the Jew Shylock who translates the divine quality of mercy into human and loses his own Jewish identity – creates *aporia* of translating letter (word-for-word) or spirit behind the letter (sense-for-sense) and carrying it across cultures/languages. How can Portia's statement "Then must the Jew be merciful" be translated, without the traces that Christianity and racism have imprinted on the history of the practice of translation? The task of the translator is not only impossible but also inflexible for Derrida as it involves: (a) "an insolvent debtedness and an oath of fidelity to a given original" (183) without transaction, a guarantee of the survival of the body of the original in a translated body. (b) The economy – laws of property and quantity. "A relevant translation is a translation whose economy, in these two senses, is the best possible, the most appropriating and the most appropriate possible" (179). (c) An incalculable equivalence, alleged correspondence between the pound of flesh and money, between letter and sense, and (d) Conversion of letter into spirit. If translation, understood in the manner of Derrida, involves transaction, monolingualism and reduction of cultural differences, what is the "relevance" of pursuing Translation Studies in the Third World? What do we gain by translating and why should we translate when we sense loss? Whatever may be the theoretical geneaology of Derrida's critique of "relevance" in translation, the essay contributes to contemporary debates in postcolonial studies on translation and supports its engagement with mammoth social, cultural and political issues involved in the task of translation, understood rigidly and derided greatly by a few translation scholars in the postcolonial world. The present article seeks to present major theoretical definitions of translation and expostulations of the task of the translator, firstly, within the Judeo-Christian tradition, and secondly, outside the Judeo-Christian tradition within the postcolonial world with a special focus on India.

These definitions and expostulations will elucidate the multifarious ways in which translation has been theorized or understood and practiced in the postcolonial world and help draw the future trajectory of translation in the postcolonial world.

The word "translation" that in its Latin etymological origin (*translatus*, past participle of the verb *transferre*, "to carry across") consists "trans-" and "latus", meaning "to carry across", assumes spatial dimension of moving from one culture into another, not just a transportation of meaning from one language into another. Even Anthony Kwame Appiah argues that the *prima facie* thought of translation as an attempt "to find ways of saying in one language something that means the same as what has been said in another" (Appiah, 2004: 418) should be resisted and expanded to an understanding of culture. It is the double bind of translatability and untranslatability that haunts a translator in carrying the task of translation with absolute fidelity. Translation, views Octavio Paz, is the principal means we have of understanding the world we live in: "On the one hand, the world is presented to us as a collection of similarities; on the other as a growing heap of texts, each slightly different from the one that came before it: translations of translations of translations. Each text is unique, yet at the same time it is the translation of another text. No text can be completely original because language itself, in its very essence, is already a translation – first from the nonverbal world, and then, because each sign and each phrase is a translation of another sign, another phrase" (Paz, 1992: 154). We must translate in order to understand the incomprehensibility of the world that could be penetrated through our engagement with language. As Eaglestone expresses through the lens of Levinas, we are responsible for those whom we do not, cannot or could not understand and therefore we must translate. It is our insolvent debt and duty, both beautiful and terrifying that, says Derrida, we must take up the task of translation. Contrary to Portia who wishes to translate the Jewish discourse of mercy into the Christian discourse of justice, Derrida himself translates into French Portia's statement "When mercy seasons justice" as "quand le pardon relève la justice (ou le droit)", applying the French term "relève" used before for translating Hegel's dialectical concept of *Aufhebung* which allows him to retain "the double motif of the elevation and the replacement that preserves what it denies or destroys..." (Derrida, 2001: 196). Edward Said himself in "The Public Role of Writers and Intellectuals" perceives the role of the intellectual as translator of what gets forgotten in the contemporary world. We need translations and translators to voice the muteness of the subaltern, or the silenced other, to translate their pain into happiness. Or as Freudian psychoanalysts would take "(in)significant" things like dreams seriously, we must take the "(in)significant" activity of translation seriously since it is in its apparent "insignificance" that its significance lies. "I translate, therefore I am," states the diasporic writer Jhumpa Lahiri on the basis of her experiences of translating India. We can reiterate this by proclaiming, "We translate, therefore we are." Translation is perceived as probably the sole medium through which the destiny of language and literature can be seen.

## TRANSLATION AND THE TASK OF THE TRANSLATOR: JUDEO-CHRISTIAN TRADITION

Translation and the task of the translator, in the long history of Translation Studies in the West and in the postcolonial world, have been perceived variously by translation theorists, a broader understanding of which can help us further theorize the essence of translation and the task of the translator more accurately, keeping practical experiences of translation and "beautiful and terrifying responsibility" (174) of the translator in mind. The Biblical story of the Fall of Man and the Tower of Babel perceives translation as "touching without taking", impossibility of accumulating universal human experience and attaining, out of many names and languages, the single language of Eden and entering the gate of God – the incompatibility between the language of God and the language of Man. Benjamin defines translation as "afterlife"/"survival" and the task of the translator as rendering the interplay of diverse ways of signifying legible by revealing how meaning exceeds from its habitual construction every time a translator ascribes meaning to a word and who, during the task of translation, realizes the possibility of approximating original in the unfolding of new meanings. "The pure language that is banned in the foreign tongue – to redeem it in one's own … that is the task of the translator" (Quoted in Berman and Wood, 2005: 76). Similarly José Ortega y Gasset expresses that, in translation, "one tries to say in a language precisely what that language tends to silence" (Gasset, 1992: 57) but the task of translation also reveals "the mutual secrets that peoples and epochs keep to themselves and which contribute so much to their separation and hostility; in short an audacious integration of Humanity." (57)

Translation, Gideon Toury thinks, is "*communication in translated messages* within a certain cultural-linguistic system, with all relevant consequences for the decomposition of the source message, the establishment of the invariant, its transfer across the cultural-linguistic border and the recomposition of the target message" (Toury, 2000: 469) as it occurs in Patrick Creagh's translation of Antonio Tabucchi's *Sostiene Pėreira*. Translation has cultural significance and Toury pleads for directing translation activities into social and cultural arenas. In this respect, Lefevere's contribution to translation is seminal who regards culture rather than word or text as the operational unit of translation, and by challenging the idea of a pure text, postulates the idea of translation as a rewriting of an original text, a rewriting which has an ideology and a poetics and which manipulates literature to function in a given society in a given way. Translation as rewriting and manipulation shapes culture and literature by bringing new concepts, genres and devices. Mary Louise Pratt, by inventing the phrase "linguistics of contact" for the processes of "appropriation, penetration or co-optation of one group's language by another" (Pratt, 1987: 61), foregrounds the definition of translation as "a linguistic "zone of contact" between the foreign and translating cultures, but also within the latter" (Venuti, 2000: 477). Such "community"/"utopian linguistics" makes the functioning of language across social differentiation as the central principle and focuses on "modes and zones of contact between dominant and dominated groups, between persons of different and multiple identities, speakers of different languages" (Pratt, 1987:60) and on constitution of speakers relationally and in difference and their enactment of differences in language. However, the formulation of concepts such as target culture/ language and source culture/language in translation theories carries a utopian dream of a common understanding between foreign and domestic cultures, envisioning an imagined community living eternally in peace, as Lawrence Venuti thinks as the proper task of the translator. But such perceptions of translation and the task of the translator imply, as Paul de Man argues, "what Benjamin calls 'die Wehen des eigenen' – the suffering of what one thinks of as one's own – the suffering of the original language. We think we are at ease in our own language, we feel a cosiness, a familiarity, a shelter in the language we call our own, in which we think that we are not alienated. What the translation reveals is that this alienation is at its strongest in our relation to our own original language, that the original language within which we are engaged is disarticulated in a way which imposes upon us a particular alienation, a particular suffering" (de Man, 1986: 84). However one may attempt to domesticate the foreign, one's alienation in one's own language raises here the issue of the ethical and the ethics in translation, when translation is thought in relation to communities and the utopian dream of the translator. Translation becomes "metaphysics of comprehension", a taking of power and a reduction of otherness, argues Eaglestone, quoting Levinas who suspected language's translatability, and hence translation as a whole, a translator's reduction of otherness into sameness: "... we have ethical grounds to be even more suspicious of the idea of translation and the way it relates to communities: 'what I translate is upset by the way I translate'" (Eaglestone, 2005: 137). The past animosity, suppressed differences between languages and cultures come to the surface at the end of translation practice that make us return to the dogma of untranslatability and together with it the idea of the original, refuted by Fuentes as "a sickness", "the sickness of modernity". To what extent then, Jean-Luc Nancy's formulation of translation as a community, a single ontological order in which any assumption of a "sacred" original is eliminated, is adequate? The gaps between languages need to be recognized to make the project of translation go on, which will confront the translator more in attempting translations from European languages to non-European ones or vice versa. The feminist interventions in translation theory in 1980s have drawn our attention to the specific gendered uses of language, and feminists like Lori Chamberlain have defined the task of the translator as "to learn to listen to the "silent" discourse – of women, as translators – in order to better articulate the relationship between what has been coded as "authoritative" discourse and what is silenced in the fear of disruption or subversion" (Chamberlain, 2000: 326).

Since Translation Studies have become more interdisciplinary in making traffics with disciplines like Gender Studies, Comparative Studies and Corpus Linguistics, the late configuration of Translation Studies with Cultural Studies (Postcolonialism particularly) popularly known as Cultural Translation and the role of translation and the task of the translator, outside Judeo-Christian tradition and the monolingual cultures of Europe, in the Third World, especially India, as understood by postcolonial translation theorists, is enormously significant.

## THE TASK OF THE POSTCOLONIAL (-SUBALTERN) TRANSLATOR

Gayatri Spivak, working within the tradition of bhakti/devotional poetry and the Derridean deconstructive idea of translation as under erasure, considers translation as the most intimate act of reading, assigning more premium and responsibility to the reader, and identifies the task of the feminist translator in the Third World as to surrender herself to the linguistic rhetoricity of the original text and to consider language as a clue to the workings of gendered agency, the sort of politics of gendered translation that Third World women translators are supposed to be more cautious. Elaborating on the differences between translation of Derrida's *De la grammatologie* and of Mahasweta Devi's *Stanadayini*, Spivak as a woman and a woman translator feels intimacy with Devi and has no fear of being judged most accurately by the readers of what she has translated and what she thinks as a woman. The idea of translation as love and surrender in Spivak's translations of non-European texts like Farhad Mazhar's *Ashoumoyer Noteboi* ("Untimely Notebook") calls upon the ethical responsibility to preserve the trace of the other, the cultural and epistemological otherness at work in language, more pressingly.

Spivak's seminal essay "Can the Subaltern Speak?", as argued by J. Maggio, is pleading for translation of the everyday culture of the subaltern by understanding the political logic of the culture of the subaltern and thus "unsilencing" the unique muteness of the subaltern. Translation, for Spivak here, is a desire to understand/respect the subaltern, which can help overcome the inaccessibility of knowledge about the subaltern without being able to signify accurately the otherness of the Other. Translation of the everyday life of the subaltern, as the subaltern uses many codes of communication which necessarily should be understood for the task of translation both by the European and the native informant, mitigates against the hierarchy in forms of communication, the standard dominant Western discourse. In this task of subaltern translation, the Western intellectual must be sensitive to the imposition of his/her dominant mode of communication upon the subaltern, therefore the task of subaltern translation becoming utmost difficult. Translating the subaltern is a matter of listening and understanding; hence it foregrounds the dialectical relationship between the Western critic and the subaltern, each one engaged reciprocally in the constitution of the subjectivity of the other. Translation is an appropriate mode than "representation" to understand the subaltern. Translation of the subaltern as thought by Spivak in the manner of Benjamin, does not attempt to "re-present" (*dartelling*) the original nor "represent" (*vertreten*), neither equivalent to the original nor completely imaginative. This sort of translation is similar to Charles Taylor's notion of "interpretation" which is non-identical and creates a distance from the source, a space wherein the subaltern can speak. Thus Spivak, reading Marx from the prism of Derrida, concludes J. Maggio, avoids the Kantian loop of the active Western "speaker" and the dominant mode of democratic representation and translates the subaltern to understand him/her, as in the Bhaduri case, neither as *dartelling* nor as *vertreven*.

Translation is a linguistic, social, cultural, political, ethical and a sensual act. The current fusion of Cultural Studies and Translation, understood as Cultural Translation, by postcolonial translation theorists like Homi Bhabha and Gayatri Spivak, have redefined each discipline and extended the definition of translation as process and condition of human migrancy. As Gayatri Spivak reads J.M. Coetzee's *Foe*, Toni Morrison's *Beloved* and Wilson Harris' *Guyana Quartet* as "cultural translations", Bhabha himself, in *The Location of Culture*, theorizes diasporic literature by Salman Rushdie (who articulated "We are translated men"), Hanif Kureishi and Jhumpa Lahiri ("I translate, therefore I am") as examples of cultural translations and their authors as cultural translators: "If hybridity is heresy, then to blaspheme is to dream. To dream not of the past or present, nor the continuous; it is not the nostalgic dream of tradition present not the Utopian dream of modern progress; it is the dream of translation as "survival" as Derrida translated the "time" of Benjamin's concept of the afterlife of translation, as *sur-vivre*, the act of living on borderlines. Rushdie translates this into the migrant's dream of survival: an initiatory *interstices*; an empowering condition of hybridity; an emergence that turns "return" into reinscription or redescription; an iteration that is not belated, but ironic and insurgent. For the migrant's survival depends, as Rushdie put it, on discovering "how newness enters the world". The focus is not making the linkages through the unstable elements of literature and life – the dangerous tryst with the "untranslatable" – rather than arriving at ready-made names" (Bhabha, 1994: 226–227). The creative potentialities of the liminal space or the space of in-betweenness have been illuminated by Sujit Mukherjee and Rita Kothari by understanding translation and translator as occupying an in-between zone of depolarization. On her English translation of *Angaliyat* ("The Stepchild", 2003), a Dalit novel in Gujarati by Joseph Macwan, Kothari (Kothari, 2010) described the cardinal function of translation as "*parakaya*" and "*parasamaaj pravesh*". Such an understanding of translation and the task of the translator echoes the words of Bhabha: "To that end we should remember that it is the 'inter' – the cutting edge of translation and renegotiation, the *in-between* space – that carries the burden of the meaning of culture. It makes it possible to begin envisaging national anti-nationalist histories of the 'people'. And by exploring this Third Space, we may elude the politics of polarity and emerge as the others of ourselves" (Bhabha, 1994: 35–39). Translation in this sense becomes "new writing" as Sujit Mukherjee defines, "a creative writing" as Susan Bassnett thinks, "a transcreation" as Haroldo de Campos argues, or "rewriting" as André Lefevere understands.

The history of translation and its practice in India from Vedic times in rewritings and localizations of *kavyas*, *puranas*, *itihasa-puranas* to the contemporary postcolonial era in Indian English Literature, Indian Literatures in English Translation and other translatory practices are more in tune with this definition, translation as *anuvad* ("saying after"), suggesting a temporal movement, than the myth of Fall and the search for origin (or, *Ur-Sprache*) in perpetual exile. The poet and translator A.K. Ramanujan considers translator as "an artist on oath", one who is caught in his double allegiance to text as its reader and as its new writer, caught between self-reflection and risk of representation, mirrors and windows, the original and the unborn, theory and praxis: "A translation has to be true to the translator no less than to the originals. He cannot jump off his own shadow. Translation is choice, interpretation, an assertion of taste, a betrayal of what answers to one's needs, one's envies" (Ramanujan, 1973: 12–13).

How do we judge translations in the Third World when postcolonial theorists like Niranjana and Cheyfitz understand text as colony, colony as translation and translation as the colonial power-play between the colonial masters and native subjects while phrasing the arguments in the same Judeo-Christian, Orientalist and Colonial traditions of translations in Europe to evaluate translations in India? It raises the question of following Western criticism of literary translation for translations in India and hence impossibility of translations in India that Ganesh Devy argues in *In Another Tongue*, or the near impossibility of "a complete calling in question of the colonial situation" (Fanon, 2001: 28) by the translator as Fanon thinks the task of the translator. At the same time what about the politics of translations of *vacanas* of Allama Prabhu by A.K. Ramanujan and translations as such that Niranjana thinks make hegemonic representations, essentialize Hinduism and condone communal violence in postcolonial India? How do we combine the double perceptions of translation as "carrying across" in the West and *anuvada* as "saying after" in India? Analyzing the role of translation in colonial period, Anuradha Dingwaney and Carol Maier too have critiqued translation as violence; and Victor Hugo's indictment of nationalism too led him to despise translation. "When you offer a translation to a nation, that nation will almost always look on the translation as an act of violence against itself" (Quoted from Lefevere, 1992: 2). How do we translate violence and understand the role of translation, as Rita Kothari says, "translation as a stepping out of the zones of (con)texts in order to hear and be heard, as a way to heal wounds and bridge distances," (Kothari) and perform the task of the translator as "to seize upon the in-between spaces" and "to diffuse polarization", when translation itself in its colonial, nationalistic and postcolonial period is perceived as violence? How do we formulate an Indian theory of translation for translating India in a disruptive/interventionist mode, or does the very "translating consciousness" of India not need its own theory of translation? (Devy, 1993 & 2000) Notwithstanding the postcolonial societies must think in their own terms but such nativist call to define translation or thinking in exclusive Indian terms (something painful which colonialism has made impossible) harbours dangers of its own and diminishes the creative potentialities of the liminal space.

## CONCLUSION: FUTURE OF TRANSLATION STUDIES IN INDIA

An urgent need to broaden the discipline of Translation Studies in both theoretical and practical aspects has been perceived. For this aim, the conceptualization of translation and the task of the translator in the Third World, particularly India, beyond the historical trajectory of Translation Studies which have remained within the domain of literary translations, must be envisioned. The flourishing of Translation projects immediately after the Independence since the Nehruvian era had been aligned with projections of nationalist ideology to present an imaginative "holistic" picture of India as one uniform nation to the masses, obliterating and homogenizing the irreducible differences among different cultures, languages and people. The scholars of Translation Studies must provide an authentic historical account of itself in India from the post-independence period to the contemporary times. Moreover, the task of translation of critical and cultural theory, though pursued in the past few decades in Western academia, thinking the engagement of theory with contemporary cultural issues in dissident styles productive for society, but not so far pursued at a greater scale in various Indian languages, becomes significant in this respect, so that we can keep our windows open to the theoretical thinking which can carry the discourse forward outside the Eurocentric centre than blown by them by our ignorance and intellectual disengagement. Friedrich Schleiermacher, Mariano Jose de Larra and Domingo Faustino Sarmiento, notes José María Rodrígues García (García, 2004: 8–9), expressed that an enlightened elite could not come into being in their nations – Germany, Spain and Argentina respectively – without the benefit of a cosmopolitan education which included translation practice as a tool to enrich the analytical precision of one's own language and habits of thought. As Lawrence Venuti observes on his translation of Derrida's remarkable essay, "A translation practice might not only advance theories of culture and translation, but join them to a politically oriented understanding that can potentially extend their impact beyond the academic institutions in which these theories are housed. This is not to say that translation, especially the translation of specialized theoretical texts, can change the world in any direct way. Rather the point is that translation can be practiced, in various genres and text types, so as to make their users aware of the social hierarchies in which languages and cultures are positioned. And with that awareness the different institutions that use and support translation, notably publishers, universities, and government agencies, can better decide how to respond to the cultural and social effects that follow upon the global dominance of English" (Venuti, 2003: 259). At the same time, Himalayan theoretical and practical issues involved in translations of critical and cultural theories, both Western and non-Western, in Indian vernaculars, possible hurdles involved in such translations and adequate remedies for them, must be offered both by the theoreticians and practitioners of translation. What should be the task of the translator in translating cultural theory in the Indian vernaculars and its political, social, cultural and literary repercussions? The question is also left to the skeptics to be answered.

Probably there is little history of translating critical theory in Indian vernaculars despite profound theoretical thinking and awareness present outside and inside the country. Though Gujarat (and I contend, most regions in India), as pointed out by Rita Kothari in her *Translating India*, has little history of translating from the regional language to English, the argument about translation pursued above intends language into traverse a more conventional path in attempting translation or translation of translation from "prime" theoretical texts written in European languages into Indian vernaculars, with a subtle difference in making initial attempts at translating and making theoretical thinking accessible in the vernacular to audience in vernacular, and vice versa. Why should the postcolonial translator translate Empire only into English and privilege it as the only suitable mode for translation as the present vogue for getting everything translated into English unmasks? True decolonization or "Swaraj" must remain awakened to what is happening elsewhere and at the same time instead of parochializing knowledge through regional fetishism, must constantly try to modify itself and its source.

Defining translation as teaching which can stimulate reading, in the academic sense that Anthony Kwame Appiah uses the term "thick translation", the purpose behind such translation endorsed here would be largely academic in nature, since at the altar of academics most translations are produced and consumed in quantity, but it also seeks to transcend the institutionalization of the practice and products of translation through the use of the vernacular for wider dissemination into social, cultural, political and other domains. The history of translation in India has always been open to thoughts concealed in "alien" texts to assimilate them within itself and enrich it, and give back her thoughts to the world; therefore the present call to translate critical and cultural theory into Indian vernaculars expects to receive a more cerebral response.

## Works Cited

Appiah, Kwame Anthony. "Thick Translation." *The Translation Studies Reader*. Ed. Lawrence Venuti. London and New York: Routledge, 2004. 389–401.

Bassnett, Susan. *Translation Studies*. London: Routledge, 1980.

Benjamin, Walter. "The Task of the Translator." *Selected Writings. Vol.1. 1913–1926*. Ed. Marcus Bullock and Michael W. Jennings. Cambridge: Harvard University Press, 1996. 253–263.

Bermann, Sandra and Michael Wood, eds. *Nation, Language, and the Ethics of Translation*. Princeton and Oxford: Princeton University Press, 2005.

Bassnett, Susan and Harish Trivedi. *Post-colonial Translation: Theory and Practice*. London and New York: Routledge, 2000.

Bhabha, Homi K. *The Location of Culture*. London and New York: Routledge, 1994.

Chamberlain, Lori. "Gender and Metaphorics of Translation." *The Translation Studies Reader*. Ed. Lawrence Venuti. London and New York: Routledge, 2000. 314–329.

Cronin, Michael. *Translation and Identity*. London and New York: Routledge, 2006.

de Man, Paul. "'Conclusions': Walter Benjamin's 'The Task of the Translator.'" *The Resistance to Theory*. Minneapolis: The University of Minnesota Press, 1986. 73–105.

Derrida, Jacques. "What Is a 'Relevant' Translation?" Trans. Lawrence Venuti, *Critical Inquiry* 27.2 (Winter 2001):174–200.

Devy, Ganesh. "Translation Theory: An Indian Perspective." *In Another Tongue: Essays on Indian English Literature*. New Delhi: Macmillan, 1993. 134–152.

———. "Translation and literary history – an Indian view." *Post-colonial Translation: Theory and Practice*. Ed. Susan Bassnett and Harish Trivedi. London and New York: Routledge, 2000. 182–188.

Dharwadker, Vinay. "A.K. Ramanujan's Theory and Practice of Translation." *Post-colonial Translation: Theory and Practice*. Ed. Susan Bassnett and Harish Trivedi. London and New York: Routledge, 2000. 114–140.

Eaglestone, Robert. "Levinas, Translation and Ethics." *Nation, Language, and the Ethics of Translation*. Princeton and Oxford: Princeton University Press, 2005. 127–138.

Fanon, Frantz. *The Wretched of the Earth.* Trans. Constance Farrington. New Delhi: Penguin, 2001.

García, José María Rodrígues. "Introduction: Literary into Cultural Translation." *Diacritics* 34.3/4 (Autumn-Winter, 2004):2–30.

Gasset, José Ortega y. "The Misery and the Splendor of Translation." *Theories of Translation: An Anthology of Essays from Dryden to Derrida.* Ed. Rainer Schulte and John Biguenet. Chicago: The University of Chicago Press, 1992. 93–112.

Jakobson, Roman. "On Linguistic Aspects of Translation." *The Translation Studies Reader.* Ed. Lawrence Venuti. London and New York: Routledge, 2004. 138–143.

Klein, Dr. Ernst. *A Comprehensive Etymological Dictionary of the English Language, Vol. I.* Amsterdam: Elsevier Publishing Company, 1966.

Kothari, Rita. *Translating India: The Cultural Politics of English.* New Delhi: Foundation Books, 2006.

———. "Diffusing Polarizations: Language and Translation at the Time of the Gujarat Riots." <http://www.eipcp.net/transversal/1107//kothari/en>.

———. "Tales of memory and music", *The Hindu*, July 3, 2010. <http://www.thehindu.com/arts/books/article498657.ece.>.

Lahiri, Jhumpa. "Intimate Alienation: Immigrant Fiction and Translation." *Translation, Text, Theory: The Paradigm of India.* Ed. Rukmini Bhaya Nair. New Delhi: Sage, 2002. 113–120.

Lefevere, André. *Translation, Rewriting and the Manipulation of Literary Fame.* London and New York: Routledge, 1992.

———, ed. *Translation, History, Culture: A Sourcebook.* London and New York: Routledge, 1992.

Maggio, J. "Can the Subaltern Be Heard?": Political Theory, Translation, Representation, and Gayatri Chakravorty Spivak." *Alternatives* 32.4 (Oct.-Dec. 2007):419–443.

Mukherjee, Sujit. "Personal Commitment: The Craft Not Sullen Art of Translation." *Translation, Text, Theory: The Paradigm of India.* Ed. Rukmini Bhaya Nair. New Delhi: Sage, 2002. 25–34.

Niranjana, Tejaswini. *Siting Translation: History, Poststructuralism and the Colonial Context.* Berkeley: University of California Press, 1992.

———. "Post-colonial Representation: Translation as Disruption." *Translation, Text, Theory: The Paradigm of India.* Ed. Rukmini Bhaya Nair. New Delhi: Sage, 2002. 55–76.

Paz, Octavio. "Translation: Literature and Letters." *Theories of Translation: An Anthology of Essays from Dryden to Derrida.* Ed. Rainer Schulte and John Biguenet. Chicago: The University of Chicago Press, 1992. 152–162.

Pierre, Paul St. "Translation in a Plurilingual Postcolonial Context: India." *Translation and Multilingualism: Postcolonial Contexts.* Ed. Santha Ramakrishna. New Delhi: Pencraft, 1997. 135–145.

Pratt, Mary Louis. "Linguistic Utopias." *The Linguistics of Writing: Arguments between Literature and Language.* Ed. Nigel Fabb, Derek Atridge et al. Manchester: Manchester University Press, 1987.

Ramanujan, A.K., trans. *Speaking of Shiva.* London: Penguin Books, 1973.

Said, Edward. "The Public Role of Writers and the Intellectual." *Nation, Language, and the Ethics of Translation.* Ed. Sandra Bermann and Michael Wood. Princeton and Oxford: Princeton University Press, 2005. 15–29.

Schulte, Rainer and John Biguenet, eds. *Theories of Translation: An Anthology of Essays from Dryden to Derrida.* Chicago: The University of Chicago Press, 1992.

Spivak, Gayatri. "The Politics of Translation." *The Translation Studies Reader.* Ed. Lawrence Venuti. London and New York: Routledge, 2000. 369–388.

———. "Translation as Culture." *In Translation: Reflections, Refractions, Transformations.* Ed. Paul St. Pierre and Prafulla C. Kar. Amsterdam/Philadelphia: John Benjamin's Publishing Company, 2007. 263–276.

Toury, Gideon. "The Nature and Role of Norms in Translation." *The Translation Studies Reader.* Ed. Lawrence Venuti. London and New York: Routledge, 2000. 205–218.

Trivedi, Harish. "India, England, France: A (Post-) Colonial Translational Triangle." *Translation and Multilingualism: Postcolonial Contexts.* Ed. Santha Ramakrishna. New Delhi: Pencraft International, 1997. 248–262.

Venuti, Lawrence. "Translation, Community, Utopia." *The Translation Studies Reader.* Ed. Lawrence Venuti. London and New York: Routledge, 2000. 482–502.

———. "Translating Derrida on Translation: Relevance and Disciplinary Resistance." *The Yale Journal of Criticism* 16.2 (2003): 237–262.

———. "Local Contingencies: Translation and the National Identities." *Nation, Language, and the Ethics of Translation.* Princeton and Oxford: Princeton University Press, 2005. 177–202.

Weber, Samuel. "A Touch of Translation: On Walter Benjamin's "Task of the Translator." *Nation, Language, and the Ethics of Translation.* Princeton and Oxford: Princeton University Press, 2005. 65–78.

# Questions of Cultural Identity

# 4

# Salman Rushdie and Cultural Translation: A Bhabhaian Reading of *Midnight's Children*

*Manish Solanki*

> It is the dispersal attendant on migrancy that disrupts and interrogates the overarching themes of modernity: the nation and its literature; *language and sense of identity*; the metropolis; the sense of centre; *the sense of psychic and cultural homogeneity*. (Emphasis mine)
>
> (Chambers, 1994: 23)

> "Home" has become such a scattered, damaged, various concept in our present travails.
>
> (Rushdie, 1994: 93)

Salman Rushdie, a writer valorized by the discourse of postcolonial studies, has come to be identified with fiction celebrating cultural eclecticism and migrant hybridity. His fiction has become almost emblematic for the body of writing known as postcolonial literatures. The present article studies Rushdie's engagement with cultural translation effected by the factors of migrancy and globalization, in light of his novel *Midnight's Children* that draws on the trajectories of respective careers of two of its characters, Saleem Sinai and Jamila Singer (or Brass Monkey).

"Displacement", "transfer", "migration", "exile" – these are the terms that have become now the parts of the standard lexicon of postcolonial studies. Postcoloniality as a *condition* of postnational global order is conceived in terms of a movement from one place to another, a movement that involves not only a one-way shift but also inevitably a bidirectional cultural hybridization. Postcolonial studies engage with the issue of cultural convergence between East and West, North and South, metropole and colony. The unprecedented flow of migrancy in contemporary times has inevitably resulted in transaction between different cultural contexts. This factor has also impacted upon the practice of literary writing, especially in the case of postcolonial literatures. Salman Rushdie, a symptomatic postcolonial writer, materializes, in his own persona as well as in his fiction, the juxtaposition caused by the past of colonization and present migration that subsequently results into the defamiliarization of cultures of both the colonizer and the colonized. This defamiliarization, in the case of a postcolonial migrant writer like Rushdie, offers the split vision enabling him to see cultures in terms of one another. Further, the rhetoric of "sameness" and "difference" associated with this body of writing also adds an emphasis on the tension between the "same" and the "other" with regard to the process of cultural translation. Through the postcolonial migrant subject, two distinct and distant cultural realities meet, interact and gradually change each other. The postcolonial aesthetics of inter (-intra) cultural hybridity and translation are shaped by the historical contingencies of colonial violence and occupation, anticolonial resistance, and postcolonial migration. It studies the complex process of acculturation of peoples brought together by geopolitical upheavals. One of the major reasons for the ascendancy of postcolonial literature in the second half of the twentieth century is the amenability of postcolonial experience to aesthetic expressions negotiating the issues such as dislocation of identities due to territorial displacement, unexpected/unpredictable conjunctions of cultures/discourses, linguistic as well as cultural hybridity, stereoscopic vision and dual consciousness enabling to see "sameness" in "difference" and vice versa. These issues are integral to the practice of postcolonial literatures and Rushdie, being not an exception to it, fictionalizes them in his novels. Rushdie's oeuvre has been seen as a celebration of the experience of cultural hybridity, along with an engagement with the resultant complex process of cultural translation and its impact on identity formation.

## MIGRATION/NARRATION AND POSTCOLONIALITY

The issue of the relationship between migrancy and its literary expression finds a theoretical treatment in Walter Benjamin's essay "The Storyteller" (Benjamin, 1992). Analysing the tradition of telling stories, Benjamin suggests a historical link to social figures as diverse as the journeyman apprentice, the pilgrim, the merchant sailor; all those who were able to leave their homes and return with straightforward or embellished narratives of the places and peoples they had seen in their wanderings. This perspective can also be applied to postcolonial literatures in their fascinations with the link between migration and narration, between cultural transaction and cultural translation. But it also requires a cautious approach as simply equating postcolonial literatures with the ancient tradition of storytelling would elide an important feature of this writing. The issues referred earlier are no doubt central to postcolonial literatures, but there is more thrust on problamatizing them as a result of which the relationship between migration and narration takes on altogether a new and a qualitatively different significance than the one offered in Benjamin's essay. One of the factors that contribute to it is the fact that the present world is witnessing greater numbers of people, moving more often and travelling greater distances than ever before in the record of human history. While celebrating cultural hybridity and migrancy, it would be too naïve to forget that all forms of migration do not entail the same experience or involve the same risks/advantages and that all exiles are equally a matter of unconstrained free choice. Nevertheless, there is a general consensus among commentators in the field of social sciences and humanities that "migration seems likely to go on growing into the new millennium, and may be one of the most important factors in global change[1]" (Castles, 1998: 4).

Migrancy has become a central trope within the field of postcolonial literatures as evidenced in the works of writers, culturally and geographically discrete, such as Gabriel García Márquez, Carlos Fuentes, Wole Soyinka, Derek Walcott, Vikram Seth and Salman Rushdie, to

1. For a detailed analysis of this issue, see also: Arjun Appadurai, *Modernity at Large*; Robin Cohen, *Global Diasporas*; Nikos Papastergiadis, *The Turbulence of Migration*; Steven Vertovec, and Robin Cohen, *Migration, Diasporas and Transnationalism*; James Clifford, "Travelling Cultures."

name just a few from the dizzying gallery of postcolonial writers. The task which befalls on a writer in a globalized post/trans-national world is succinctly encapsulated by the postcolonial migrant writer, Ben Okri, in his view that we live in a world in which there are no longer set centres, definite horizons, or clear limits on things. Therefore it falls to the postcolonial writer to rediscover the role of the cultural frontiersperson. Okri suggests that we need now more than ever the individual who can explore in art and writing what life is like in a world where everything is becoming borderspace. For Okri, this fluid cultural landscape seems an inviting prospect when he goes as far as to discern in it the glimmering of a "first universal golden age" (Okri, 1997: 31). Here migrancy becomes the name, not of an *act*, but for the *condition* of human life in a present day world. In other words, it refers to the way how we exist and understand ourselves in the contemporary time of *borderless location*. For the same reasons, Benita Parry has argued that postcolonial theory is a form of "immanent critique"(Parry, 1987: 11): criticism from the inside out. This body of theory celebrates the idea that the postcolonial migrant is in a position of peculiar insight, blessed with a specific awareness of the relativity of all cultural formations. The theoretical impetus of this version of migrancy, as reflected in the writings of Homi Bhabha and Salman Rushdie, is its association of migration and exile with the establishment of the truth that *truth is relative*, that *no knowledge can ever be certain*. Rushdie himself becomes, in many respects, the archetypal migrant who, in his own words, has "...been forced by cultural displacement to accept the provisional nature of all truths, all certainties..." (Rushdie, 1991: 12). Scholars in postcolonial studies have been fascinated by the idea that cultural facts and values, being historically contingent, are mutable, contested and shaped in and through the act of narration. Rushdie makes it clear that it is the "double perspective" of the migrant writer that is instrumental in exposing this cultural *relativity*.

## POSTCOLONIAL MIGRANCY AND CULTURAL TRANSLATION: HOMI BHABHA

The postcolonial cultural theorist Homi Bhabha has a far reaching influence on this debate on migrancy within postcolonial cultural studies. In his seminal text *The Location of Culture* (1994), Bhabha begins with the recognition that there is "no necessary or eternal belongingness" (Bhabha, 1994: 179). Generally, in day-to-day life, one tends to think of one's identity, whether ethnic, religious or national, as pre-given and stable. But for Bhabha, this comfortable feeling of self-sufficiency of personal identity is an illusory construction that has come to have "cultural compulsion" (Bhabha, 1990: 1). He further elaborates: "[C]ultures come to be represented by virtue of processes of *iteration* and *translation* through which their meanings are *vicariously* addressed to – through – an *Other. This erases any essentialist claims for the inherent authenticity or purity of cultures*" (My emphasis) (Bhabha, 1994: 59). Bhabha is highly dismissive of dialectical pairs – colonizer/colonized, local/immigrant, for example – since such pairings are only ruses of the powerful, the attempts to create unequal structures of order. Such hierarchical pairings are upset and threatened when one looks closely at the borderline between communities, situated at the threshold of "cultural difference", and realizes how different identities are implicated in and with each other. Bhabha explains, "[I]t is the 'inter' – the cutting edge of translation and negotiation, the in-between space – that carries the burden of the meaning of culture" (38). Since, in this respect, culture is constituted from the edges rather than by virtue of a self-enclosed and an inherent centre, the position of the migrant becomes peculiarly symptomatic. For Bhabha, the "newness" or "untranslatability" of immigrant community dramatizes the flaw in the pluralistic dream of a multicultural society where difference is smoothly assimilated. The migrant represents the "signifying position of the minority that resists totalization" (194) undermining the liberal dream of a single national body under command from the centre and marking up in its stead the "menacing agonistic boundary of cultural difference that never quite adds up, always less than one nation and double" (168). The presence of migrant, or "borderline community" as called by Bhabha, shows us how, despite the attempt to fix others (and also ourselves) with stereotypes of sameness and essence, cultures are not closed and complete in themselves, but split, anxious and even contradictory. Like Okri, Bhabha implies that the migrant (especially the migrant intellectual and writer) is therefore a forerunner of a new type of politics in which groups no longer mobilize on the basis of the old dichotomies of opposition, but move together in and through hybridity and difference.

Bhabha's theoretical stance on postcolonial migrancy is also shared by Rushdie whose fiction foregrounds the relationship between migration and narrative. By the incessant flow of migration in our world, previous assumptions regarding human beings as citizens of nations or as blood members of ethnic groupings are exposed as theoretically insufficient and practically inadequate ways of identifying oneself. It reveals the fact that these identities are actually stories which are acted out in life but which are not unchangeable. It also shows how such constructions of identity often smother and silence other competing and conflicting stories. Migrants become emblematic figures in postcolonial fictions such as Rushdie's precisely because they represent a removal from "old" foundations and from previous "grounded" ways of thinking characteristic of Western humanistic discourse (Krishnaswamy, 1995). An earlier approach to migrancy promoted the idea of a search for lost "roots". Postcolonial approach to migrancy is however characterized by a deep-laid suspicion to such notions of quest for an "originary past". It rejects both the West's Orientalist nostalgia for Eastern origins and the East's nativist nostalgia for a precolonial uncontaminated past. Frantz Fanon warned against fetishising and embalming the precolonial past; artists who "turn their backs on foreign culture, deny it and set out to look for a true national culture… forget that the forms of thought and what it feeds on, together with modern techniques of information, language and dress have dialectically reorganized the people's intelligences and that the constant principles which acted as safeguards during the colonial period are now undergoing extremely radical changes" (Fanon, 2001: 181). Such desire to recuperate the precolonial pristine past is not amenable to postcolonial attitude to migrancy. This is repeatedly shown in Rushdie's fiction where the migrants, unhoused by modernity and colonialism on the one hand and education and migration on the other, find themselves incapable to rest securely (and squarely) in what Bhabha calls the idea of culture "as a homogenizing, unifying force, authenticated by the originary past" (Bhabha, 1994: 37). Instead they symptomize the postcolonial condition of migrancy that Bhabha terms as "unhomeliness – that is the condition of extraterritorial and cross-cultural initiations." (9) Housed in homelessness, such postcolonial migrants know that cultural identity is, as Stuart Hall aptly puts, "…not a fixed essence… It is not a fixed origin to which we can make some final and absolute Return" (Hall, 1997: 113). Such a suspicion is also expressed by Gayatri Chakravorty Spivak in an interview: "If there's one thing I distrust, in fact more than distrust, despise and have contempt for, it is people looking for roots. Because anyone who can conceive of looking for roots should already, you know, be growing rutabagas (turnips)" (Spivak, 1990: 93). Thus, the earlier formations of identity, based on ancestry, nationality or geography, are called into question for their apparent fixity by postcolonial approaches to migrancy. Rushdie adopts this stance on migrancy in his works as a postcolonial writer, trying to re-cathect the precolonial past as a powerful locus of identity, yet self-consciously probing the multiplicity and the constructedness of identity effected by territorial displacement and cultural re(-de)location. In spite of the much applause accorded to migrancy in postcolonial literary and theoretical discourses, the writers and theorists are not oblivious of the serious lacuna besetting this approach.[2] Real political action becomes awkward in this situation, partly because it would be hard to find the basis on which to judge the validity for any particular stance. For some theorists, class-or race-or sex-based anti-systemic movements are seen to have lost their authority; oppositionality is now seen to consist most sharply in an individualist cosmopolitanism.[3] If there is a space left for unity and political action, it is an awkward one in which what we share is, as it were, a strangeness, the common fact of having little definite in common. To quote Bhabha again: "It is by living on the borderline of history and language, on the limits of race and gender, that we are in a position to translate the differences between them into a kind of solidarity" (Bhabha, 1994: 170). Migration, therefore, occupies centre space in what is grouped as postcolonial literatures and in its theoretical analysis.

2. For theoretical objections against this celebratory discourse on postcolonial migrancy, see: Aijaz Ahmed, "The Politics of Literary Postcoloniality."; Arif Dirlik, "The Postcolonial Aura: Third World Criticism in the Age of Global Capitalism."; Ella Shohat, "Notes on the Postcolonial."; Anne McClintock, "The Angel of Progress: Pitfalls of the Term Postcolonial."; Benita Parry, "Problems in Current Theories of Colonial Discourse."

3. For this see: Iain Chambers, *Migrancy, Identity and Culture*; Ulf Hannerz, *Transnational Connections*; Ulf Hannerz, "Cosmopolitans and Locals in World Culture."

## *MIDNIGHT'S CHILDREN*: RUSHDIE, MIGRANCY AND CULTURAL TRANSLATION

Salman Rushdie's fiction engages with this theoretical debate on postcolonial migrancy as exemplified by his symptomatic novel *Midnight's Children*. The winner of the Booker Prize in the year of its publication (1981) as well as the Booker of Bookers in 1993 as the best novel to have won the Booker Prize in its first twenty five years, *Midnight's Children* is a watershed in the post-independence development of Indian English novel. The novel proved indeed influential to subsequent journey charted by Indian English fiction during post eighties as evidenced by the fact that the term "Post-Rushdie" has now come to refer to the decade or so after its publication in which a resurgent wave of novels appeared by established as well as young writers. Highly irreverent to traditional ideological investments and promiscuously self-conscious of its own status as an artefact, this novel registers the creative tensions between personal and national collective identity. Through the trajectories of respective careers of two of its characters, Saleem Sinai and Jamila Singer (or Brass Monkey), Rushdie problamatizes the issue of identity (personal as well as cultural) and shows the complex process (disruptive or otherwise) of cultural translation of self due to the factor of migrancy in postcolonial cultures. In this, Rushdie clearly fictionalizes the Bhabhaian concept of postcolonial migrancy with all its contours in a postnational globalized world. The careers of both these characters offer a parallel to each other, whereby both of them, in spite of being diametrically opposed to each other, reciprocally illuminate each other and bring to the light the issue of cultural translation.

Through the persona of the narrator-protagonist, Saleem Sinai, the novel critically engages with the relationship between narration and migration. Since it is Saleem who is attempting to tell his story from the vantage point of his individual perspective, the novel poses a challenge to the collective discourse of national history. But since this perspective is continually as well as continuously destabilized throughout the novel due to Saleem's own scepticism regarding the validity of his experience, the novel confounds any hope invested in its narrative for offering any unified vision (and version) as a reliable alternative to the Western discourse of collective history by undercutting Saleem's narrative. Saleem, by beginning the narration of his story *in medias res*, undermines the Western discourse of history whose governing structural principles are chronology and linearity with their (illusory?) promise of imposing a semblance of reality on historical narrative constructions and obtaining an unproblematic validity for them. This Western outlook on history is ultimately rooted in the logical fallacy *post hoc ergo propler hoc* ("after which, therefore, because of which"), thus grounding its faith in sequentiality and causation. Rushdie mockingly refers to such historical faith as "what-happened-nextism" (Rushdie, 2006: 45).

Rushdie wants to interrogate with this ingrained Western historical faith in his offering of an alternative history, which does not seek authenticity but flaunts its own constructedness, and thereby calls into question the instrumentality of causation as a basis for history-writing. The novel being highly self-conscious of its own status as a fiction brought forth by discursive strategies repeatedly draws attention to its own artificiality as an artefact. The chief device used by Saleem in telling his story is that of his individual memory which is, he keeps on reminding us, fallible, wanton, volatile and autonomous in its unwillingness to obey external demands put upon it. Rushdie has said that he was writing a novel "of memory and about memory" (Rushdie, 1991: 10). The narrative thus constructed also becomes a suspect as far its truth-value is concerned. But this is exactly the point that Rushdie wants to make in this novel; no narrative, historical or fictional, can claim to be the authoritative version of the past. Saleem wants to offer a family chronicle which can, in its turn, destabilize the national history, without seeking to replace it as a more authenticated version. He wants to offer a worthwhile testimony of private experience as an alternative to public history. He does so by taking recourse to his individual memory as his chief structural device through which he intends to reconstruct/recover episodes from collective history. Simultaneously he is also aware of the risks involved in this project since he knows that "past is not only what you remember, it is also what you imagine you remember, convince yourself [and others] that you remember, pretend to remember" (Adler, 1979: 198). Narrative thus brought forth cannot claim a truth-value except only as an imaginative fabrication. Nonetheless, Rushdie is of the opinion that the individual recollections and assessments of historical reality are ultimately self-validating. Individual versions of reality provide a version of "truth" for the individual. Rushdie forefronts the role of memory in his depiction of India in this novel by justifying it as thus: "We remake the past to suit our present purposes, using memory as our tool" (Rushdie,

1991: 24). Saleem makes virtue of this hindrance and tells his story in an episodic structure full of digressions and shows his disregard for sequentiality/linearity, but, at the same time, never allows it to assume the status of authoritative macronarrative by consistently undercutting it through his constant reminder of the instrumentality of his fallible memory in it. This craving for offering a history and an accompanying scepticism for such a project results in Saleem's stereoscopic vision which is emblematic of postcolonial migrancy as discussed earlier. In other words, Saleem conceives of himself as a perpetual migrant, no matter wherever he is geographically/culturally located.

Saleem's postcolonial migrancy is further reinforced in his alternative genealogies. After narrating the story of his ancestry that traces his cultural roots back to a Kashmiri Muslim family, Saleem undercuts this by offering the biological genealogy that traces his lineage back to William Methwold, the departing British colonialist, and Vanita, the wife of the street singer Wee Willie Winkie. This is further accentuated when he avers that William Methwold is a half-British, his grandmother being French. Thus, even at the biological level, Saleem materializes, in his cross-pollination, the meeting point of distant cultural realities. Later on he comes to grow in Sinai household due to Mary Pereira's act of swapping Sinai's baby with Vanita's baby at Dr Narlikar's nursing home. This fact is revealed by Saleem only in the last chapter of Book One, after relating himself to a Kashmiri Muslim family in the foregoing pages. With this revelation, the apparent fixity of familial/cultural lineage is exploded by biological genealogy which is, in its own turn, not stable either. Saleem's complexity exemplifies cultural translation and syncretism, as unstoppable as ever, and shows that individuality is constructed forth by multiple cultural influences which, Saleem is convinced, remain untraceable in the final analysis.

Thus, a son of a British (who is himself a product of mixed breed and thus indicative of cultural translation effected at the level of biology) and Vanita (the wife of a Hindu street singer) is inserted into a cultural milieu of a Muslim family in Bombay. Read allegorically, Saleem's personal story also represents the story of India's independence and partition. Vanita, as a biological mother of Saleem, allegorizes Mother India; William Methwold allegorizes colonialist England; both of them have brought forth Saleem who, due to his insertion into a Muslim culture, allegorizes Pakistan. Even Saleem's physiognomic features further mock the notion of a stable self relatable to fixed origin. His eyes are "as blue as Kashmiri sky – which were also eyes as blue as Methwold's – and a nose as dramatic as a Kashmiri grandfather's – which was also the nose of a grandmother from France" (Rushdie, 2006: 157). Saleem symptomatically represents his creator Rushdie who, being born in India, bred in Muslim culture and blossoming on English soil, considers himself as a migrant and a traveller across borders. Rushdie has also, as a writer writing in English, entered into an alien land with alien culture and alien language. While commenting upon Günter Grass, Rushdie puts succinctly this complex process of triple disruption that the postcolonial migrant undergoes: "...denied all three, [the migrant] is obliged to find new ways of describing himself, new ways of becoming human" (Rushdie, 1991: 278). Like his creator, Saleem also conceives of himself as a perpetual outsider living on the borderlines of cultures. This may be a distressing phenomenon disruptive of the liberal humanist notion of the stable self, but Saleem makes, much like Rushdie himself, a virtue of this historically contingent experience by bringing to light its advantages. (One of the major benefits for Saleem is that he can keep himself free from cultural parochialism in spite of the fact of being bred in a Muslim culture.) The cultural unbelongingness provides him with split vision and dual consciousness, allowing him to be on the margins of a culture and, at the same time, to resist any restrictive identification with that culture. Indeed, Rushdie celebrates, in the persona of Saleem, who is not tied to any fixed cultural location, the cultural in-betweenness that allows Saleem to have an insider's view of a culture and yet to remain a perpetual outsider to it. The novel shows Saleem inhabiting different cultures at different stages of life. He grows in India, migrates to Pakistan, flees to East Pakistan (later Bangladesh) and finally returns to India. The trajectory of his journey finds him in different cultural ambience and Saleem narrates his experience through this journey as a traveller of and in multiple cultures. Thus, Saleem comes to embody the Bhabhaian postcolonial migrant.

The trajectory of Saleem's journey is offered an added thrust by Rushdie in the novel through the depiction of a journey of Sinai's biological daughter, Jamila Singer (or Brass Monkey) which offers a sharp contrast to that of Saleem's. In the novel's narrative and theoretical framework, she has been offered more as an aberration. This is suggested even by the names that are used for her by Rushdie. We never come to know her real name, Jamila Singer, indicative of her religio-cultural identity/location, until the 20th Chapter in Book Two when she is in

Pakistan (Rushdie, 2006: 407). As long as she is in India in the earlier section of the novel, she is referred to by the name(?) Brass Monkey. The animal taxonomy is intended by Rushdie as an oblique indication of her aberration as a cultural misfit and a deviant. Rushdie has often been criticized for his tendency to demonize female sexuality in his fiction. The case of Brass Monkey appears to fall in with this line. But a closer analysis would nullify such a criticism. As long as she is in India, she is called Brass Monkey, a term displaying her animality that seems to undercut her humanity. But in Rushdie's narrative framework, it is clearly shown that this feature of her is not imposed on her by Indian culture symbolized in eclecticism of Sinai household. Rather, it is the result of a failure on her part to relate herself with that culture in a meaningful manner, as done by Saleem. Theoretical implications of this failure may be interpreted in the light of Bhabha's critique of the quest for an originary past as the basis for stable identity. She is, contrary to Saleem, a biological heir of Ahmed and Mumtaz-turned-Amina. Thus, her genealogy connects her back to dominant Islamic Kashmiri culture. But since Sinai household comes to represent a crucible of cultural eclecticism in post-independence India, their daughter fails to find an accommodation within it. She is allegorizing what Saleem has described, though in a different context: "In a kind of collective failure of imagination, we learned that we simply could not think our way out of our pasts" (158). Her aberrationality is repeatedly emphasized throughout the earlier part of the novel dealing with Sinais' stay in Bombay. According to the testimony of Saleem himself, her conception coincides with the event of freezing of Sinais' assets. She was born in September, 1948, a year and a month after Saleem's birth, at a time when, says Saleem: "... we were all exhausted" (187). The reason for her being referred to as Brass Monkey is "... her thick thatch of red-gold hair" (205) further reinforcing her inability to negotiate her place in the Sinai household. She also develops a curious habit of setting fire to footwear as a means for fighting for parental and sibling attention. She is driven to such destructive activities as she is "...possessed by her need to place herself at the centre of events..." (207). She never even makes any attempt to conceal her crimes in order to make people notice that "... she [is] there" (207). She is as beautiful as Saleem is ugly; but she is also "... mischievous as a whirlwind and noisy as a crowd" (208). Due to this, Mary Pereira is led to say: "That one! That Monkey! Should have been born with four legs!" (208) She has "bad table manners; she tramples flowerbeds;" as a result, "she acquire[s] the tag of problem-child" (209). As she was born second and unheralded, unlike Saleem, she reacts violently to any declaration of affection. She is believed to speak the languages of birds and cats, but the words of affection and love rouse in her an almost animal rage. Her treatment of Sonny Ibrahim on expressing his teenage crush for her is indicative of this (209 & 254).

Brass Monkey's failure to locate herself culturally may also be theorized in the light of Spivak's views. As referred earlier (Spivak, 1990), Spivak is highly distrustful of attempts to search for cultural roots. Brass Monkey's aberration should be placed in this Spivakian framework. She is the biological heir of Sinais whose religio-cultural lineage goes back to Kashmiri Muslim culture. As a result, Brass Monkey attempts to define herself by resorting to the culturally purist notion of identity. But she makes a mistake not to realize the historical specificity of her own familial genealogy. Her grandfather and Amina's father, Aadam Aziz, is a doctor by profession who returned to India after securing his medical degree from Heidelberg University, Germany. His five-year stay in Germany, one of the epicentres of modernity, changed his outlook to such an extent that, after his return to Kashmir, he could not reconcile his educated, stethoscoped return to his familial religion. He could not bring himself to offer *namaz* (the Muslim prayer) which has now, for him at least, become nothing more than "Mecca-turned parroting" (Rushdie, 2006: 6). Subsequently he loses faith in Islam and is left with a permanent hole in him following the event of offering *namaz* (7). Moreover, the Sinai household represents a cultural ambience that is tolerant of diversity and plurality as suggested by their undiminished love for Saleem, even after the truth regarding his real parentage is revealed, as well as for Brass Monkey, in spite of her repeated disruptive behaviour. Thus it is represented as accommodative of differences and heterogeneity. In such an atmosphere, Brass Monkey, searching for purist identity, is bound to feel frustrated as her attempts are rendered futile. She is looking for a homogenizing culture authenticated by the originary and unitary past which does not exist and is non-recuperable to her in a way and manner she desires. She presents herself as a staunch believer in the idea of cultural monism and as such fails to reconcile to the fact that cultures are dialogic by nature which renders the quest such as her futile right from its outset. This is demonstrated, albeit diametrically, by Saleem's ability to travel across cultural borders due to his acceptance that, cultures are not watertight compartments but are always porous and absorptive. He also practises, while in India, his gift of telepathy as a contribution towards this idea of culture. He considers himself as "Akashwani" or "*All India Radio*" where divergent and mutually conflicting voices are offered a space of accommodation. He also conceives of his Midnight Children's Conference (M.C.C.) as a sort of "... loose federation of equals, all points of view given free expression" (305). This is the reason why, in spite of all travails, Saleem considers his childhood stay in Bombay as the most pleasant. His position is sharply contrasted with Brass Monkey's attitude of sheer obstinacy.

Rushdie further punctuates the mutual contrariness in their cultural attitudes through their subsequent stay in Pakistan after Sinais' migration. Here also we find conspicuous difference between their respective attitudes to the complexity of cultural negotiations. Coming to Pakistan is, for Brass Monkey, like returning to the Promised Land. Pakistan, etymologically, the Land of Purity, comes to symbolize the pristine Muslim culture that she is looking for. As a consequence, she soon embraces it wholeheartedly and finds herself adequately accommodated into it. We must note that Rushdie reveals her real name, Jamila, which unproblamatically connects her to Muslim culture, after this event only. In other words, she comes to realize her identity as a human being only amidst the majoritarian Islamic culture represented by her uncle General Zulfikar's household in Rawalpindi, Pakistan. Insertion and accommodation into this cultural milieu results into her getting rid of her earlier aberration as manifested in the change of her name; Brass Monkey is now transformed into Jamila. Saleem's attitude to their migration to Pakistan and their stay in Zulfikar's house is diametrically opposed. He acknowledges his feeling of comfortlessness when he describes it as "... a dull, lifeless house, for all its military airs..." (396). Moreover, Saleem is also surprised by her sister's metamorphoses after her insertion to the God-ridden country. Brass Monkey, now turned Jamila, once so rebellious and wild, adopts expressions of demureness and submission. She also learns to cook, to keep house and to buy spices at the market. Her domestication is completed when she makes the final break with the legacy of her grandfather, Aadam Aziz, by learning prayers in Arabic and saying them at all prescribed times. The wild monkey of India reveals the streak of puritan fanaticism as Jamila of Pakistan by asking for a nun's outfit. As Saleem says: "[S]he, who spurned all offers of worldly love, was seduced by the love of that God who had been named after a carved idol in a pagan shrine built around a giant meteorite" (406). Rushdie's intention, through the portrayal of Jamila in this manner, is to highlight the basic difference between India and Pakistan and their respective cultures. Pakistan, as a postcolonial nation, is founded upon, unlike India, the religious base and so nation and religion become identical for Pakistan's Islamic culture that offers the promise to Jamila to realize her identity in culturally purist terms. Jamila's wholehearted embrace of such a cultural milieu also results into her achieving professional identity as a Singer. She earns names "Pakistan's Angel" and "Bulbul-of-the-Faith." What is noteworthy in her professional success is that, in Pakistan, love for nation is synonymous with love for god as in Pakistan's political scenario nation and god are one and the same.

If Jamila comes to fruition of her abilities in such a culture, Saleem finds himself losing all his abilities. He loses his gift of telepathy and cannot organize Midnight Children's Conference as geographical frontiers between India and Pakistan jam the transmission of waves. Later on he also loses his memory and his very humanity, underscoring the fact that Saleem can be Saleem only in India with its non-sectarian pluralistic culture and not in Pakistan with its monolithic culture. Saleem comes to look upon his stay in Pakistan as a period of exile. He cannot consider himself as the citizen of Pakistan; instead he sees himself more as a refugee. He compares his earlier stay in India with that of Pakistan and comes to the conclusion that Pakistan is a land of monistic purity, reflected in its religious fundamentalism politically attested; whereas India is a land of contaminated plurality where "...population of deities rivalled the numbers of its people" (431). Saleem underscores the claustrophobic cultural zealotry in Pakistan when he, while commenting upon his education in his aunt's college, says, "...not even learning could make me feel a part of this country..., in which my fellow students took out processions to demand a stricter, more Islamic society – proving that they had contrived to become the antithesis of students everywhere else on earth, by demanding more-rules-not-less" (431). As Jamila's career as a singer takes off, Saleem's career comes down. She, now Jamila Singer, goes on to give public concerts and achieves her fame, earning titles such as "Pakistan's Angel," "Bulbul-e-Din" or "nightingale-of-the-faith" (435) and "Voice-Of-Pakistan," (436) the latter being the name of the Pakistani government broadcaster.

This reminds us of Saleem's earlier claim that he was once, in India, "All India Radio", with all its connotations of cultural polyphony and heterogeneity. Jamila becomes a sort of mirror of the Islamic nation, a sort of collective property of the entire populace. Her voice becomes "...a sword of purity... a weapon... [that] clean[s] men's souls" (437). Thus her career in Pakistan is offered as an antithesis to Saleem's career earlier in India. With the loss of telepathic power, as if in compensation, he gets the power to smell emotions, feelings and thoughts. Jamila's voice and Saleem's olfactory power are also diametrically opposed to each other as they perform different functions. Jamila, through her voice, dedicates herself to patriotism (which is also symptomatic of her total surrender to Islamic culture); while Saleem squanders his power in his preference for uglier and impure smells (which is also a gesture of defiance against cultural demands for purity). Saleem encapsulates their respective positions by saying: "...while she rose into the clouds, I fell into the gutter" (438).

The surface reading of these antithetical careers would create an impression that Saleem is, like Brass Monkey in India, a cultural misfit, finding it utterly impossible to ingratiate himself in Pakistani culture. Similarly, Jamila may appear as, due to her complete absorption in and identification with this culture, reaping the harvest of professional success. But this reading is only partially true since Rushdie intends to foreground the contrast between them for entirely different reasons. Saleem's apparent failure and Jamila's professional success have more to do with wider circumstances rather than with their individual traits. Saleem may be viewed as an alienated figure in Pakistani culture but it is not due to his individual failure. Rather it is his ability, as a *mohajir* (migrant), to distance himself from the disruptive absorption into such a stifling cultural milieu. Born and bred in India's pluralistic society respecting heterogeneity, Saleem is able to see through cultural ruses of the collective religio-nationalistic project of Pakistan aiming to bind people into a unitary community whereby differences are smoothly (and sometimes with gruesome consequences) glided over for the sake of apparent sameness. This is the metaphorical meaning of his preference for uglier smells in the Land of Purity. He divines that it is the cultural monologism that is masquerading as purity in Pakistan, a fact never perceived by Jamila. She may have achieved professional glories as a patriotic singer, but on analysing the nature and condition of her success, one comes to know that this success will not prove to be a profitable bargain in the longer run. In other words, Jamila has been assimilated in Pakistani culture on the terms and conditions dictated by it. The very situation of her public concert highlights the ambivalent nature of her professional success. Jamila sits, while giving public concerts, demurely behind an all-concealing white silk chadar used as a curtain or veil. It is heavily embroidered in gold brocade-work and religious calligraphy. This curtain has a hole made in its centre against which Jamila presses her lips and performs her singing (435). This arrangement is made with a view to keeping Jamila hidden from public eyes and to allow the audience to have an access to her voice only. This can be interpreted as cultural selectivity looking only for convenient constituents contributing to homogeneity. Jamila is allowed an access to the centre of culture provided that only her voice would be foregrounded, in its representation of the ideal of purity for Pakistan, while the rest of her personality would either be rendered invisible or subsequently be erased completely. Jamila's success bought on such terms and conditions can hardly be justified when one is reminded of her earlier life in India as Brass Monkey. During her stay in India she is seen more as an aberration underscored by the animal taxonomy. Yet the pluralistic society represented by Sinai household allows her an individual space and the right to exist on her own terms, destructive though they may be, never trying to erase her as an exorbitant misfit. Moreover, such a cultural atmosphere also offers space for vehement cultural oppositions couched in Brass Monkey's incendiary activities. She is allowed to be what she wants to be and is, as Saleem reminds, never punished for her such acts of symbolic transgression. Conversely, her stay in Pakistan may have offered a personal name, indicative of her humanity, and public fame and glory, but simultaneously her whole personality is put under total effacement for the sake of this cultural purchase. Only by conceding to the majoritarian culture's demand for complete identification to it, on its terms and conditions that, Jamila could have an access to it. Having done this, she can have professional success bestowed upon her. But for this she has to compromise her individual self and surrender herself to the demands of cultural purity. Such a wilfully blind embrace to culture can be fatal in the longer run as suggested by her decision, in the later stage of her career, to serve the hidden religious order of Santa Ignacia in Karachi, Pakistan. Here she bakes bread and sings sweetly to the secret nuns and thus ends up exchanging one form of invisibility for another (549–550). No doubt, as Brass Monkey in India, she defiantly flirted with Christianity, but, now in Pakistan, her decision to serve Christianity has more to do with her attempts to keep herself wilfully insulated as clad in black burqa. The life which is available to Jamila in Pakistan is that of a nun which, in the last analysis within the novel's framework, is symptomatic of cultural putrefaction. As long as Saleem is amidst such a stifling culture, he remains the victim of amnesia. He also loses his sense of "feeling" due to such cultural asphyxiation. It is only after coming back to India that he regains his memory and sensory power to feel. The end of his career is also diametrically opposed to that of Jamila's. While Jamila prefers secrecy and invisibility by insulating herself within the high walls with bolted doors of the hidden order of Santa Ignacia, which is more a form of imprisonment than a sanctuary, and thus opting for illusory fixity, Saleem, on the contrary, explodes as a bomb and is splintered into as many pieces as the total number of Indian population, thus metaphorically securing his release into unpredictable and uncontrollable pluralities of Indian culture. Saleem expresses his experience of the difference between his Indian childhood and Pakistani adolescence respectively thus: "... in the first I was beset by an infinity if alternative realities, while in the second I was adrift, disorientated, amid an equally infinite number of falsenesses, unrealities and lies" (453).

## CONCLUSION

Interpreted in Bhabhaian concept of postcolonial migrancy, Saleem represents the migrant who is perpetually travelling, in and out of cultures, and always inhabiting the interstitial space (what Bhabha terms as liminal space) that allows him to have the double consciousness facilitating him in the complex process of cultural translation. Jamila represents, in complete contrast to Saleem, a quest for unitary and originary past that, in its regards for homogeneity, attempts to resists cultural translation. She materializes Saleem's diagnosis of failure of imagination as she "... simply could not think [her] way out of [her] pasts"(158). The quest that she is engaged in is, as demonstrated by Spivak, not only unfeasible but also undesirable in our present postnational globalized world in which cultural exchanges are as unstoppable as ever and cannot be prevented through linguistic, racial-religious and geopolitical barriers. In his alternative as well as parallel treatment of careers of Saleem and Jamila, Rushdie seems to share the Bhabhaian concept of postcolonial migrancy favouring cultural translation and Spivak's refusal to accord any value to the search for originary cultural roots. The trajectories of their careers, in spite of being antithetical to each other, illuminate each other in a reciprocal manner to a great extent highlighting the complex process of cultural translation in postcolonial cultures.

In *Midnight's Children* Rushdie becomes the spokesperson of the postcolonial migrancy by revealing, through Saleem, that marginality of the migrant is not to be grieved over but to be appreciated in its promising prospect of stereoscopic vision opening a highly interrogative interstitial space facilitating the creative/theoretical exploration of cultural translation. Rushdiean political aesthetics is founded upon the conviction that the postcolonial dislocation highlights the continuity-in-change of human identity. Rushdie is of the view that the postcolonial experience of cultural dislocation and migration forces genuine constancy into view—the constancy of mutability—of all cultural formations. As Rushdie writes, the "migrant's-eye view of the world," the "experience of uprooting, disjuncture and metamorphosis (slow or rapid, painful or pleasurable)," can stand as "a metaphor for all humanity" (Rushdie, 1991: 394).

## Works Cited

Adler, Thomas P. "From Flux to Fixity: Art and Death in Pinter's *No Man's Land*." *The Arizona Quarterly* 35.3 (Autumn, 1979): 197–204.

Ahmed, Aijaz. "The Politics of Literary Postcoloniality." *Contemporary Postcolonial Theory: A Reader*. Ed. Padmini Mongia. New Delhi: Oxford, 1997. 276–293.

Almansi, Guido and Simon Henderson. *Harold Pinter*. London: Methuen & Co, 1983.

Appadurai, Arjun. *Modernity at Large: Cultural Dimensions of Globalization*. Minneapolis and London: University of Minnesota Press, 1996.

Benjamin, Walter. "The Storyteller: Reflections on the Works of Nikolai Leskov." *Illuminations*. Trans. Harry Zohn. London: Fontana Press, 1992. 83–107.

Bhabha, Homi K., ed. *Nation and Narration*. London and New York: Routledge, 1990.

———. *The Location of Culture*. London and New York: Routledge, 1994.

Castles, Stephen. *The Age of Migration: International Population Movements in the Modern World*. 2nd ed. Basingstoke: Macmillan, 1998.

Chambers, Iain. *Migrancy, Culture, Identity*. London: Routledge, 1994.

Clifford, James. "Travelling Cultures." *Cultural Studies*. Ed. Lawrence Grossberg, Cary Nelson, and PoulaTreicher. London and New York: Routledge, 1992. 96–116.

Cohen, Robin. *Global Diasporas: An Introduction*. Seattle: University of Washington Press, 1997.

Dirlik, Arif. "The Postcolonial Aura: Third World Capitalism in the Age of Global Capitalism." *Contemporary Postcolonial Theory: A Reader*. Ed. Padmini Mongia. New Delhi: Oxford, 1997. 294–320.

Fanon, Frantz. *The Wretched of the Earth*. Trans. Constance Farrington. London: Penguin, 2001.

Hall, Stuart. "Cultural Identity and Diaspora." *Contemporary Postcolonial Theory: A Reader*. Ed. Padmini Mongia. New Delhi: Oxford, 1997. 110–121.

Hannerz, Ulf. "Cosmopolitans and Locals in World Culture." *Global Culture: Nationalism, Globalization and Modernity*. Ed. Mike Featherstone. London: Sage, 1990. 237–251.

———. *Transnational Connections: Culture, People, Places*. London and New York: Routledge, 1996.

Krishnaswamy, Revathi. "Mythologies of Migrancy: Postcolonialism, Postmodernism and the Politics of (Dis)location." *Ariel: A Review of International English Literature* 26.1 (1995):125–146.

McClintock, Anne. "The Angel of Progress: Pitfalls of the Term Postcolonial." *Social Text* 31–32 (1992):84–98.

Okri, Ben. *A Way of Being Free*. London: Phoenix House, 1997.

Papastergiadis, Nikos. *The Turbulence of Migration: Globalization, Deterritorialization and Hybridity*. Cambridge: Polity, 2000.

Parry, Benita. "Problems in Current Theories of Colonial Discourse." *Oxford Literary Review* 9.1-2 (1987):27–58.

Parry, Benita. "The Postcolonial: Conceptual Category or Chimera?" *Yearbook of English Studies* 27 (1997):3–21.

Rushdie, Salman. *Imaginary Homelands: Essays and Criticism 1981–1991*. London: Granta, 1991.

———. *East, West*. London: Jonathan Cape, 1994.

———. *Midnight's Children*. London: Vintage, 2006.

Shohat, Ella. "Notes on the Postcolonial." *Contemporary Postcolonial Theory: A Reader*. Ed. Padmini Mongia. New Delhi: Oxford. 1997. 321–334.

Spivak, Gayatri Chakravorty. *The Post-Colonial Critic: Interviews, Strategies, Dialogues*. Ed. Sarah Harasym. London and New York: Routledge, 1990.

Vertovec, Steven and Robin Cohen, eds. *Migration, Diasporas and Transnationalism*. Cheltenham and Northampton: Edward Elgar Publishing, 1999.

# 5

# We, the Castaways of History: Translating the Passion for South Africa of the 'Interregnum'

*Aroma Kharsiing*

## TRANSLATION: A METAPHOR FOR POSTCOLONIAL WRITING

As Maria Tymoczko (Bassnett and Trivedi, 1992:19–20) observes, reading translation as a metaphor for postcolonial writing brings us closer to the etymological meaning of the word, which is "translation" as an activity of carrying across, of transporting and relocating certain aspects, be it a material culture, a socio-cultural system, or history, which may constitute the ethos of a particular cultural group. In this sense, as a background to their literary texts, postcolonial writers carry across a culture that should be understood as a language, that is, as a cognitive system that informs the writing of the text: "The culture or tradition of the postcolonial writer acts as a metatext which is rewritten – explicitly and implicitly, as both background and foreground – in the act of literary creation" (21). Such cross cultural and linguistic transfer have led critics such as Homi Bhabha to define post-colonial authors as interpreters of the nation, while regarding translation as a metaphor for postcolonial writing (Bhabha, 1990). The phenomenon of "cultural translation" has a social and political impact which acquires a special significance in the historic process of nation building. Furthermore, a central endeavour in the practice of reading literature emerging from postcolonial territories is the examination of the relationships between language and power across cultural boundaries, especially in the redefinition of cultural and ethnic identities. Analysis of such texts therefore call for an active engagement with minority culture writing that often involves negotiation with, and transfer of significant cultural and linguistic codes across cultural and linguistic divides.

A significant aspect inherent in cross-cultural transfer that marks the writing of postcolonial literature is, as Gayatri Chakravorty Spivak observes in her works (1988, 1993), the active role that these cross-cultural transfers play in the dissemination of an ideologically motivated image of the colonized people, which in turn reinforces and legitimizes the structure of imperial hierarchy. The act of writing and cultural translation therefore converge together into a creative practice in what Mary Louise Pratt calls the "contact zone" (1992: 6). The "contact zone" is the site where two or more distinct cultures meet and overlap to establish ongoing relations, which are more often than not, characterized by "conditions of coercion, radical inequality and intractable conflict" (6), that is best exemplified in the historical enterprise of colonization.

Corresponding to Mary Louise Pratt's "contact zone" is Homi Bhabha's concept of the third space of enunciation". In *Location of Culture* Bhabha says that all cultural statements and systems are constructed in a contradictory and ambivalent space that he names as the "third space of enunciation". This space is characterized by "liminality". The term "liminal" is derived from the Latin "limen" meaning "threshold" and it refers to a transitory, in-between state of indeterminacy that is invested with a potential for change and subversion. Bhabha's third space of enunciation which emerges from the interstices, the overlap and displacement of a variety of competing cultural categories such as race, class, caste, gender, and cultural traditions, is identified as the site of cultural translation. Postcolonial literature, or, to use Bhabha's metaphor, postcolonial translation, in this sense transcends a purely linguistic horizon to become a cultural and political phenomenon which takes shape in the subversive political zone of the liminal.

This article takes up the South African author J.M. Coetzee's *In the Heart of the Country* to theorize, metaphorically, Coetzee as a cultural translator, who attempts to break free from the "unfreedom" of white writing in South Africa that is characterized by a lack of love for the people and polity of the country. For its framework it invokes Bhabha's use of translation as a metaphor for postcolonial literature and the implications of writing from within the politically subversive liminal and hybrid space. It also invokes Spivak's emphasis on a critical self-awareness of the investigating subject, her concept of "ethical singularity" to discuss Coetzee's scrupulous ethical position on the condition of writing in a country like South Africa.

## THE POSTCOLONIALITY OF SOUTH AFRICA: COETZEE AS CULTURAL TRANSLATOR

In the multi-lingual, multi-ethnic mosaic of South African society it is indeed relevant to consider postcolonial literature as cultural translation that is carried out in a highly complex contact zone. The situation of South Africa is even more difficult to map onto the postcolonial framework. South Africa, as many critics claim, has become postcolonial several times over, each time for a distinctly different population. The first instance was the creation of the Union of South Africa in 1910, by the Afrikaner community, the second was the victory of the Afrikaner based National Party and the birth of the apartheid state; the third was the declaration of the Republic status after independence from Britain in 1961 and lastly the end of apartheid rule in 1990. The prevailing narrative of postcoloniality that underlines a single break from colonialism and the model of the postcolonial as a diasporic formation are therefore not strictly applicable in the South African context.

Furthermore, South Africa is a highly pluralistic society characterized by an extraordinarily high level of internal conflict, contradiction, and dysfunction. The country is compartmentalized into several political systems, economies, and linguistic, religious, and racial groups which are maintained along a system of racial segregation and stratification based on a paternalistic, master-servant model of social relations. The policies of South African governments have paralleled rather closely those of other European powers in Africa during most of colonial history. It is therefore crucial to interpret South Africa in the broader perspective of Western imperialism. With the end of apartheid in the 1990s and the establishment of the "Rainbow Nation", a painful change in the relationships between the races of Post-apartheid South Africa becomes one of the central concerns of the South African writers. South African writers like Nadine Gordimer and J.M. Coetzee, find themselves in an ambiguous position. The social, political and economic fabric of South Africa is so deeply fraught with the residual memories of the violence and injustice of apartheid that the issue of reconciliation between the majority blacks and the white minority remains a sensitive and problematic one. In the face of such racial hostility, the white authors are not only made aware of their complicity with the violence of apartheid, whose ideology and methodology is remarkably similar to that of imperialism, but also of their unique positioning. Theirs is a position of necessary marginality, as they are caught between the compulsion to "write" their concerns for the marginalized black population and implications of their racial background. The creative writers belonging to both races in South Africa not only find themselves inhabiting a liminal position, they are also unsure of their voice and articulation. The uncertainty of narrative authority instead of vitiating articulation opens a new perspective of "narrative in-betweenness". Writers are thus compelled to search for an "as-yet-undefined site of creativity" from which one can render the ethical nuances of their positionality. The quest for this "as-yet-undefined site of creativity" plays an important part in understanding the interim position of the white authors like J.M. Coetzee, whose works according to critics such as Dominic Head may be studied in relation to a particular context of postcolonial writing, that of the literature of the "post-colonizer" (Dominic Head, 1997).

## IN-BETWEEN SPACE OF CULTURE: THE MASTER-CASTE AND THE MIDDLE VOICE

According to Bhabha, "liminality" is a category related to the concept of cultural hybridity. The liminal for Bhabha is an interstitial passage between fixed identifications which entertains difference without an assumed or imposed hierarchy. Taking his cue from Derrida, Bhabha attributes the inability of culture to be located in a fixed space to its inherent quality of "liminality". Bhabha takes up Derrida's notion of *différance*, splitting it up to account for sameness while simultaneously creating space for its *differend* to set into motion a discourse on similarities and differentiation. Through this concept, Bhabha makes a case for the interstitial spaces that culture occupies in the imagination of the nation. "What emerges as an effect of such "incomplete signification" is a turning of boundaries and limits into the in-between spaces through which meanings of cultural and political authority are negotiated" (1990: 5). Moreover, the zone of the political is not the "public" sphere of material relations between the colonizer and the colonized, but the shifting, often unconscious and affective area "in between" the dominant and subordinate cultures. This is a site that is marked by the unstable traffic of continuously (re)negotiated psychic identifications and political (re)positioning necessary to bring about a radical transformation in socio-cultural fabrics which are scored by coercion, inequality and conflict. As Bhabha says: "The place of difference and otherness, or the space of the adversarial...is never entirely on the outside or implacably oppositional...The contour of difference is agnostic, shifting, splitting" (1994: 109).

It is from within this politically charged liminal, in-between space of culture that authors like J. M. Coetzee write. Coetzee's novels, with their diverse locales and period, are oblique fictional enquiry into his country's moral and political crisis. His works are an enquiry into the Afrikaner society's embattled national myths and authoritarian modes of literary discourse, as he tries to grapple with the hermeneutical dilemma forced upon the white author by the legacy of apartheid. Coetzee writes from a displaced and marginalized position. In the course of his investigations, he challenges traditional assumptions about authority and agency in fiction and targets some of its key ingredients, such as myth, ideology, and historical vision.

By virtue of belonging to the white race, Coetzee is associated with the hegemonic authority of the white race. However, Coetzee consciously rejects the cultural authority of the white man, "The Master Caste" along with its implications of racial superiority – a concept that he continually tries to dismantle in his works. Nevertheless, in the complex and fractured society of South Africa, where the category of race with its consequences of economic and political privilege and deprivation has played an important formative influence, Coetzee realizes that it is impossible to escape one's social class. Coetzee responds to the accusation of complicity by self-reflexively examining the specific form of marginality that he represents and thereby highlighting the crisis of authority in writing in South Africa. He strives to highlight his crisis of authority and marginality by being critically aware of his "writing self" by writing in what he calls in the "middle voice", which is indicative of writing that is self-referential. His "writing self" is constantly under suspicion and interrogation hence it acquires an impersonal and detached force by virtue of the phenomenon of the "middle voice", a writing position that is in between the active and the passive. According to Coetzee, the phenomenon of the "middle voice" incorporates the idea of carrying out an action, with reference to the self. In the instance of writing, writing in the "middle voice" is indicative of writing that is self-referential.

Coetzee's notion of writing in the "middle voice" in writing is akin to Barthes' analogy of the act of writing as the writer's attempt to "make oneself the centre of the action of *la parole*... to leave the writer (*le scripteur*) inside the writing, not as a psychological subject...but as an agent of action" (1970: 142). Writing in this sense is thus not an art, but an activity; the only space there is for the one who writes to inhabit; and narrative is a historical product as it engages with the contingent forces of culture and history. Coetzee's focus on the problem of authority in the South African scene of writing brings the notion of agency, as well as the writer's relationship with his social environment into question. In the context of a fragmented nation-state like South Africa, the notion of agency is more closely aligned with the concepts of nationhood, legitimacy and authority within the framework of a broader national narrative. Coetzee posits a wary, marginal narrative subject who, as David Attwell says, "deftly negotiates the interstices of power, maintaining its ethical integrity, but avoiding not only appeals for inclusion but also any overstatement of its own legitimacy and authority" (1993: 25–6).

Coetzee's engagement with the nature and crisis of fiction writing in the South Africa of what a fellow South African writer, Nadine Gordimer (1988) has called as the "interregnum" leads Coetzee into a rigorous enquiry into the ontology of fictional discourse as well as an attempt to locate a position from which to speak. His works are characterized by a reflexive self-consciousness which is not simply a reminder of the constitutive functions of language; rather, it is a mode of self-consciousness that informs the understanding of the linguistic, formal, historical and political forces that determine the scene of writing in South Africa. The act of writing and textuality sets into motion a certain play of signifiers, which in turn contains the ghostly traces of history and any attempt to escape historical reflexivity would lead to the erasure of the horrors and injustices of the legacy of apartheid. Coetzee is of the opinion that once radical Metafiction does away with the tyranny of the "real", it has few options. It can simply bequeath a legacy of failed attempts at transcendence; or in a spirit of defiance, turn this impasse into a virtue by celebrating the notion of plurality and play. Coetzee is aware that the linguistic condition governing the available forms of association, such as identity, agency and intention, is more complex and pronounced in postcolonial writings and in writings on South Africa in particular. In the postcolonial context, writing cannot divorce itself from concrete historical conjunctures. Since Coetzee's oeuvre is reflections on an encounter in which the legacies of European postmodernism comes into contact with colonialism and apartheid, his works take the form of a compelling postcoloniality that brings its metropolitan heritage into a charged and complex relationship with the historical crisis in which it finds itself. According to Coetzee, the issue of authority and possible forms of address in the absence of self-reflexivity forms the representative crisis of postmodernism and its crippling paralysis before history. He therefore seeks a means within fiction to interrogate the postmodern paralysis and to move beyond this impasse to a reconstructed position in which fiction can speak to the political concerns in South Africa.

## *IN THE HEART OF THE COUNTRY*: MAGDA'S MARGINAL SUBJECTIVITY

Coetzee's 1977 novel *In the Heart of the Country* displays a wary marginal narrative subject who attempts to intervene and subvert the dominant narrative of colonialism through the vector of gender. As a parody of the white South African frontier narratives and pioneer histories, the novel subverts colonial pastoralism. The story of Magda, Coetzee's female protagonist, throws into sharp relief not only the inherent problems and eventual breakdown of colonial patriarchy, but also constitutes a strategic position of weakness from which Coetzee can dismantle colonial authority. As a displaced subject who is poised on the verge of unreason, Coetzee's Magda not only dramatizes his own crisis of authority and representation in writing, but also provides him with a model of marginality that necessarily disrupts the attempts of the hegemonic power to frame and signify him, which itself is a historical act.

Coetzee's *In the Heart of the Country*, published in 1977 examines the conventions of the South African "plaasroman", or farm novel. The novel follows the convention of confessional writing. It is written in the form of a personal journal; its numbered paragraphs modelled on the interior monologue of its author, who is also the central character of the novel. Influenced by the "nouveau roman" or the colonial pastoral and its equivalent in film, *In the Heart of the Country* tests the limits of a late modernist consciousness in the savage torpor of settler colonialism. The novel is composed as a series of numbered paragraphs which underscores its own fictiveness. The metafictional commentary here focuses on the literature of colonial pastoralism in South Africa and on the liberal romantic novel of the "plaasroman" which can be traced back to Olive Schreiner's *The Story of an African Farm*. Magda, the protagonist is a self confessed "spinster" living with her Afrikaner father in a farm in the out-backs of South Africa. She is jealous of her father's black mistress, who also happens to be the Black servant Hendrik's wife and in her bid to cope with her resentment she writes the novel in which she lets her mind flow, describes the plans she makes to assassinate the concubine and cries for her frustrated desire of becoming a woman. In the midst of this stream of consciousness, she informs us of how she actually killed her father and had sexual encounters with servant Hendrik. At the end of the story, she has lost her mind, alone in her home in the middle of nowhere. *In the Heart of the Country* blurs the thin line between insanity and reality through the eyes of the protagonist. This rapid thrust between lucid dreams and everyday life, however, merely provides the reader with a wholly unreliable narrator. This type of narration consumes the novel, as Magda does not actually recount what has occurred, but rather what she wishes to occur, or perhaps her fantasies of such situations. The reader is challenged when presented with the text in a blur of reckless accounts. We first believe Magda to have murdered her father and his wife with an axe, but after her father reappears in the novel, it becomes clear that she has in fact merely fantasized about such an act. The line between reality and fantasy is no longer visible, and the reader is compelled to take it upon himself or herself to determine not only what Magda actually does, but what she wants us to know.

*In the Heart of the Country* is Coetzee's attempt to search for "an as-yet-undefined site of creativity" that dramatizes the vicissitudes of his liminality and settler-postcoloniality. For Coetzee, the act of writing is a mode of self preservation in a highly politicized society like South Africa. In order to foreground a certain truth in writing, Coetzee distinguishes between two forms, one that he calls as truth to fact and the other that reaches beyond the factual. The latter according to Coetzee, unfolds only in writing, as it "is related to silence, to reflection, to the practice of writing" (1992: 65–6). Embedded in the practice of writing, this truth has the underpinnings of Coetzee's ethical and humane vision. This vision holds the key not only to the establishing of an equal and reciprocal exchange between the races, but also the truth about one's self. This vision calls for a critical self examination and an unflinching awareness, followed by forgiveness when dealing with the historical burden of South Africa's shameful legacy of colonialism and apartheid.

For Coetzee, the novel of traditional liberal positivism and realism cannot produce this form of truth telling, as this task requires a degree of reflexivity that is necessary to expose the facticity and political underpinnings that govern the conditions of writing. He maintains that confession and introspection, no matter how rigorous, is not enough to arrive at the truth. As Attwell says, Coetzee's "self of writing" therefore attempts to arrive at this truth by drawing the scepticism and symptomatic sensitivity of poststructuralism into writing, as a means for searching ways in which the novel might recover an ethical basis, while acknowledging the political context of South Africa (1992: 4).

This stance enables Coetzee to deal with the problem of narrative authority in his fictions. His involvement with the problem of authority leads him, as Attwell says, to acknowledge two observations regarding authority. Firstly, he observes that the brute facticity of power has the effect of confining and limiting writing. Secondly, if authority is ultimately an effect of power, it should be possible, through fiction's capacity to reconfigure the rules of discourse, to find a speaking position outside power relations. This is the central concern of Coetzee's endeavour to "imagine the unimaginable" (1992: 11), which is an attempt to retrieve an unreconstructed position outside power relations from which he can voice his authorial concerns. Nevertheless, this authorial position situated outside power relations is not free from Coetzee's self-imposed complicity with the history of colonialism and apartheid rule. Coetzee's search for a means of bringing about an ethical reconstruction of South Africa begins with a negation of unbridgeable historical constraints that constantly undermine his efforts.

Magda, in *In the Heart of the Country*, is instrumental in demonstrating Coetzee's stance both as a linguistic and critical-cultural theorist in his concept of the "self" as a decentered and displaced construct. As a critical-creative author, Coetzee inherits the poststructuralist scepticism of liberal positivism and realism, which can be traced back to the Western project of Enlightenment and rationality. Coetzee displays this scepticism by critiquing the Cartesian self as a fictitious construct that coincides with the period of imperial expansionism that is nevertheless nearing its extinction with the onset of decolonization. For Coetzee, the issue of historicity entails the implications of living in a particular historical culture. From this perspective, writing and fiction can no longer be considered as an unreflexive and ambivalent medium of reaction to historical givens; rather, it is a site where historical discourse and fictionality begin to compete for authority.

Coetzee's critical treatment of history and rationalism leads to the emergence of the displaced authorial subject, who is the result of his struggle with colonialism. A displaced subject as a narrator is locked in a struggle with the historical burden of colonialism that is oppressive and defining; giving shape to a particular consciousness and existential condition. Inhabiting the fringes of an oppressive colonial system that he/she cannot actively relate to, but is forced to endure, the displaced subject is compelled to move alternately between a self-conscious recognition of its complicity with the colonial discourse and denial of its colonial moorings which negates the self-reflexivity of the first stance.

In *In the Heart of the Country*, Magda is such a displaced subject. Magda is not a conventional mother-martyr and sustainer of racial purity of the South African "plaasroman" or farm novel. She is a spinster, caught up in her neurotic fantasies where she constantly kills and buries her Afrikaner father, as well as the regime that he represents. She searches for a reciprocal relationship with her black servants, yet remains trapped within the very racist patterns of dominance and subservience that she tries to subvert. Magda claims to be "a spinster with a locked diary", having an "uneasy consciousness", frantically resisting the possibility of becoming "one of the forgotten ones of history" (1999: 11). As a displaced subject, her desperate attempts to seek and construct a life for herself become the only means to resist her fate. She realizes that in a colonial condition, all forms of relationship and communication – filial, societal, marital as well as the colonial structures of kinship – lack authenticity and reciprocity. In such a situation, she realizes the need to create a new order of authenticity that is possible only by subverting the old racist regime of colonialism. However, in the absence of a cultural mechanism that functions as a mirror that throws back the reflections of the self by others, Magda is bereft of a crucial factor in constituting a stable identity. As a result, she is completely alienated. Cut off from the world that she inhabits, Magda turns to a schizophrenic interior monologue, which displays a breakdown of the signifying chain that is responsible for bringing about cohesion and meaning in the language of social interaction. The consequence of this breakdown is a schizophrenic and fragmented discourse that fails to display a unified personal identity connecting to different segments of time. The numbered units of her discourse reflect Magda's lack of a reciprocal exchange with others, as well as the fictiveness of her discourse. Denied of a reciprocal exchange and relationship with her Afrikaner father, as well as her black servants: Hendrik and his wife Klein-Anna, Magda retreats and is trapped in her internal monologue of neurotic and morbid fantasies: "This monologue of the self is a maze of words out of which I shall not find a way until someone else gives me a lead" (1999: 17).

The fictiveness of Magda's monologue is a metafictional commentary on the literature of colonial pastoral realism in South Africa, as well as on the tradition of the liberal Romantic novel of isolation that can be traced to Olive Schriener. Coetzee does not subscribe to the genre of realism and the belief that a realistic documentation of colonial and apartheid's oppression is the unquestioned means of telling the truth about South Africa. Coetzee is sceptical of the liberalism of the white realist writers, as they have failed to engender a literature of equal and reciprocal relationship between the races. In the unproblematic realism of South Africa's literary culture, Coetzee claims to find a "failure, almost a refusal to create a structure in which there is some centre of intelligence" (Cited in an interview with A. Thorold and R. Wicksteed), for they cannot convey his ethical concept of truth-telling about the politics and culture of South Africa. In this sense, Coetzee's writing is a metafictional commentary on the "nausea of writing without conviction, without desire" (1992: 19).

Magda's fictive monologue is not an indication of a degeneration into a post-Romantic impasse brought about by the recognition of its factitiousness; rather it is a reflection on the self's negotiation between its existential-ethical dimensions of consciousness and the linguistic rules of language that define it. Coetzee acknowledges the impossibility of existing and expressing oneself outside of language. This is more pronounced in a colonial situation, where the linguistic conditions governing the available forms of exchange and association are more rigid. The endeavour to search out a form of linguistic expression that is capable of bearing the complex nuances of his concern for an equal and reciprocal exchange between the races, as well as addressing the implicit question of identity in postcolonial, multiethnic South Africa leads Coetzee to have an active engagement with what he calls "poetics of reciprocity" and "poetics of failure." Coetzee's "poetics of reciprocity" deals with the possibility of an existing reciprocal linguistic exchange between the races.

## "POETICS OF RECIPROCITY"

As a linguist, Coetzee is particularly concerned with people as a grammatical category, especially the relation between the pronouns "I" and "You" and how their existential implications signify in language. Coetzee explores the "I-You" relationship, which is an integral part of his "poetics of reciprocity" in his essay on Gerrit Achterberg's "Ballade van de gasfitter." In this essay, Coetzee draws upon Sartre's existentialism, Martin Buber's theological myth of the primal "I-Thou" relationship, Wallace Stevens' post-Romantic concept of selfhood, as well as the linguistic descriptions in Benveniste and Jakobson of the unstable patterns of reference in pronouns and shifters, to focus on the self's relation to language and to others. On the level of semantics, the pronouns "I" and "You" are in Jakobson's terms "shifters" (1957: 2), what Benveniste describes as a "set of 'empty' signs...which are 'filled' as the speaker adopts them", entering the referential system as mere "abbreviative substitutes" (1966: 254–56). Simultaneously on the existential level, Coetzee draws from Martin Buber's primal "I-Thou" relationship to emphasize on the mutual existential dependence of the "I" and "You." According to Buber's myth, the primary word is not "I", but "I-Thou", the word of "natural combination" (1959: 3, 24), which indicates a primordial relationship between "I" and "You", that precedes their signification in language. With the objectification of the "You" into "It" that leads to the isolation of the "I"; the "I" is thrown into a perpetual search for the "You" to resolve its existential incompleteness. An attempt to convey this reciprocal dependence of the "I" and "You" in linguistic discourse forms the central concern of Coetzee's "poetics of reciprocity". This existential search of the "I" for a primal "You" compels it to cut through the complex signifiers of names to get through to a real "You". At this juncture, Coetzee refers to Achterberg's "Ballade van de gasfitter" in terms of an unqualified romantic "I" searching for an equally enigmatic "You". Convinced that a pure "You" lies beyond the disguise of names, the "I" in the ballad picks up a disguise of a gasfitter as a manoeuvre to get closer to the elusive "You". The gas is metaphorically significant as the knowledge of a pure "You". Released in its pure state in the atmosphere, gas expands formlessly to infinity and can prove to be destructive by causing death by asphyxiation or explosion. However, when mixed with other elements of the atmosphere and subject to the synthesis of controlled combustion, gas is an invaluable source of light and warmth. Similarly, by analogy, a pure and unrestrained "You" has destructive portentions. Just as the gasfitter has to seal the "dichten" or hole through which gas infiltrates the atmosphere, the "I" is also compelled to seal and contain the spillage of the pure "You". For Coetzee, language is the only means to block the hole through which the overwhelming pure essence of "You" threatens to spill out in the form of an unqualified romantic selfhood. The neglect of the art and craft of dichten of sealing the hole, according to Coetzee, stems from a "metaphorical overwhelming to carry us to a state of being beyond names or identities, that is, beyond language, to the forest where things have no names" (1992: 78). There is an affinity between Achterberg's gas and dichten imagery and Sartre's imagery of consciousness as a hole through which nothingness pours out into the world in *Being and Nothingness* (1966: 59). Coetzee therefore likens the search of the "I" for the primal "You" to the story of the search of the Christian knight for the way to the cross of Calvary, whose consummation of the search for the "Thou" is a moment in the presence of both his nothingness and an infinitely remote God. Since a primal "I" and "You" cannot be reinstated nor contained in the field of linguistics, the existential void of the "I" cannot be resolved.

In Coetzee's *In the Heart of the Country*, Magda dramatizes the altercations and negotiations of the linguistic and existential aspects of the "I-You" relationship. She displays the implications of the "I-You" relation for the subject in a society as divided as South Africa, where possibility of a language of equal exchange does not seem to be attainable. She recognizes that the language that she speaks with her black servants has been contaminated by her Afrikaner father and the regime that he represents: "The language that should pass between myself and these people was subverted by my father and cannot be recovered. What passes between us is now a parody. I was born into a language of hierarchy, of distance and perspective. It was my father-tongue..." (1999: 195).

Magda's obsession with how language constitutes the self and her determination to get beyond the "names" that keep her from bursting "...through the screen of names into the goatseye view of Armoede and the stone desert" (1999: 19), leads her to reflect on the relationship between desire, language and social relations. Language is a social medium of exchange but, ironically, it cannot portray the passion that she feels for the land and the people: "Words are coin. Words alienate. Language is no medium for desire. Desire is rapture, not exchange. It is only by alienating the desire that language masters it" (1999: 28).

Magda's attempts to cut through the rigid colonial linguistic hierarchy in her search for a language of equal exchange fails, yet at the same time she realizes that this inadequate and contaminated language that is her legacy from her white settler father, is her only means of exchange with the black servants. Burdened by the political legacy of her Afrikaner father and the pathological master-servant relations in the farm, Magda describes her predicament as: "Aching to form the words that will translate me into the land of myth and hero, here I am still my dowdy self in a dull summer heat that will not transcend itself" (1999: 4).

In such circumstances, Magda undertakes some of her most intense ontological introspection. She imagines herself as existing outside the boundaries of human society, in a primordial state of "unthinking animal integrity" (44) and she thinks of herself alternately as a beetle "who lays no eggs and blinks in the sun" (20); a snake "licking the eggslime off herself" (41) before crawling off to the farmhouse; and a black widow spider that hides in a corner to "engulf whoever passes by in [my] venom" (43). She also conceives of herself as inhabiting a world outside of consciousness altogether in a condition akin to the Sartrean "being-in-itself": "I am lost in the being of my being. This is what I was meant to be: a poetess of interiority, an explorer of the inwardness of stones, the emotions of ants, the consciousness of the thinking parts of the brain. It seems to be the only career, if we accept death, for which life in the desert has fitted me" (1999: 38).

At the same time, Magda is also acutely aware of an internalized absence of meaning. She describes herself as "a hole with a body draped around it... a hole crying to be whole" (1999: 44). In his Achterberg essay, Coetzee quotes from Wallace Stevens' "Nanzia Nunzio" that approximates Magda's condition: "I am the woman stripped more nakedly/Than nakedness.../Speak to me that, which spoken, will array me..." (1955: 395–6).

## "POETICS OF FAILURE"

As Magda lacks reciprocity, her sense of the self has to be created by auto-suggestion that Coetzee dramatizes by saying that: "All versions of the I are fictions of the I. The primal I is not recoverable. Neither of the words I and You can exist pure in the medium of language" (1992: 75).

In the absence of reciprocity, Magda is compelled to resort to fictional self construction. She concocts a pastoral comedy in which she features as a wife to a farmer and the mother of "a litter of ratlike, runty girls, all the spit image of myself, scowling into the sun, tripping over their own feet, identically dressed in bottle green smocks and snubnosed black shoes" (1999: 46). Alternatively, she imagines herself as the defender of the feudal codes that her father disregards in his illicit relation with the wife of his black servant. Magda's endeavours to create a story with "a beginning, a middle and an end" (1999: 46) is indicative of her self-preservation instincts. She has to resort to fiction as the only means of self representation whereby she can construct a subject position for herself within history. Magda's stories of a childhood, spent in the schoolhouse learning the fundamentals of culture with the siblings of her fantasy is chaotic in nature. The siblings degenerate quickly into cruel step-brothers and step-sisters who ostracize her. However, as none of Magda's fictions can be sustained for a substantial period, Magda hides and takes recourse to a denial of her situation that is characteristic of a displaced subject: "Whose shell I presently skulk in does not matter, it is the shell of a dead creature. What matters is that my anxious self should have a refuge from the predators of the deep" (1999: 47).

Rather than dissolving the issue of the self's relation to language and to others in its existential-historical dimension into a postmodernist "play", Coetzee emphasizes on the possibilities and limits of discursive prose. This is particularly true when the question of true passion is concerned. Referring to Nizhinsky's diaries, Coetzee says that whenever a real passion of feeling is loosened in discursive prose, one feels as though one is reading the utterances of a madman (1992: 60). Magda's madness is an indication of her passion, a passion that Coetzee speaks of in his Jerusalem Prize speech – a passion for South Africa that does not valorize land above people and polity, a passion for the country and its people which is woefully lacking in the European settlers and their descendants. Magda's passion is what makes her an anomalous figure, for as Coetzee says, "her passion doesn't belong in the genre in which she finds herself" (1992: 62). Magda allows Coetzee to stage his passions, for as he says, "Magda may be mad, but I, behind her, am merely passionate" (1992: 61).

The failure for reciprocity, in his own words, as "poetics of failure", "involves a history of self-cancelling literature which in John Barthe, Nabokov and Beckett has projected the failure of the romantic-liberal notion of the self" (1992: 61). The "poetics of failure" is a form of self-reflexive writing that is suspicious of an unproblematic, romantic liberal notion of the self. Coetzee's poetics of failure is a metafictional commentary on the fictionality of the self. It is an endeavour which consists of a deliberate display of the constructedness of the artefact of an "authentic" self, out of "an endlessly regressive, etiolated self consciousness lost in the labyrinth of language and endlessly failing to erect itself into autonomy" (1992: 87).

The poetics of failure deliberately parades the failure of the Cartesian self to reach autonomy, so as to emphasize on the fictitiousness of an autonomous and essential self and demonstrates the overwhelming role of language in the formation of the self. The poetics of failure is evident in Achterberg's "Ballade van de gasfitter", where the endeavour of the "I" to constitute a pure "You" meets with failure. Having failed, the "I" is split off and discarded by a "real" "I", who can only assert that his mere survival, the fact that the ballad exists, is proof enough of its non-failure. The poetics of failure is therefore a system of closure that resembles the traditional hermeneutics of closure. It follows a manoeuvre in which through a denial and denouncing of the self, writing and textuality achieve closure by cutting off the link between the real world of authors, writing and sequence of signs on the paper on the one hand and a fictive world of characters, actions and passions on the other.

Coetzee's poetics of failure is reminiscent of Beckett's concept of art, which is an "expression that there is nothing to express" (Cited in Coetzee, ed. Attwell 1992: 87). Having failed to bridge the chasm between her father as well as the black servants and herself, Magda speculates about what other kinds of literature she could have constructed for herself. She mentions the genre of the colonial-pastoral, but ultimately rejects it. According to Coetzee, the colonial-pastoral constructs an isolated space, where things that normally seem improbable in the wide world and the cities can be achieved. This concept of a constructed space as a local solution to complex issues is, according to Coetzee, artificial and ineffective. He displays his rejection of the colonial pastoral novel through Magda, who is sceptical of the South African pastoral genre that is loaded with the notion of humanism in South Africa. According to Coetzee, humanism in South Africa is a part of British liberal culture that has not only failed to engender a literature of equal and reciprocal relations between the races, but also has failed to persuade the British as well as the Dutch colonialists that such a relation is something worth sacrificing for (1992: 62).

The consequence of such a failure is the establishment of a South African society that is burdened with the pathologies of the master and slave relation. It is a society where neither the master nor the slave is free; master is not free as he cannot do without his slave, while the slave is not free as he is not his own master. The colonial pastoral genre exemplifies this stunted and deformed human relation and demonstrates what Coetzee calls in his Jerusalem Prize speech a "literature in bondage":

> South African literature is a literature in bondage, as it reveals in even its highest moments, shot through as they are with feelings of homelessness and yearnings for a nameless liberation. It is less than fully human literature, unnaturally preoccupied with power and the torsions of power, unable to move from elementary relations of contestation, domination, and subjugation to the vast and complex human world that lies beyond them. It is exactly the kind of literature you would expect people to write from a prison (1992: 98).

Following Coetzee, Magda also rejects the colonial pastoral genre and claims that " I have uttered my life in my own voice throughout, what a consolation that is I have chosen at every moment my own destiny, which is to die here in the petrified garden" (1999: 151). In Magda's declaration there is a hint of a palpable selfhood in an existential-historical realm of possibility. However, the subjecthood hinted at is simultaneously aware of its facticity and arbitrariness, of its dependence upon language. The duality of this position is, as Attwell says, a demonstration of Coetzee's reflexivity and scrupulous position which ensures that the existential-historical dimensions are never totally eclipsed by the field of language (1993: 59).

## TRANSLATION/TRANSGRESSION

As a novel which is impelled by the poetics of failure, *In the Heart of the Country* is, in another sense, a work of transgression. Transgression is a manoeuvre by which Coetzee exposes the limits of the structures of South Africa's settler colonialism and legacy of apartheid. There are no actual events as such that take place in the novel. What takes place in the novel is an act of consciousness and of language; and what historicizes this act is the fact that it is deeply transgressive. The transgressions in *In the Heart of the Country* are mainly anthropological in nature. According to Mary Douglas (1985), societal and anthropological taboos define the boundaries of legitimate social behaviour. When they are broken, these boundaries as well as the social structures that they support are exposed. Magda's transgressive consciousness in *In the Heart of the Country* reveals the pathological undertone of the structure of relationships in the settler-colonial context. Through Magda's transgressive consciousness, Coetzee exposes the social codes of South Africa's settler colonialism to the scrutiny of the readers. In the novel, Magda's transgressions compile through sequential episodes in the narrative. In the first sequence, Magda's transgression exposes the deformed family relations in a colonial set-up. From Magda's standpoint, the conspicuous absence of the mother in the family throws Magda and her father into a relationship that is tinged with Oedipal implications. Pondering her relationship with her father, Magda concludes that the colonial daughters who are wooed by their "masterful fathers" are "bitter vestals, spoiled for life" (1999: 4). She calls this power of the white settler fathers over their daughters as "The childhood rape" (1999: 4). According to Attwell, two sets of consequences arise from this situation of the family that can be discussed in anthropological terms (1993). The first sequence is the establishment of the father's role as the bearer of what Bronislaw Malinowski (Cited in Attwell, 1993) calls the "principle of legitimacy", which bestows an identity and a name to the offspring thereby providing a notion of order and identity. In the absence of the mother, the role of the father becomes a terrifying legitimizing factor that seeps into Magda's consciousness of herself, locating her firmly in the historical destiny of the colonizer. Severed from the nurturing figure of a mother, Magda's world is a "lost world" that is characterized by stark masculine sterility: "My lost world is a world of men, of cold nights, woodfire, gleaming eyes and a long tale of dead heroes in a language

I have not unlearned" (1999: 7). Magda's family structure is an allegory of the effect of colonialism on the continent. Colonialism in South Africa brought about the separation between the indigenes and their homogenous culture thereby forcing them into an alien territory that was divided among the white settlers.

The second consequence of Magda's family situation is what Slater calls "libidinal withdrawal" (Cited in Attwell, 1993), which undermines the establishment of exogamous relations. Magda conceives of herself as a spinster who is lost to history because unlike her father, she does not have any role to play in reproducing history, through marriage. She is lost to history, as she cannot gain access to a position from which she can represent herself within the feudal system that her father symbolizes. As a white woman within the patriarchal regime of settler-colonialism of her father, Magda finds herself in a position of marginality: "To my father I have been an absence all my life. Therefore instead of being the womanly warmth at the heart of the house I have been a zero, null, vacuum towards which all collapses inward" (1999: 2). However, Magda's bitter acceptance of her non-position in her father's household is eclipsed by her fear of total displacement with the arrival of her father's bride. Though the courtship and marriage of her father is her own construction, Magda's imaginary step-mother poses a threat to the only close relationship and social identity that Magda enjoys by virtue of belonging to her father's household. Magda is resentful of the patriarchal imperialist structure of her world, but at the same time, she realizes that her father and the imperial system that he symbolizes is the only available social identity for her. Caught is such a situation, Magda is plagued by ontological-existential anxieties which compel her to confront the naked truth about her position as a white woman in South Africa: "What are pain, jealousy, loneliness doing in the African night? Does a woman looking through a window into the dark mean anything? I stare out through a sheet of glass into a darkness that is complete, that lives in itself....There is no act I know of that will liberate me into the world. There is no act I know of that will bring the world into me" (1999: 10).

The first act of parricide in the sequence is Magda's attempt to break free from the impasse of absence and displacement that she is subjected to in her father's household. The imaginary murder of the bridal couple is symbolic of Magda's rebellion against the rule of her father as well as the colonial history that he represents.

In the second sequence of the novel, Coetzee exposes the hidden pathologies underlying the master and servant relationship in the colonial family. As Attwell says, "a principle of equivalence" (1993: 62), is erected between the colonial family in the farmhouse and that of Hendrik, the black servant when he brings home his new bride Klein-Anna, in a move that is reminiscent of the beginning of the first sequence where Magda's father brings his bride home. According to Attwell, this equivalence creates a tension that is manifested in two scenarios; in the first scenario, Magda's father is substituted for Hendrik in the servants' marriage; while in the second scenario, Hendrik is substituted for the father in a quasi-incestuous relationship with Magda. The first scenario breaks the bar against miscegenation and unlocks the liminal apprehensions in Magda when she is confronted with her father's illicit desires. Her father's illegitimate relation with Hendrik's wife forces Magda to face the harsh truth that the exogamous relations defined by her father's colonial decree cannot ensure equal and reciprocal relation between the races. However, this does not diminish the possibility of easy sexual gratification for the dominant white masters that is not governed by institutionalized forms of social exchange. Repelled by such hypocrisy, Magda murders her father in the second sequence of the novel. The act of parricide in the second sequence is symbolic of Magda's rebellion against the duplicity of her father as well as the conventions of her social structure. After the imaginary murder of her father, Magda attempts to domesticate the illicit sexuality unleashed by her father by bringing Hendrik and Klein-Anna to live with her in the farmhouse while attempting to enter into a liaison with Hendrik. Her effort to draw near to the black servant falls through and she is raped. With the failure of her attempts to establish an equal and reciprocal relation, Magda discovers that the racial conflict underlying the master-servant relationship is more pronounced and consequential than she has imagined it to be.

Magda's two-fold failure, the failure to secure a subject position within history by creating fiction of the self; and her failure to establish an equal and reciprocal relation between the races is dramatized in her disorientation towards the end of the novel, where she steadily loses her grasp over time. Magda's disorientation begins in the second sequence, after she brings the servants into the house following the imaginary murder of her father. As the novel moves towards closure,

Magda's disorientation is sharply contrasted by the resurgence of a more conventional and chronological sense of time in the novel. However, this conventional sense of time weighs down on Magda and she begins to live more and more sporadically: "Once I lived in time as a fish in water, breathing it, drinking it, sustained by it. Now I kill time and time kills me" (1999: 87). The outside world, which impinges on Magda's interior world of fantasy through external agents of temporality in the form of the visitors to the farm, an assertive Hendrik who demands his wages and the boy who arrives with a message demanding payment of taxes, demonstrate Magda's loss of monopoly on the time of her fictive constructions and narrative perspective.

In an interview in 1978, Coetzee speaking of both Jacobus Coetzee and Magda said that they lack the stature to transform Buber's "It" into "You"; to create a society in which reciprocity exists. Therefore, both have condemned themselves "to desperate gestures towards establishing intimacy" ("Speaking", 1978: 23). The poetics of failure builds up to a crescendo in the final sequence of the novel, which depicts Magda labouring to attain reciprocity in the realm of myth. She gives up on any possibility of human exchange after being abandoned by Hendrik and Klein-Anna and chases away the boy carrying the tax message, who is similar to the boy who appears at the end of each act in *Waiting for Godot*, claiming to have a message from the elusive and enigmatic Godot. Cast aside by the community of humans, Magda is forced to resort to communion with the elusive sky-gods, in her effort to find a language that is unmediated by social division. However, the language of "pure meaning" (1999: 137) uttered by the mystical sky-gods is a metaphysical discourse, to which Magda has no access. In her attempt to seek transfiguration through a reciprocal dialogue with the mythical sky-gods, Magda tries to communicate with them by shouting skywards, placing stones in the field to form letters, writing entreaties and cryptic poems; yet all her efforts fall through, leaving her in a state of thwarted passion and poignant despair: "Why will no one speak to me in the true language of the heart? The medium, the median-that is what I wanted to be. Neither master nor slave, neither parent nor child, but the bridge between, so that in me the contraries should be reconciled" (1999: 145).

## THE VOICE OF THE WHITE WOMAN

Transcendence, Magda eventually realizes, is something that proves to be unattainable: "We are the castaways of God as we are the castaways of history. That is the origin of our feeling of solitude" (1999: 147). Through Magda, Coetzee also demonstrates the complex ramifications of the settler postcoloniality and his positionality as a white male author in South Africa. For Coetzee, the voice of the white woman is the most effective vehicle, whereby he can dismantle the prevalent structure of power, authority and language. The feminine narrative voice combines the twin strategies of the lack of an adequate vantage point, as well as lack of absolute authority. Drawing from the dominant patriarchal ideology that defines the white woman's possession of the "word" as unstable, unauthorized and outside the general masculine "canon", Coetzee adopts the figure of the white woman whose awareness of the limitation of their narration as well as their limited access to narration, best exemplifies the suspicion and self-reflexivity of Coetzee's own writing position. The voice of the white woman narrator closely approximates to Coetzee's strategy of "writing in the middle voice" – a self-reflexive writing position that is situated between the active and passive position. Magda's passionate desire in *In the Heart of the Country*, Magda's to be "The medium, the median" (1999: 145), corresponds to the in-between position of the middle voice, that has the potential to bridge the gap between the contraries of a South African society torn by apartheid. As the white woman inhabits the interstices of colonial power, her ambivalent position in between the white masters and black slaves, corresponds to Coetzee's equivocal position of power and powerlessness. Coetzee conceives of his position as a white male in South Africa occupying a "lonely throne", shrouded by a "veiled unfreedom" (1992: 97) that is manifested in the scene of writing, where he finds himself without the moorings of authority. He conceives of himself "without authority" (1992: 392), because he rejects the authoritarian connotations that are linked to his position as a white male in South Africa. Coetzee therefore makes a deliberate choice of aligning himself to a position of necessary complicit marginality that is best demonstrated in his white woman narrator.

In one of his interviews, Coetzee emphasizes that one cannot question power from a position of power, but from its opposite position, which is the position of weakness (Morphett, 1987: 456). Therefore,

Coetzee avoids the possibility of replicating power by judiciously refusing to compete with it on its own terms. In his study of the failure of the pastoral novel in South Africa in White Writing, Coetzee highlights the dangerous potential of subversive writing to become dominant:

> Our ears today are finely attuned to modes of silence....Our craft is all in reading the other: gaps, inverses, undersides; the veiled; the dark, the buried, the feminine; alterities....It is a mode of reading which, subverting the dominant, is in peril, like all triumphant subversions, of becoming the dominant in turn. (1988: 81)

The non-position of the white woman narrator, who is placed outside the premises of authority and writing, forms Coetzee's strategic position of weakness from which he can dismantle authority. This notion draws its inspiration from Derrida's and the French Feminists' claim of the unique disruptive and subversive power of the feminine, which stems from its strategic location outside logocentrism. Coetzee's self-reflexivity and constant interrogation of the authority of the "writing self" leads him to Desiderius Erasmus' *The Praise of the Folie* (1549). In *Giving Offence* (1996: 60), Coetzee discusses Erasmus' use of the figure of the mad woman as a narrative strategy to escape the confining binaries, as well as to gain a position from which to address the debate between Papacy and Lutheran reformers. Moira, Erasmus' mad woman narrator does not need to be taken seriously for, as she points out, she is a woman who is aware of her limitations and position on the verge of unreason. She is therefore enabled by her non-position to state without inhibition her criticism about those who claim possession of wisdom, as well as wisdom itself. Magda in *In the Heart of the Country* is Coetzee's Moira, whose position as a white colonial daughter enables her to address the follies of colonialism's perceived wisdom. Like Moira, Magda's voice dominates the narrative in *In the Heart of the Country*, and like Moira, she is aware of her unique position between unreason and insight. Magda realizes her limitation and undermines the seriousness of her own narrative: "I am not a philosopher. Women are not philosophers and I am a woman" (1999: 130).

Coetzee's reliance on feminism as Fiona Probyn points out has its roots in the poststructuralist and postcolonial use of the feminine as "crisis" and necessary disruptive of narrative (2002), but is not coterminous with a feminist interest in the position of woman.

According to Michael du Plessis, rather than writing a "feminist" text, Coetzee indulges in the "textual enunciation of femininity" to "test the limits of meaning" (1988: 120). The use of the feminine is based on the notion that the female subjectivity as diffuseness, plurality, fluidity and subversiveness, can best represent the decentered and fragmented postmodern subject. As a displaced subject, poised on the verge of unreason, Magda thus dramatizes Coetzee's crisis of authority and representation in writing and provides him with a model of marginality that necessarily disrupts the attempts of the hegemonic power to frame and signify him.

## CONCLUSION

A study of Coetzee's *In the Heart of the Country* exemplifies his impulse to "imagine the unimaginable" (1992: 11), for creating a speaking position outside power relations by reconfiguring the rules of discourse through fiction. From this position of liminality, Coetzee explores the predicament of the white complicit-marginalized self while struggling for an ethical reconstruction and integration in a country that renders all such efforts futile. In his essay, "Into the Dark Chamber: The Writer and the South African State" (1986, 1992), Coetzee deals with the representation of torture in South African literature and emphasizes on the ethical vision in Gordimer's *Burger's Daughter* that anticipates a dispensation when "all human acts...will be returned to the ambit of moral judgement. In such a society, it will once again be *meaningful* for the gaze of the author, the gaze of authority and authoritative judgement, to be turned upon scenes of torture" (1992: 368). Though this ethical vision also informs Coetzee's works, he brings up his ethical reconstruction at "some as-yet-unimagined historical moment", with a movement that begins with abnegation. He acknowledges the unbridgeable historical constraints of colonialism and apartheid, as well as the constraints of the postmodern decentered and dispersed self in the ethical mission of reconstruction and integration of the races (1992: 12).

## Works Cited


Attwell, David. *J.M. Coetzee: South Africa and the Politics of Writing.* Berkeley, Cape Town: University of California Press, 1993.

Bassnett, Susan and Harish Trivedi eds. *Post-colonial Translation: Theory and Practice.* London and New York: Routledge, 1999.

Benveniste, Emile. "La Nature des pronoms." *Problemes de linguistique generale.* Paris: Gallimard, 1966.

Bhabha, Homi K. "Dissemination: Time, Narrative, and the Margins of the Modern Nation." *Nation and Narration.* Ed. Homi K. Bhabha. London and New York: Routledge, 1990. 291–322.

________. *The Location of Culture.* London and New York: Routledge, 1994.

Coetzee, J.M. "Speaking: J.M. Coetzee." Interview. Stephen Watson. *Speak* 1.3 (1978): 23–24.

________. *White Writing: On the Culture of Letters in South Africa.* Johannesburg: Radix (in association with Yale UP), 1988.

________. *Doubling the Point: Essays and Interviews.* Ed. David Attwell. Cambridge: Harvard University Press, 1992.

________. *Giving Offence: Essays on Censorship.* Chicago: U of Chicago Press. 1996.

________. *In the Heart of the Country.* Vintage, 1999.

________. "Grubbing for the Ideological Implications: A Clash (More or Less) with J.M. Coetzee." Interview. A. Thorold and R. Wicksteed. *Sjambok.* University of Cape Town, n.d.

Douglas, Mary. *Purity and Danger: An Analysis of the Concepts of Pollution and Taboo.* London: Routledge, 1966.

du Plessis, Michael. "Bodies and Signs: Inscriptions of Femininity in John Coetzee and Wilma Stockenstrom." *Journal of Literary Studies* 4.1 (March, 1988):118–129.

During, Simon. "Postmodernism or Postcolonialism?" *Landfall* 39.3 (Sept. 1985):366–80.

Erasmus, Desiderius. *The Praise of Folie.* Trans. Sir Thomas Chaloner. Ed. Clarence H. Miller. London: Oxford University Press, 1965.

Gordimer, Nadine. "Living in the Interregnum." *The Essential Gesture: Writing, Politics and Places.* Ed. Stephen Clingman. New York: Knopf, 1988.

Head, Dominic. *J.M. Coetzee: Cambridge Studies in African and Caribbean Literature.* Cambridge: Cambridge University Press, 1997.

Jakobson, Roman. *Shifters, Verbal Categories, and the Russian Verb.* Cambridge, Mass.: Harvard University Russian Language Project, 1957.

Morphett, Tony. "Two Interviews with J.M. Coetzee: 1983 and 1987." *Triquaterly* 69. (1987):454–65.

Pratt, M.L. *Imperial Eyes: Travel Writing and Transculturation.* London and New York: Routledge, 1992.

Probyn, Fiona. "J.M. Coetzee: Writing with/out Authority." JOUVERT: Journal of Postcolonial Studies, 7.1, 2002. <http://social.chass.ncsu.edu/jouvert/v7is1/Probyn.htm> (dt. 15/08/2005)

Sartre, Jean-Paul. *Being and Nothingness.* Trans. Hazel E. Barnes. New York: Washington Square Press, 1966.

Spivak, Gayatri C. *In Other Worlds: Essays in Cultural Politics.* London and New York: Routledge, 1988.

________. Spivak, Gayatri C. "In a Word: Interview." *Outside in the Teaching Machine.* London and New York: Routledge, 1993: 1–24.

Stevens, Wallace. "Notes towards a Supreme Fiction." *Collected Poems.* New York: Knopf, 1955. 406–407.

# 6

# Translating the Culture of the Subaltern in Elias's Novels

*Nazia Sultana*

> The insertion of India into colonialism is generally defined as a change from semi-feudalism into capitalist subjection. Such a definition theorizes the change within the great narrative of the modes of production and, by uneasy implication, within the narrative of the transition from feudalism to capitalism. Concurrently, this change is seen as the inauguration of politicization for the colonized. The colonial subject is seen as emerging from those parts of the indigenous élite which come to be loosely described as "bourgeois nationalist". The Subaltern Studies group seems to me to be revising this general definition and its theorization by proposing at least two things: first, that the moment(s) of change be pluralized and plotted as confrontations rather than transition (they would thus be seen in relation to histories of domination and exploitation rather than within the great modes-of-production narrative) and, secondly, that such changes are signalled or marked by a functional change in sign-systems... The most significant outcome of this revision or shift in perspective is that the agency of change is located in the insurgent or the "subaltern". (Spivak, 1987: 197)

## TRANSLATION OF THE SUBALTERN CULTURE

Who are the subalterns? Are the subalterns just a group of people who are connected through experience? Or the label "subaltern" has any other political dimension? How are they represented in texts? The representation of the subaltern is always problematic; always complicated by their position in politics and history. Indian feminist deconstructive critic Gayatri Chakravorty Spivak (1987) suggests in her book *In Other Worlds: Essays in Cultural Politics* that the phased development of the subaltern is complicated by the imperialist project. At the same time, she attempts to formulate a critical vocabulary that is appropriate to describe the experiences and histories of particular individuals and social groups who are historically repressed and exploited by the European colonialism (Morton, 2003: 47). For Spivak, words like "the colonized", "woman", and "the worker" may seem to provide a coherent political identity for disempowered individuals and groups to unite against the oppressors. These master signifiers do not do any justice to the lives and histories of those people who were frequently ignored and subsequently forgotten by anti-colonial national independence movements. Against such master signifiers, Spivak proposes to use the word subaltern to conceptualize a range of different subject positions which are not predefined by dominant political discourses (45). As Spivak claims in an interview published in *Polygraph:*

> I like the word "subaltern" for one reason. It is truly situational. "Subaltern" began as a description of a certain rank in the military. The word was used under censorship by Gramci: he called Marxism "monism," and was obliged to call the proletarian "subaltern." That word, used under duress, has been transformed into the description of everything that doesn't fall under a strict class analysis. I like that, because it has no theoretical rigor. (Spivak, 1990: 141)

If we look at Spivak's formulation carefully, we become able to understand that she believes that people or the groups which are marginalized, which cannot raise their voice collectively and have no political consciousness, are "subalterns". The task of understanding who they are, therefore, is crucial for understanding the politics of subaltern representation.

The term "subaltern" came into political discourse through Antonio Gramsci. Historically, subaltern referred to junior ranking officers in the British army (OED 1189). Notable early 20$^{th}$ century Italian Marxist theorist and politician Antonio Gramsci used the term to refer in particular to the unorganized groups of rural peasants based in Southern

Italy, who had no social or political consciousness as a group, and were therefore susceptible to the domination of the ruling ideas, culture and leadership of the state (Hawthorn, 248). In literary and cultural theory, subaltern thus refers to the members of those marginalized groups in society who are subjected to the hegemony of the ruling classes (Ashcroft, Tiffin et al., 218). In Gramsci's work, the subaltern serves as a coded way of referring to classes such as the peasantry. It is important to note that Gramsci uses the term in the plural form and uses it to refer to a class. For Gramsci, the subaltern classes are those who by definition are not unified and cannot unite until they become a state (Hawthorn, 235). Further, he directs attention towards both the way in which these groups are called into being by developments and transformations occurring in the sphere of economic production and their active or passive affiliation to the dominant political formation. His tentative conclusion is that subaltern groups "are always subject to the activity of ruling groups, even when they rebel and rise up; only permanent victory breaks up their subordination, and that not immediately" (Hawthorn, 344). For Gramsci, the history of subaltern social groups is necessarily fragmented and episodic, since they are always subject to the activity of ruling groups, even when they rebel. Clearly they have less access to the means by which they may control their own representation, and less access to cultural and social institutions (Ashcroft, Tiffin et al., 216). What is more, Gramsci emphasized that the oppression of the rural peasantry in Southern Italy could be subverted through the development of class consciousness among the peasants. To this extent, Gramsci's account of the subaltern resembled Karl Marx's earlier proclamation in the nineteenth century that the industrial working class in Europe carried the future potential for collective social and political change (216). Unlike Marx's model of social and political change, however, Gramsci stressed that the social and political practices of the rural peasantry were not systematic or coherent in their opposition to the state. It is this lack of coherence that distinguishes Gramsci's notion of the subaltern from the traditional Marxist perception of the industrial working class which is unified and coherent. Furthermore, this lack of a coherent political identity in Gramsci's description of the subaltern is also crucial to Spivak's discussion of subaltern in postcolonial world.

It is, however, imperative to note that in postcolonial theory, the concept of subaltern is an overused term, randomly used to refer to anyone who is politically or economically marginalized. Such academic co-options of the term have led Spivak to criticize academic opportunism that seeks to gain a privileged space in the name of subaltern representation. In her seminal essay on the issue "Can the Subaltern Speak?" Spivak claims that the historical and structural condition of political representation does not guarantee that the interests of the particular subaltern groups will be recognized or that their voice will be heard. She further mentions that the general difference between aesthetic and political structures of representation is that aesthetic representation tends to foreground its status as a re-presentation of the real, whereas political representation denies this structure of representation. Subaltern is a person without lines of social mobility.

"Can the Subaltern Speak?" pleads for translation rather than representation of the everyday culture of the subaltern by understanding the political logic of the culture of the subaltern and, in this way, "unsilencing" the unique muteness of the subaltern. Translation is an appropriate mode than "representation" to understand the subaltern. Translation of the subaltern, thought by Spivak in the manner of Benjamin, does not attempt to "re-present" (*dartelling*) the original, nor "represent" (*vertreten*), neither equivalent to the original, nor completely imaginative. This sort of translation is non-identical and creates a distance from the source, a space wherein the subaltern can speak. Translation is a desire to understand or respect the subaltern, an understanding or respect which helps in overcoming the inaccessibility of knowledge about the subaltern without eroding his/her otherness. The subaltern employs many codes of communication which should be understood for the task of translation. Translation of the everyday life of the subaltern, as it brings subaltern's codes of communication, mitigates against the hierarchy in forms of communication. The dominant mode of communication is not imposed upon the subaltern because it makes the task of subaltern translation absolutely difficult. Since translating the culture of subaltern is a matter of listening and understanding him/her, it foregrounds the dialectical relationship between the translator and the subaltern and engages both reciprocally in the constitution of the subjectivity of the other. Thus, Spivak translates the subaltern to understand him/her, as in the Bhaduri case, neither as *dartelling* nor as *vertreven* (Maggio, 2007).

Furthermore, Spivak claims that the narrativizations of history are structured or textured like what is called literature (Spivak, 1987: 244).

The production of historical accounts is the discursive narrativization of events. When historiography is self-consciously "non-theoretical" it sees its task, with respect to rival historical accounts of the same period, as bringing forth "what really happened" in a value-neutral prose. That history deals with real events and literature with imagined ones may now be seen as a difference in degree rather than a kind. The difference between cases of historical and literary events will always be there as a differential moment in terms of what is called "the effect of the real" (244). In fact the ways in which the difference is articulated between history and literature also has a hidden agenda. The historians's resistance to fiction relates the fact that the writing of history and of literature has social connotation even when these activities do not resemble what we understand by them today; and that historiography and literary pedagogy are disciplines.

Since official history discourses tend to privilege men and the ruling class as main actors of revolutionary politics, Spivak suggests that literature can provide a different space to articulate subaltern women, peasant, urban labourer's insurgency and resistance in the social text in postcolonial literature. So, Spivak suggests that literary texts can provide an alternative rhetorical site for articulating the histories of the subaltern. In this regard Elias's own relationship to historical discourse seems clear. He has always been gripped by the individual in history. *Chilekothar Sepai* (1986) and *Khoabnama* (1996) bend into full-fledged "historical fiction", history imagined into fiction where he depicts history with actors who seek to change it. Indeed, his repeated claim to legitimacy is that he researches thoroughly everything he represents in fiction. The plausibility of a Khijir and *Jummoner Maa* (*Chilekothar Sepai*), a Tamij, Fuljan and Kulsum (*Khoabnama*) is that they could have existed as subalterns in a specific historical moment imagined and tested by orthodox assumptions. A subalternist historian writer imagines a historical moment in order to narrate that event and creates some characters putting them at that insurgency (Spivak, 1987: 244). By the mechanics of writing as translation, a writer can also translate the subaltern within a historical moment and Elias has tried to do that. Elias's *Chilekothar Sepai* and *Khoabnama* emerge as a counter-narrative that challenges official histories. He shows Khijir's involvement in the 1969 mass insurgency and Tamij's dream of *Tevaaga* movement and indicates how these subalterns's dream and revolution have effaced gradually from the history. In *Khoabnama*, the book Khoabnama transfers from

Tamijer *Baap* to Sharafat's son. This transfer of the book Khoabnama symbolizes that the rising middle class ruling power snatches away the dream of the subaltern. This transfer is also symbolic from the historical point of view as well, because for Elias, history is collective. Hasan Al Zayed points out in his essay "Late Style as Politics" that Elias's novel traverses the long path of history but remains unnostalgic about the past and it is anchored in the struggles of the masses" (32).

However, the formation of a class is artificial and the economic agency or interest is impersonal because it is systematic and heterogeneous. So to Spivak, the concept of subaltern is far away from the concept of class. According to Spivak (1999: 29), Marx is not working to create an undivided subject where desire and interest coincide. Class consciousness does not operate toward that goal. Similarly, Elias in his *Chilekothar Sepai* and *Khoabnama* has gone far away from only dealing with the class struggle and economic problems of the poor people. To him, class is not always constant and there is class conflict within the class (we find peasants' conflict with the fishermen in *Khoabnama* and Khijir's quarrel with Bazlu and his wife in *Chilekothar Sepai* who belong to same social and economical class). Elias understands the micro politics and the dialectic of class. So, he translates the subalterns as they are and does not reduce them into stereotypes. In other words, Elias does not deprive his characters of complexities and contradictions and disinherit them from their claim to history. Such attitude to translation leads Elias to conclude that reality cannot be adequately explained through a formulaic method or philosophy, and one must place oneself squarely within the Real to understand reality.

Elias says:

> I do not see reality by sticking to any theory or philosophy. I want to see reality within it. Yet I am not a journalist. What I can see as reality is not that simple. I see dream, hopes, inspiration, and promise, all in the depth of reality. For instance, my character Khijir, he is naïve as well as weak and rough. He is a thief and a revolutionary as well. When the local goon hijacks his passenger's wife to rape, he wants his rental fee. (Mazumder, 168)

Nevertheless, to Elias, the whole life of the subaltern, both negative and positive, is important and unlike Spivak, he does not look for the aesthetic heroism in the life of the subaltern. That is why he delineates the subtle intricacies of common people, farmers, peasants, and labour class people's daily life through both his novels. Elias says in this regard, "Many writers are there who do not want to show the sexual lives of a farmer, they want to show them only as a great struggler. Why? Can't be there any kind of deception and hypocrisy in that farmer? He himself answers, these are kind of canny" (Kamran, 111). To him, the life of human being is basically positive. Elias further mentions that where people are living amidst thousand pains, there is no meaning of making them positive separately. Therefore, Elias portrays Tamij; he creates Khijir; who raise their voices against the oppressor in spite of having their own devious nature. These characters are not superhuman beings; nonetheless we see Tamij to seduce Fuljan in an open field in *Khoabnama*. Even we see him getting attracted to his own stepmother Kulsum. Khijir also kicks his wife and uses slang so often. Moreover, Elias has started his novel *Chilekothar Sepai* by depicting the masturbation of Osman. To Elias, these all are not apart from life. By showing sexual imagination, Elias shows the class consciousness. He says in this concern, "I see the class and the society behind the sex" (Kamran, 117). On the other hand, the novelist Elias does not take any position for his characters in his novels *Khoabnama* and *Chilekothar Sepai*. His position is nonaligned. He does not take any side and he does not speak for his characters rather he translates them with their both positive and negative aspects of life. That is why Elias not only deals with the subaltern as an oppressed class but he also translates their culture, pain, happiness and even their language. Elias (2004) says in *Rachana Samagra*:

> By only showing the poverty, we cannot recognize the subaltern. In their life, there are humanitarian values and these could not be uprooted by the thousand years of oppression. So, to identify them and evaluate them in proper way, to know their cultural aspect is a must. (24)

Through the novels of Elias, some of the key questions for this essay are raised. Perhaps the most significant of these would be: What are the positions of the subaltern in historical insurgency? How does Elias capture the lives of the subalterns and translate them in his novels? What is Elias's position in re-presenting the subalterns's contribution in two historical moments like *Tevaaga* and 1969 mass revolution? What is the role of women as subalterns in the patriarchy? In both *Chilekothar Sepai* and *Khoabnama*, there are revolutionary moments or insurgencies with the involvement of the masses. Elias's handling of these issues are nuanced and thought-provoking, and do not undermine the role of these people such as Khijir, Tamij, Fuljan in those historical moments. He does, however, downplay the complexities of Khijir's role in 1969 insurgency and Tamij in *Tevaaga* movement. For Elias, the characters – Fuljan, Tamij, Kulsum, and Keramat Ali – all fight against the oppressors from his/her own position but cannot raise collectively against the oppressors. Elias further exposes the contribution of these people in historical events through his novels *Khoabnama* and *Chilekothar Sepai* as a counter-narrativization of the official history. He has written both of his novels within the context of two historical moments: *Tevaaga* insurgency of early 1940s and the mass revolution of 1969. In both movements the subaltern had a great role but they could not unite collectively due to political unconsciousness, according to Spivak. None of Elias's novels shows the collective consciousness of the subalterns. Khijir in *Chilekothar Sepai* desires the downfall of *Mahajan*, yet he does not know how to proceed on with his revolution as an unconscious proletariat or urban rootless subaltern. He dies. Like him, Chengtu does not know what to do further regarding his own agitation against Khaibar Gazi. He waits for Anwar or Ali Box for further step. At the same time, Tamij in *Khoabnama* looks for a dream alone to be an *Adhiar*. Afterwards, these people are effaced from the official history of Bangladesh and all dreams of these subalterns could not be united as an entity to make a further revolution locally. These are actually examples of how Elias has provided an alternative rhetorical site for articulating the histories of the subalterns. In *Chilekothar Sepai*, Elias engages reader's view and conscience by the dialectic of the lifehood. How a manual labourer subaltern can be big, and become a symbol of power, hope and inspiration, has been shown in *Chilekothar Sepai* through *Haddi* Khijir. *Haddi* Khijir may have been lost, yet his agony and passion cannot be taken away rather it enables others to take a vow with strong arms towards the open sky. On the other hand *Khoabnama* evolves with the dream of Tamij and Fuljan for a less oppressive society with an urge for equal rights by denying the "hegemonic power". Yet they also cannot emerge as sovereign political subject in control of their own destiny.

On a final note, unlike other writers Elias has not dealt with middle class bourgeoisie, rather he dealt with different historical issues where he has included fishermen, peasants, urban workers, their lives, pains, sorrows everything as well as their positive and negative self to translate the dynamics of their life and resistance. As a very conscious writer, Elias has understood that translating these people by keeping himself apart from them is a tough job. Elias has tried to do that by his writings and his two novels are tremendous examples of good writing where he has tried to translate the subaltern in a Spivakian sense by not being a re-presenter or a representer of the subalterns, neither as *dartelling* nor as *vertreven*.

Additionally, in both *Chilekothar Sepai* and in *Khoabnama*, Elias has seen politics in-depth, yet he was not an active politician anywhere, not even a theoretician (Elias, 69). At the same time none of his main characters are politicians (69). Elias does not evaluate political history rather he has shown how politics has shaped the life of ordinary people, the life of rural peasants, fishermen and urban destitute. Elias also expands his reality beyond the conventional outlook and intellect and shows all the evidences of subalterns's history by identifying that national bourgeoisie used their epistemological power along with politics and religion to subjugate the subalterns. Similarly, Elias does not become the representative of the subalterns with an intention of proclaiming himself as subaltern rather he recounts history and brings the history and life of the subalterns such as peasants, fishermen, urban destitute and gendered subalterns like Kulsum, Fuljan and *Jummoner Maa* through his novels to give readers a counter-narrative of the official history with a true portrayal of the subaltern life. Elias also solidifies himself with those revolutions and dreams of the subalterns by keeping him aside as only a narrator. Thus, this essay contends that these two novels demonstrate a mature handling of question of class, economy and politics in terms of translating the life of the oppressed people/subalterns.

## *CHILEKOTHAR SEPAI:* HADDI KHIJIR AND HIS REVOLUTION

> A functional change in a sign-system is a violent event. Even when it is perceived as "gradual," or "failed," or yet "reversing itself," the change itself can only be operated by the force of a crisis. What Paul de Man writes of criticism can here be extended to a subalternity that is turning things "upside down": "In periods that are not periods of crisis, or in individuals bent upon avoiding crisis at all cost, there can

> be all kinds of approaches to [the social]...but there can be no [insurgency]." Yet, if the space for a change (necessarily also an addition) had not been there in the prior function of the sign-system, the crisis could not have made the change happen. The change in signification-function supplements the previous function. (Spivak, 1987: 197–198)

Spivak's approach to the history of the subaltern insurgency as a functional change in a sign system is an approach that expands and deepens the Marxist approach of the subaltern historians to include women, as well as rural peasants and the urban proletariats in literature. However, the novel *Chilekothar Sepai* explores a violent historical event of the Mass uprising of 1969[1] where Elias includes urban proletariat Khijir with landless farmhand Chengtu and house maid of Rahmatullah's house *Jummoner Maa* as well as *Khijirer Maa* who are oppressed by the ruling bourgeois. Yet they dream for changes and contribute to the insurgency to change the social, political and economic system of the society. But these contributions of the subalterns or the disempowered people are effaced from the official history. Hence, Elias tries to look at those functional changes of the society through his novel *Chilekothar Sepai.*

1969 – Dhaka, East Pakistan. Osman wakes up in the morning after dreaming his own death. After getting up from sleep he comes to know that his neighbour Abu Taleb was shot dead by military bullet. Osman, dead Abu Taleb's family and Rahmatullah *Mahajan* live in Rahmatullah *Mahajan*'s old three storeyed building in old Dhaka whereas urban labourer Khijir lives in Rahmatullah's slum accompanied by Bazlu – a blacker of cinema hall. Khijir is one of the main characters of the novel. He is a long and weak young guy raised up in Rahmatullah's garage and married to *Jummoner Maa*, an abandoned woman. He does not

1. *Unosoturer Gonoovvuthan* or the Mass insurgency of 1969 in East Pakistan (November 1968 – March 1969) is an explosive positive revolt against military dictatorship of Aiyub regime. The economical and political oppression of the military government on Bengali nation led people to agitate against the military rule. Sheikh Mujib and 35 others were accused of conspiracy as well (Maniruzzaman 59). But it was not the only reason for the mass revolution rather it had economical and social orientations. Sheikh Mujib put forward six point demands in that upheaval too.

know his father's name even. Elias names him *Haddi*[2] Khijir. Elias introduces Khijir in the novel *Chilekothar Sepai* in this way: "Khijir enters to the room following Alauddin. Khijir is in charge of taking care of Alauddin's two auto rickshaws and some rickshaws. This man is very tall yet he achieves this title "haddi" because of his skinny body. He always keeps a screwdriver and a plier in his hands"(7). Osman finds Khijir when he goes to the dead Taleb's house. He identifies Khijir as very active in the procession, in the meeting and everywhere. When university students come to take Taleb's dead body for the procession against Aiyub Khan Government[3], Khijir takes side of the students and starts giving slogans until *Mahajan* stops him. However, Osman goes to office by ignoring the strike and finds the same enthusiasm among the street children like Khijir against the military government. They take part in the strike on the street. Even any cycle or rickshaw cannot avoid this *hartal* ("strike") because of these street children. If someone does not follow the strike, these street children inform the strikers. We find their involvement and enthusiasm by Elias's illustration: "We told to close the shop; we already told...another street boy says, that lame boltu says strike! What strike? Fuck the strike...after hearing that the boys who are senior at age and in paternal identities run straight with bat in hand to close the shops" (15). More interestingly, after reaching the office, Osman comes to know none of the class four employees have come to the office. Not only fourth class employees but the rickshaw pullers, drivers, porters – all have joined and cooperated with the strike. Officers do not understand the meaning of cooperating with the strike by these subalterns. Elias illustrates the situation in this way: "One says, why you are only talking about the peons (four class employees)? Have you seen the spirit/strengths of the rickshaw pullers, bus conductors, drivers, porters? Hey, what will be your benefits if Aiyub government collapses? Will you be the ministers? Or will you sit on these chairs after returning?" (17). The involvement of the subalterns becomes clearer

---

2. *Haddi* is a bangla word for bone. Here Elias, to illustrate the sickly body of Khijir, uses the word *Haddi* as his body merely consists of bone. Khijir is weak and poor and his physical structure reflects his social and economical position. That is why Elias names Khijir *Haddi* Khijir who represents his class.

3. Aiyub khan Government was a military government came into power in 1958 by a military *coup d'etat*. The mass uprising against Aiyub regime that took place between November 1968 to March 1969 necessitated and forced this elite power of Pakistan to quit (Maniruzzaman, 11).

when Kamal, a colleague of Osman informs: "They organize processions everyday as they do not have any other works. They throw stones as soon as they see any police vehicles" (19). These people make the movement successful and by agitating and protesting on the streets of Dhaka against the autocracy of military government. Curfew, strikes by the agitators, processions, meetings – all are keeping Dhaka very hot and volatile. This agitation of the people against the government becomes more violent day by day. Angry mob torches Muslim League[4] office in Gulistan. Khijir also takes part actively in that torching. Nowadays he is more interested in the insurgency and processions than anything else. He even violates the curfew and does not care for driving and rickshaw pulling for his earning. On the other hand, Osman cannot get out from his middle class barriers and does not join in the insurgency actively, though he is very passionate about that. Khijir protests *Mahajan* aggressively and gives slogans against *Mahajan* in the meeting of rickshaw pullers organized by Awami League[5] leader Alauddin. That is why, Khijir's wife *Jummoner Maa* is very angry with her husband and scolds him for his guts to agitate against *Mahajan*. On the other hand, *Mahajan* proposes *Jummoner Maa* to remarry Kamruddin, *Jummoner Maa's* former husband as he sees Khijir's acts as an imminent

4. Established in 1906, Muslim League played a pivotal role in securing an independent land for Muslims. After independence, however, League continued as a minor party. It was a political party led by Muhammad Ali Jinnah. This party made an aspiration of a new sovereign country based on religion among the subcontinent people and gave hope of oppressionless society for the common people. Yet Muslim League looks like one "Muslim People" irrespective of class or ethnic difference, according to Kamal (331). In the pre-independence days the Muslim League concentrated all activities and energy on building a separate national identity but it did not develop any serious critique of the colonial state nor did it discuss in any of its forums the nature of the state that was to be (336).

5. The Awami League was founded in Dhaka, the former capital of the Pakistani province of East Bengal, in 1949 by Bengali nationalists Maulana Abdul Hamid Khan Bhashani, Shamsul Huq, and later Huseyn Shaheed Suhrawardy. The Awami League was established as the Bengali alternative to the domination of the Muslim League in Pakistan. The party quickly gained massive popular support in East Bengal, later named East Pakistan, and eventually led the forces of Bengali nationalism in the struggle against West Pakistan's military and political establishment. The party under the leadership of Sheikh Mujibur Rahman, the founding father of Bangladesh, would lead the struggle for independence, first through massive populist and civil disobedience movements, such as the Six Point Movement and mass upheaval of 1969. (Source: www.albd.org)

threat to his autocracy and his maltreatment towards the subaltern. Yet Khijir continues his fight against both military government and *Mahajan*. Finally, one day in the middle of that insurgency when Khijir is taking part in the procession by violating the curfew, one bullet takes away Khijir's life. But before his death Khijir has given his Plier and Screwdriver to his stepson Jummon and Khijir's role in the novel does not end by his death. Rather the dead Khijir emerges as more violent and powerful than the live one and starts haunting Osman to get away from the *Chilekotha* ( "the attic") to break all the political, economic and social shackles of the society. At the end of the novel, Osman emerges as a schizophrenic. But his schizophrenia is not a hopeless status for him, rather, it is that which helps to recant him from his middle class bondage and attachment.

The second part of the novel lies in the heart of rural Bengal. Elias takes us to the bank of Jamuna River by leftist politician Anwar. Anwar goes to his ancestral village to see the oppression of the rural people by the landlords after getting his maternal uncle's letter. After reaching the village, Anwar comes to know that oxen and cows are often stolen from the village and especially landless peasants's oxen are stolen which are the only assets of those farmers. The only assets of the peasants are stolen by Khaibar Gazi's people to make *khoar*[6] in *Dakatmarar Char* (alluvial land) of Jamuna River. Anwar does not understand the village politics yet he understands that the micro politics of the village has a far reaching effect in the society. Here he comes close to Chengtu, a local peasant and a resistant of Khaibar Gazi's act. This young Chengtu is inspired by Ali box, a local leader who made a mass tribunal in *Sinduriar* Char. Now the local people of Chengtu's village are also getting together for collective resistance against Khaibar Gazi and his pupil under the leadership of Ali Box. *Jotdar* Khaibar Gazi oppresses people for long especially peasants and *Borgachasi*[7] in many

6. *Khoar* is a place or custody for domestic animals. If the domestic animals, for instance cows or goats ravage crop field, they are kept in *Khoar* for certain time as a punishment. The peasants or the owners of the animals have to give fine to get return of those.

7. *Borgachasis* are farmers or peasants who cultivate other's land. But there is a subtle difference between the *borgachasi* and the *adhiar*. *Adhiars* are the share croppers who share the crops with the land owner with 2:2 proportion. On the other, *Borgachasis* take the land on lease from the land owner by money for a season or a year, and generally they do not share crops with the land owner nowadays.

ways. Now he steals peasants' oxen and sells those to the East of the Jamuna River. If someone can reach to the *Dakatmarar Char* to get return of those stolen cows from the *Khoar*, the supervisor of that *Khoar* Hossen Ali would have demanded 100 taka for each cow in the name of government tax. Two oxen and a cow owned by Pochar *Baap*, a local resident of the village have been stolen from his own house. Somehow he has reached to the *Khoar* with the money but he could not return from there alive. People have found his dead body. This is a common scenario in that area. That is why the young people have organized for a collective resistance. Chengtu is a born resistant. He makes his vow against Khaibar Gazi and Hossen Ali while Chengtu's father is very obedient to the *jotdars*. But Chengtu is not as good as his father. He argues with his father: "huh is there plenty of rice in your home? Will your master/local landlord give you more share of crops/rice if you slay me?" Chengtu is not afraid to resist the oppressors as he does not have anything to lose. He says: "What is our risk? We do not have land, no home, no rice, no *chili* – what is our loss if there is any danger or threat?" (109). Chengtu is not afraid to resist the oppressors as he does not have anything to lose. So one day they attack Hossen Ali in *Dakatmarar Char* and set him on fire. They also set up a mass tribunal for Khaibar Gazi but somehow Khaibar Gazi manages to escape when the Awami League leaders come to the village for meeting and appeal for unity. They appeal to the villagers to work under a single leadership and for one single national demand in the name of nationalism by ignoring the local peasants's vow and resistance against the local oppressors. In this way, the collective resistance of the local people of Jamuna area also shatters in the name of nationalism. At the same time Chengtu's dead body has been found in the rice field who used to agitate local peasants and farmers against their oppressor Khaibar Gazi.

However, this essay has tried to look at the novel from two perspectives: One is to translate the subaltern from the sense of translating the true life of the subaltern and the other to show Elias's notion of counter-narrativization of history. In *Chilekothar Sepai*, Elias narrates the struggles and compromises of both urban and rural labourers and shows their life and contributions in the mass uprising of 1969 and in local insurgency. But the simple ongoing life of the subalterns is not kept apart by the novelist. We find not only the agitating mood of Khijir and Osman but their normal everyday lives where Osman looks for Ranju's sister Ranu with an intention of making love and Khijir often quarrels with his neighbour Bazlu and his wife in *Mahajan*'s slum. Elias's portrayal of Khijir's activities on Eid day is also very important to comprehend the subaltern's life. *Haddi* Khijir and Chengtu fit well into Spivak's typology of "subaltern" because of their positions in the society, economically, socially and politically. In fact, *Chilekothar Sepai* is such a novel where Elias translates a true subaltern life through the characters of *Haddi* Khijir, Chengtu, Bazlu, and *Jummoner Maa* by portraying both their revolutionary and absolute human characteristics. In this regard, Elias asserts the theoretical Spivakian definition of the subaltern. Like Spivak's subaltern, Elias's subaltern characters are not only revolutionaries but they have pain, sorrow, happiness, fault, hypocrisy, disgrace, abomination, etc. which are common in human life. To translate the life of the subaltern, Elias creates the character *Haddi* Khijir and makes him his weapon for his counter-narrative of the historical moment of 1969. For Elias, Khijir is both a revolutionary and a thief. Khijir becomes Elias's weapon by not even being the central character of the novel. According to Anu Mohammad, "no one is a hero in Elias's novel" (30). Yet Khijir attracts readers' attention for his strong characteristics as a human and a revolutionary. Here Elias's attempt is not to portray Khijir as a noble character but to re-present him as he is in the society. In this regard Elias himself mentions in his biographical article "Attokothon":

> I want to see the reality in depth. I don't want to impose any idea of mine upon the reality. If I do that it will be a wishful thinking and wishful thinking is a thing I am the last person to go with… I can not impose my wish on reality. For example my haddi Khijir, he has his own struggle/battle, simplicity, he also steals and irreverent and weak. When the local goon hijacks his passenger's wife to rape, even that time he wants his rent. I want to see him with his good and worst side and I feel that with all these Khijir is immense. (Kamran, 23)

Yet, Elias translates the subaltern without any personal involvement, without claiming to be the perfect translator of the subaltern. Subaltern in Elias appears with in the chronoscopic space. In *Chilekothar Sepai* through the character Khijir, Elias mentions that just because some one is poor/subaltern, he is not innocent. When Khijir constantly abuses *Jummoner Maa*, we understand his unworthy manner. When Khijir sighs as he could not con Mahajan's 3 taka on Eid day, we identify his greedy nature and immorality. On many occasions he steals *Mahajan*'s money. He cheats other rickshaw puller on Eid day. Khijir also cannot tolerate the idea that Jummon will live with them despite his own same experience with Faalu *mistri*. At the beginning he has to endure Jummon. Khijir's all enthusiasm on Eid day goes away as soon as *Jummoner Maa* wants to see her son. He makes angry utterances. Khijir, like his own stepfather, misbehaves with Jummon and *Jummoner Maa* regarding her son. Khijir is selfish and pragmatic too. When he goes outside in curfew he observes and enjoys people's misery. He tells an incident humorously to Osman. Khijir feels good about other's humiliation and embarrassment because he does not have social status and material power. Therefore he enjoys a gentleman's misery who often holds a better social status and economic power in the society. When Osman shows anger and rebukes Khijir for this attitude, Khijir shows his pragmatic side. So, Elias does not create this character Khijir only to fight against his class enemy and to turn him into immortal revolutionary figure. Rather he portrays a human being, a subaltern who with his dignity and falsity takes part in the revolution.

Now the question is why does Khijir want the downfall of military government along with those street children? Do they have any political aim or ideology behind this aspiration? If the Aiyub Khan government falls, what would be the benefit of these street children who actively participate in the strike on the street? Why do the slum dwellers make procession against the government everyday and throw bricks at the police vehicles? And why does Chengtu make resistance against Khaibar Gazi and Hossen Ali Fakir? To get the answers of these questions we need not make any sociological or psychological analysis. We find the clear answer of these questions through Khijir's aspiration for the downfall of Aiyub Khan Government and Chengtu's vow to take revenge against Khaibar Gazi. The lifelong material and social exploitation of this group of people who are defined as subaltern by Spivak and Gramsci and who are susceptible to ruling class's exploitation, give them the audacity to raise against their oppressors. Khijir's involvement in the mass revolution is symbolic as he believes that the downfall of the military government will bring a far-reaching effect for him and for the society. He hopes for a social change and that is why he joins the insurgency. We see Khijir's visible revolution against the military government, yet it carries his anger towards *Mahajan*. His insurgency is not only against the military rule but also against the

*Mahajan* who exploits him, his mother, and tries to exploit his wife. *Mahajan* and Aiyub Khan Government are synonymous to him. The resentment and the revolution of Khijir against both these oppressors do not happen by a single day. The military government has exploited Bengali nation economically and politically for long, while *Mahajan* is exploiting Khijir and others materially. Khijir's class position creates this resentment towards *Mahajan* as well as to the system. Rahmatullah's exploitation and oppression marginalize him by keeping him in the economical periphery. He does not know where he was born and who his father is. He does not even have a house to live in; Alauddin's garage is his only shelter. He does not belong to any particular occupation as well; sometimes he is a rickshaw puller, sometimes a scooter driver and sometimes just the caretaker of Rahmatullah's garage. This is Khijir's life. He leads most of his life like this. "Khijir is a lumpen proletariat, Elias names him *Haddi* Khijir" (37). His mother and wife both are exploited by *Mahajan*. His mother along with him takes shelter in Mahajan's house as a maid after leaving Faalu *Mistri* and has carried the illegal child of Rahmatullah *Mahajan*. Afterwards she dies due to illegal abortion arranged by *Mahajan*. In a way, *Mahajan* kills Khijir's mother after fulfilling his sexual appetite. *Mahajan*'s wife also blames his husband for this killing in front of teenage Khijir. But Mahajan blames Khijir's mother in spite of his direct involvement. *Mahajan* further abuses Khijir as he does not know his father's name. This incident haunts Khijir till his death. He knows his mother was once exploited by Rahmatullah *Mahajan* and now he notices that he is trying to exploit his wife. Bazlu's wife teases Khijir. Both these situations and material exploitation create awareness in Khijir's mind about his marginalization and give him strength to stand against both the military government and Rahmatullah *Mahajan*. That is why Khijir and other street children join in the mass insurgency of 1969 with the aspiration for new days where there will be no oppression and there will be no more Rahmatullah *Mahajan*.

In contrast, Chengtu is also involved in an agitation in rural Bengal though it is not directly connected to mass revolution of 1969. Rather it is a peasant movement against the local landlords and *Jotdars* who exploited the *Borgachasi*. Chengtu is well aware of this oppression and repression unlike his father. His father feels proud because Anwar's grandfather once beat him by his shoes. Chengtu and other local peasants have suffered long enough of this inequality by local bourgeois.

But when he along with Ali Box has found that there is no remedy of this oppression by political leaders, they have stated to take action by themselves through a violent local insurgency which is similar to *Naxalite* Movement[8]. Chengtu and others cannot believe in nationalistic dream, so they do consider their local problem as their own problem and say to the Awami League leaders when they come and pledge to work on a single platform: "What have you started? Why are you pulling our men?" (249). But Chengtu does not believe in the national leaders's words. His dream of oppressionless society by discarding Khaibar Gazi and Hossen Ali is shattered by the nationalist movement. From this point of view, we can say that both Chengtu and Khijir aspire for the same dream of an oppressionless society where there would not be any material marginalization and class struggle. However, Rahmatullah and Khaibar Gazi remain in the same place in a new guise while Chengtu and Khijir die and have effaced from the history with the course of time.

Yet, *Chilekothar Sepai* introduces the reader to Khijir and Chengtu and a series of events that crisscrosses the disadvantaged people's lives and the mass insurgency. The novel does not carry any central character yet it is the story of Khijir, Chengtu and other poor oppressed people through whom Elias has translated the most important insurgency of Bengali history, 1969 mass revolution. Khijir acts as a liaison between the mass insurgency and the subaltern in the urban area where Chengtu's role exposes how the peasants were also integrated themselves in that revolution. Anu Mohammad says, "People are keen for a change, they are dreaming for something new. Labour class people of Bangladesh never have dreamt for a change in such an immense manner"(83). It has already been mentioned that *Chilekothar Sepai* is Elias's first novel published in 1986 and the context of the novel is 1969 mass revolution. Through the narrator's story telling about Osman, Khijir and Chengtu, the story travels from volatile and hostile metropolitan Dhaka to the social reality of rural area which has been built up on the bank of Jamuna River – both the plots are entangled with a central issue of fighting against the oppressors. The story also crisscrosses with a certain time

8. Naxalite movement is an Indian revolutionary movement named after the village of Naxalbari in the Himalayan foothills in West Bengal, where it first began. The communist party CPI (M-L) first organized several armed risings of landless agricultural labourers, especially in eastern India in 1967. It subsequently developed into an urban guerrilla movement, especially in Calcutta. Its programme of terror was suppressed with considerable violence.

and context – this is a story of Osman and Khijir in the mass revolution in Dhaka and Chengtu and others's collective struggle against the oppressor Khaibar Gazi in rural Bengal. Elias has written the history of that oppression through his characters like middle class Osman, Leftist Anwar, urban landless labourer Khijir, landless farmhand or *Borgachasi* Chengtu, maid *Jummoner Maa*, Bazlu and so on. Elias shows through his novel *Chilekothar Sepai* that how all classes of people come to a platform from their own point against their oppressors but remain isolated for a specific goal as Elias himself states by his character Anwar, "Peasants and labourers cannot recognize/identify right person and they do not have any political lesson"(105). The boundaries between the oppressors and the oppressed are somewhat fluid in the novel. Khijir, over the course of the novel, becomes the link that connects the various characters of the novel, including Rahmatullah *Mahajan*, Osman, *Jummoner Maa* and secular nationalist Alauddin. Eventually, through Khijir's life and his involvement in the mass revolution, Elias tries to re-examine his idea of the role of the subalterns in the insurgency of 1969. He also tries to give a counter-narrative of history by the novel *Chilekothar Sepai* and through his characters Khijir, Chengtu and others. Khijir, one of the main characters of the novel, an urban landless labourer denies and refuses the oppression of Rahmatullah *Mahajan* along with his agitation against the Military Aiyub Khan government. Khijir and Chengtu, both of their lives are examples of life-long oppression, Khijir by urban Rahmatullah *Mahajan* and Chengtu by Khaibar Gazi and Hossen Ali. Khijir's long anticipation proves his desperateness for *Mahajan*'s downfall. He denies *Mahajan*'s autocracy and joins in the procession against the military government with a hope of Mahajan's defeat. In fact most of Khijir's revolution is against his class enemy *Mahajan*. He embraces his life as an active participant of the insurgency on the Dhaka Street because this gives him a hope for oppressionless society. However, at the end of the novel, which culminates in the death of both Chengtu and Khijir in two different situations, Elias demands the readers to share his understanding of the role of the subalterns in historical events. Chengtu's and Khijir's death proves that in each and every historical insurgency the subalterns have great contributions. Without their effort a revolution like mass revolution would not happen. So, this is Elias's way of delineating the involvement of the subalterns in 1969 insurgency to his readers by keeping his focus on Khijir and Chengtu who are the representatives of the subalterns.

However, mass uprising of 1969 is a great experience of Bengali nation. People of Bangladesh do have experience of *Tevaaga* movement, *Hajong* Movement, Peasant movement and language movement. But the spontaneous movement like 1969 mass uprising is a rare case in Bengali history (Mohammad, 83). Anu Mohammad further says that the mass revolution of Bangladesh is not a simple incident; it was a sudden flow of sweat, blood which was accumulating for long. Elias looks at this mass uprising in depth and translates this historical moment as a counter-narrativization of the history. Along with the true translation of the subaltern life, he shows and portrays the engagement and contribution of the subalterns in the historical moment of the mass uprising of 1969. Elias shows the involvement of the subalterns in 1969 insurgency by keeping his eye on Khijir and Chengtu. He shows without the involvement of these subalterns, a successful mass revolution might not occur in 1969. The novelist through an unknown character asks, "Who die? We have been observing the meetings, processions since the British period. Who die...where there none of the leaders have to die by the bullet! Only..." (8). Finally, the 1969 upheaval was not only a student upsurge but a mass uprising. But in the history of Bangladesh revolution, this is ignored very often. In political history of Bangladesh, it is quite often mentioned that mass upheaval is the result of student movement and is a political success of Bangladesh Awami League. And the unity of the mass movement broke down after the release of Sheikh Mujib (Maniruzzaman, 62). But what are the positions of Chengtu, Khijir, Taleb and young children of the Dhaka Street in the history who have joined actively in the procession and protested military government? They are effaced gradually from the history. Even after their spontaneous response and involvement in the mass revolution, the subalterns like Khijir, Chengtu's name are lost somewhere in the pages of history. On the other hand, still Alauddin and Khaibar Gazi are in their own positions in a new phase. The office boss, who was annoyed with the undisciplined chaos of 1969 insurgency, is now busy with his elite life. Alauddin takes the position of Rahmatullah *Mahajan*, and Khaibar Gazi is still in his same position. We can understand the dream of the subaltern through destitute rickshaw puller Khijir's dream, and Chengtu's agitation against Khaibar Gazi. The main desire of these people was not the fall of Aiyub Khan, but an oppressionless society. In this regard Elias has tried to give us a counter-narrativie of the history where he not only intends to show the revolutionary side of the subalterns but their lives, their falsity, their weakness, their passion, their fraudulent attitude and fakeness. With all these, a subaltern is a true human being and Elias has tried to translate this whole life of the subaltern by this novel *Chilekothar Sepai*, not an isolated heroic feature of subaltern life.

## *KHOABNAMA:* TAMIJ AND HIS DREAM

*Khoabnama* is the second and the last novel of Akhtaruzzaman Elias. It is set in the British colonial period and narrates incidents that take place in three years before and after independence. Characters and geographies represented in this novel revolve around with two historical issues of *Tevaaga* insurgency[9] and Pakistan movement[10]. The narrative space of the novel is populated by the characters Tamij, nameless Tamijer *Baap*, Fuljan, Keramat, Shrafat Mandal, Kalam Majhi, Abdul Qader and Ismael. These characters are important to comprehend the peasants's and fishermen's lives and the peasants's and fishermen's lives have got significant importance in Elias's narrative style. These two historical incidents create a space in the lives of the subalterns. Elias places his four main characters Tamijer Baap, Kulsum, Fuljan and Tamij into these events and narrates the life of the subalterns through them. So far, these four characters of this novel are either peasants or fishermen.

9. *Tevaaga* insurgency is a serious peasant uprising. It is historic *Tevaaga* or share-croppers's struggle and movement against landlords, *Jaminder* and *Jotdars*. Most of the areas of erstwhile Eastern Bengal and part of Assam, mainly the Sylhet district were in the grip of peasant movements of variable intensity and nature in the decade preceding political independence. All these movements originated in the pre-independence socio-political situation of East Bengal. This movement is popularly known as *Tevaagar Larai* and it was about the reduction of the landlord's demand from half of the production to one third (Kamal, 346).

10. Pakistan movement was a movement against British rule for a sovereign Muslim country. With the birth of Pakistan on the midnight of 14 August 1947, a new state emerged in the world and liberated from British colonialism, which was a culmination of Pakistan movement. Muslim League activists led by Muhammad Ali Jinnah who worked up for a vision of Pakistan for East Bengal Muslims failed to define the ideology of the new state in any precise terms even while they were engaged in outlining the principles of a new constitution. There was a liberal view of nationhood in Pakistan movement. Nationalist leaders termed the independence of Pakistan as "Pakistan Revolution". The birth of Pakistan was asserted as "complete sovereignty of the constituent Assembly" by Jinnah (349).

However, Elias has tried to deal with these peasants and fishermen whose lives have been determined and regulated by dreams. Elias reviews the lives of the rural people and their micro-politics of village for his narrative *Khoabnama*. Two historical events like *Tevaaga* movement and Pakistan movement had a great influence in developing the plot of the novel. By revolving around these two incidents, different classes of people such as *Jaminder*, Petty landlords, politicians etc. emerge in the novel. However, how these two movements influence, control and shape the life of the subalterns is also an important issue of the novel. Elias also narrates the struggles and compromises of the landless farmers whose labour is exploited by local land-owning bourgeoisie. In this sense, Elias's *Khoabnama* demonstrates a mature handling of questions of class, economy and politics.

The novel *Khoabnama* revolves around the life of the people of the *Jamuna-Korotoya* region[11]. To translate the lives of the people of this area, Elias observes them from a decent distance. And, sometimes the characters are built up independently. Tamij is one of those independent characters of the novel *Khoabnama*. He lives in Girirdanga village in the west bank of *Katlahar Bill*. He is a landless farmhand or *adhiar*[12], despite having his fishing lineage. Tamij lives with his father and stepmother Kulsum, a much younger woman married to the old, allusive Tamijer *Baap*. Both Tamij and Tamijer *Baap* are hard-working labourers. They work on others's land. Despite being an ordinary landless labourer, everybody respects Tamijer *Baap*. Villagers believe that he has a connection with Munsi Baitullah and Pakur tree which have a mythical and religious importance among the villagers. Tamij is more pragmatic than his father. He works and sells his labour in the rice fields of *Khiar* area. From there he comes to know about the *Tevaaga* movement of the peasants which inspires him to be an *adhiar*. Tamij dreams to become an *adhiar*. But Abdul Qader, a secular nationalist who is also the son of a prosperous landed bourgeois named Sharafat

11. Jamuna-Korotoya region is primarily situated in the North Bengal of Bangladesh. Bogra is the district which built up in the bank of Jamuna and Korotoya River. The setting of *Khoabnama* is Jamuna – Korotoya region or rural village of Bogra district.

12. *Adhiars* are the share croppers or those peasants who cultivate in other people's land. Earlier the crop used to be equally shared by the owner of the land and peasants who cultivate in the land. But the *adhiars* mobilized a peasant movement in the 1940s demanding two thirds of the crop.

Mandal exploits Tamij by wheedling him to work and campaign for Muslim League. Hasan Al Zayed in his essay "Late Style as Politics" (2008) claims that Qader fits well into Franz Fanon's typology of national bourgeois who exploits the surplus labour of the agricultural labourers under the pretext of national liberation, a false promise never to be fulfilled. Qader's promise of land reform that, the properties of landlords will be confiscated and then redistributed among their subjects, keeps Tamij on the brink of hope. He begins to believe that if Pakistan, a separate nation state for Muslims, is established "*Tevaaga* will be implemented and landless farmers will get two thirds of the crop" (260). When that does not happen and the bill which is supposed to confiscate the properties of the landlords is deferred, Tamij gradually comes to understand that he has no other choice but to go in search of *Tevaaga* to fulfill his dream. Thus, Zayed (2008) says that Tamij's journey to the *Tevaaga* area constitutes a metaphor which can be interpreted as a journey in search of a real revolution that is to come.

However, *Khoabnama* requires the readers's attention because it concentrates on the struggle of the subalterns. This novel is not at all a national allegory celebrating the heroism of the postcolonial bourgeoisie. Rather it is an ontologization of collective emancipatory struggle of unity as well as of betrayal. Thus, through this narrative, Elias mainly tries to recuperate an insurrectionary moment of history. All humanitarian sides such as poverty, pain, sex, and hope – all are integrated in that dream. Nameless Tamijer *Baap* dreams all over the night and walks in his dream as well. Tamij dreams for land and becomes a fugitive due to charge of lake robbery. Kulsum, after dreaming whole night, sees her old husband sleeping like dead and his stepson Tamij is talking to naughty woman Abiton. In this way, by keeping the center of *Katlahar bill*, a narrative of dream and reality evolves.

*Khoabnama*, besides being a rewriting of nationalist history is also a story of subaltern life. The landless farmers, fishermen, craftsmen are the ones who dominate the novel's chronotopic space. Tamij learns the process of farming by coming into contact with Fuljan and his father Harmatullah. Katlahar bill changes by time. New alluvial land awakes and Sharafat occupies it. Tamij thought he would have got that land to cultivate but he does not even get a chance to become an *adhiar* of that land. So, he runs to *Khiar* area where there is a tight fight against the *Jotdars* (petty landlord) with the *adhiars*. A single *Jotdar* has 5000 *Bigha* land there. As long as the eye sight goes, Tamij can see the rice field. Tamij becomes a manual labourer in *Khiar* area with bearing the hope of *Tevaaga* movement. He says, "The wholesalers go where by rail after buying ton after ton of rice" (20). Tamij returns home and Sharafat Mandal does not tolerate Tamij as he dreams to be an *adhiar*. Sharafat Mandal is afraid of these peasants of *Tevaaga* movement as he sees them as threat to his wealth and prosperity. His son Ajij, a government employee, is well known about the impact of *Tevaaga* movement. So, he does not want to give Tamij any land for cultivating crops. Abdul Ajij says, "Peasants are keeping no limit. How long it will take to come across this raging and fuming from the town by crossing the Korotoya River? The peasants of Khiar area want two portions of the crops, they will take two portions of the crops and will give one part of the crop to the land owner's granary" (45). Sharafat Mandal, Kalam *Majhi* and Abdul Ajij buy migrated Hindus's land and Tamij and others see dream to be *adhiar* of those lands. With the emergence of Pakistan, they see a dream of a povertyless society and this dream becomes bigger when the political leader like Ismael tries to integrate *Tevaaga* movement as a part of Pakistan movement. When in Jaypur, peasants take position against *Jaminders* and landlords, Muslim landlords come to the Muslim League political leader Ismael Hussein. *Tevaaga* makes them worried because they think if *Tevaaga* becomes successful; the *Jamindari* system will be thrown away. That is why when landlords and politicians get together at Qader's home, every landlord gives his opinion against *Tevaaga* to Ismael. Muslim peasants are taking 2/3 of the paddy of their land and they have united whereas these peasants were Muslim League supporters before. The landlord Altaf Mondol who owns 3000 *bigha* land whines, "We have been totally ruined by these adhiars. Humph/hallow! My own landless farmers have taken away the crops of my own land in their home and we hear these are the party members of our own party. What are you doing?...These treacherous workers are instigating our landless peasants. I am totally ruined" (302). That is why, Ismael looks for Keramat. Keramat is a singer of *Tevaaga* who inspires the *adhiar*. This vagabond works with *Tevaaga* leaders and inflames the peasants of Jaypur, Panchbibi, Akkelpur through his songs. Ismael tries to use Keramat and his songs for his party purposes and for Pakistan movement. Muslim League leader Ismael also gives hope to the peasants by telling, "Have patience, as long as Pakistan will be established these land bourgeois will be kept tight. There will be Tevaaga bill along with ejecting Jaminderi system in the assembly"

(143). In this way Muslim League leaders try to get the support of the peasants and they campaign that *Tevaaga* movement is a part of Pakistan movement and try to make the peasants to understand that, "the state Pakistan is demanded for the poor" (143). When Muslim League wins in the election, communal riot spreads all over East Bengal, the peasants assemble there by neglecting that riot and give slogans like, "Hindu Muslims are brothers, there is no caste no class for the laborious/ toilsome people, demolish the land bourgeoisies, pass the Tevaaga bill" (265). Budha, Shamser Pramanik, Judhistir, Tamijer *Baap* stand with Ismael and communist leaders with several demands. And the leaders claim, "Tenancy bill has moved to the assembly, the bill of abolishing Jamindari system and Tevaaga bill will be passed together" (265). By seeing the big victory procession for the independence of Pakistan Tamij thinks that *Tevaaga* will be implemented. He also joins the procession and gives slogan on behalf of Pakistan and *Tevaaga*. Tamij and others also hope that there will not be any *Jamindari* system in Pakistan. After being released from jail, Tamij again goes to lake for fishing. He is defiant as he thinks that in Pakistan *Jaminders* are redundant. He says, "Who cares the Jaminders or the landlords in Pakistan!" (297). He does not know that Kalam *Majhi*, who was a fisherman before, has slipped into the shoes of the *Jaminder*. Again problem occurs when Tamij does not listen to the new owner of the *bill* and starts fishing in the marsh. He does not understand the rationale behind Kalam *Majhi*'s control. That is why he asks Kader, "Didn't you tell that a bill will be passed to implement the right of the landless peasants on the land? If that is so, how do your father throw away Fuljan's father from the land which he cultivates" (336).

So, could Tamij and others fulfill their dreams? Rather it creates a new myth, a new environment of oppression. When Tamij and others want to know about the right of *Tevaaga* (right of two thirds of the crops) as an assembly bill, they get answers that "There was a term like that but this time it has deducted to talk about the landless peasants from the assembly" (336). That is why he left his home in search of *Tevaaga* with a new spirit. Finally, I would like to say that *Khoabnama* is not a novel about an individual with time. History for Elias is collective. Elias's characters emerge out of a collective resistance; thrive in explosive junctures of the revolutions. The novel *Khoabnama* is not about any individual or society, yet it is a preparation to find out the dream and life of many Tamijs. So, Tamij's dream is not an individual dream rather it reflects and represents the collective dream of many Tamijs. Tamij is the last person in *Khoabnama* who dreams. In his dream, there is no past like his father and Boikuntha; there is no mythical figure like Munsi or Vobani Pathok, no feelings of mystery. He only knows his present and sees the future. He hates those rural exploiting class who are delighted and rejoiced on the hope of Pakistan. In this way with the hope, dream and life of Tamij, Elias shows the rotation of 40 years of political agenda within the village life, recycling of class relations, and the saturation of party culture in social phenomenon. Elias makes authentic translation of the subaltern lives and their roles in historical event in *Khoabnama* by portraying poverty, oppression, people's belief in myth. Tamij and his dream play a pivotal role to understand the lives of these subalterns.

Nonetheless, we must admit that *Khoabnama* is not a novel about *Tevaaga* movement; rather it has only the shade of that momentous event that has occurred around the year 1943 and ended in 1950. But this particular historical movement gives us the idea about how the dream of the subalterns has been betrayed by the national bourgeoisie. Tamij dreams of a classless society by joining in *Tevaaga* movement and sees it fades because of the betrayal of people like Ismael, Kalam *Majhi* and Abdul Qader. That is why he again looks for a new path. Though his fate is not clearly shown, but we can understand that there is no possibility of his return. His legacy stays alive through the dream of his daughter Sakhina.

## TRANSLATION OF THE GENDERED SUBALTERN: KULSUM, FULJAN AND *JUMMONER MAA*

In the classic Marxist theory of labour, there is a sexual division of labour between productive labour and reproductive labour (feminine) which is based on an essential notion of sexual difference. This sexual division of labour has conventionally devalued and ignored the material specificity of women's domestic work, including childbirth and mothering, because these forms of work directly do not produce exchange value of money. In *Chilekothar Sepai*, however, the character *Jummoner Maa* signifies how a subaltern woman's reproductive body is employed to produce economic value. *Jummoner Maa*'s labour in Mahajan's home to support Khijir effectively reverses this traditional sexual division of labour between men and women. On the other hand, in the novel *Khoabnama,* Fuljan's hard work in her father's paddy field is also unrecognized as she is an abandoned woman. According to Spivak, (1987: 252) woman's employment as professional worker crucially invokes the singularity of gendered subaltern. In this manner, *Jummoner Maa* and Fuljan both problematize the male-centered definition of the working class subject.

In *Khoabnama* and *Chilekothar Sepai*, Elias articulates the histories and struggles of subaltern women with a political commitment. Both the novels highlight the particular social oppression of the subaltern women in the context of pre/postcolonial nationalism. In the novel *Khoabnama,* we find two female characters, one is Kulsum and the other is Fuljan. Kulsum is the grand daughter of Cherag Ali *Fakir* and the second wife of Tamijer *Baap*. She holds the characteristics of Fakir, fishermen, peasants and women. There is an illusion in Kulsum's character. But the other woman character of the novel Fuljan is very strong character. She is an abandoned woman who constantly gives her labour to her father's land yet does not get any recognition of her labour. She emerges as a beloved of Tamij and gives him inspiration. The love between Tamij and Fuljan creates cogitation in the society in the distinction of fisherman and peasants. On the other hand *Jummoner Maa* in *Chilekothar Sepai* is also a very important character. She is a house maid in Rahmatullah's house and married to an urban labourer Khijir.

Both *Jummoner Maa* and Fuljan's reproductive body become a matter of economical exploitation. *Jummoner Maa* is exploited by the *Mahajan* while Fuljan's constant labour on her father's land does not get any recognition as she is an abandoned lady. On the other hand, Kulsum remains a silent figure in the novel *Khoabnama* while we find the articulation of subaltern women's agency and resistance through the characters of Fuljan and *Jummoner Maa*. In fact Elias has shown multiple female characters to illustrate gendered subaltern and their role in patriarchy and society. Yet, along with presenting the life of the farmers and urban labourers, Elias presents the oppressed women in the society. Women have got importance in Elias's novels like any other oppressed class of the society because they are also subjugated by the patriarchal, male dominated society. That is why the economical and physical exploitation of the women have got emphasis in translating the life of the gendered subaltern in Elias's writings.

However, Elias's women characters are not showcased as merely beautiful ladies. Rather he portrays them as strong women but often exploited by the ruling bourgeois and domination of patriarchy. Elias's character *Jummoner Maa* in *Chilekothar Sepai* is exploited physically like her mother-in-law, Khijir's mother. But when Tamij in *Khoabnama*, is involved with his stepmother in a sexual intercourse, this is not overlooked by the novelist. Neither the subalterns's physical relationship nor their sorrow and pain are overemphasized by Elias in both novels. Somehow, he translates them as they are in society. So, from this point of view Elias's gendered subalterns are not naïve or innocent but they are powerful with their voice and attitude. However, Fuljan in *Khoabnama* is much stronger than Tamij; she works more than Tamij in her father's paddy field. *Jummoner Maa* is also vocal and strong in taking her decision.

None of the women characters of Elias are beautiful. Elias's women characters are not narrated as beautiful showcased lady. Elias does not create them as very beautiful women. Elias describes *Jummoner Maa* as "Jummoner Maa has used snow-powder after washing her face thoroughly/tightly by using soap. The design/diagram of her broken cheeks have changed; the ash colour is glowing over her dark complexion, but this charm dissolves due to her keen/sharp and pointed voice" (47). On the other hand in *Khoabnama* Elias describes Kulsum's physical beauty in this way, "Kulsum sees the right sight of her cheeks one time and the left part again by keeping the small round mirror on her right hand. There is no distance/wide interval between the two cheeks, the deep dark colour becomes pale so the complexion seems a bit light/fair. Though the nose is not aquiline but it is high, the front of the nose is bit larger" (17). And *Khoabnama*'s Fuljan is physically disabled. But everybody runs with their dream. *Jummoner Maa* works in Rahmatullah's home with a hope that *Mahajan* will make a good fortune for his son Jummon. Both *Jummoner Maa* and Fuljan are labourers, one gives her labour as a domestic help to other's house and the other gives her labour on her own father's rice field and home. But the labours of both are unrecognized in the society as a means of productive labour, Elias shows this subtly.

Thus, through the characters of Elias's novels we have found the social culture of the subalterns. For instance, the unnamed *Jummoner Maa* has been married twice which is a frequent phenomenon in the life of the subaltern and often is seen in the society. On the other hand, teenage Kulsum is married to old Tamijer *Baap*, and Fuljan is involved in extra-marital relationship with Tamij in an open field, which are not uncommon matter in a subaltern's life. These incidents are illustrated by Elias not to humiliate these people but to give a true picture of the subaltern's life and society.

How patriarchy is involved in the lives of the marginalized people we come to understand that in the narration of Kulsum's life as well. Kulsum is dominated by her old husband and his stepson. Elias illustrates this patriarchal domination through these lines: "Some dal has slightly fallen down on the floor from the plate of Tamijer Baap. No, not any thing other than that. What a rage/anger of this man for that! He leaps up from eating and tightly stiffens 'you give your foot to my rice? Now how do I eat this impure rice? At once the fisticuffs of that hand starts on the back of Kulsum"(19). In a way a petty bourgeois like Kalam *Majhi* tries to capture Kulsum is also significant to understand the position of women in society. As long as Kulsum's husband was alive, she was secure. Her old husband's death is the starting of her unsecured life. Keramat and Kalam Majhi try to take the advantage of the absence of Kulsum's guardian. Kulsum's life is immobile too like any other rural women of the society; Elias did not overlook this as well. All kinds of conservativeness keep women like Kulsum immobile, dark and deaf. This immobility is part of poor landless subaltern women's lives. When Tamij tells his story of Khiar area, rail station, landlords, and many things, Kulsum feels of the outside world for the first time of her life. Through the character Kulsum, Elias gives us a true translation of the gendered subaltern whose voice is not heard. When Kulsum asks about the war, what is the relation of war and *Jotdars*, Tamij remains silent, and he starts another story by neglecting Kulsum's passion to know about *Tevaaga*.

From this point of view we can come to a conclusion that Elias's women characters are those oppressed people who are at the centre of social, economic and patriarchal domination. Yet, he translates them not only as an oppressed class but he demonstrates their insecurity in society through the character of *Jummoner Maa* as she says to her husband Khijir when he proposes her to leave *Mahajan*'s house: "Ho! Is this a word of a man/are you telling this like a man! Mahajan will give rickshaw to my son. I have to stay within your chest/bosom by leaving all these, right? Huh! while there is nothing but only some bones. Will you be able to keep me in that skinny bonny cage? A vagabond man!" (88). *Jummoner Maa* cannot believe that Khijir would give her protection, food and shelter. In the same way, we find this insecurity in Kulsum's character. As long as Tamijer *Baap* was alive, Kulsum was fine in her husband's house. When Tamijer *Baap* dies, she is attacked by Kalam *Majhi* and attracted by Keramat. At the same time, it is not negligible to take into account that *Jummoner Maa* accepts the physical exploitation of *Mahajan* with the hope that *Mahajan* will ensure her and her son's better future. In a way she is also manipulating *Mahajan* for her purposes by using her body. Kulsum also has engaged in physical relationship with her stepson Tamij.

At the end, it can be said that Elias's women characters live in the middle of social, economic and patriarchal domination. But he does not translate them as showcased beautiful lady of the society. He does not translate them as totally naïve and innocent. Rather Elias's women characters are those who prevail in the society with the social and patriarchal domination. Their domestic labour is not recognized by the family and society as well as their voice cannot be heard. They remain in the social and economical periphery. That is why they are the gendered subalterns (subalterns within the subalterns).

## LANGUAGE OF THE SUBALTERN: *CHILEKOTHAR SEPAI* AND *KHOABNAMA*

Elias deals with the subaltern's language in his two novels – *Chilekothar Sepai* and *Khoabnama*. To him, subaltern's language and culture are very important and he mentioned it frequently in his interviews and articles. He said, "We can not recognize the lives of the subalterns by only showing their poverty. In their lives, there are humanitarian values and those could not be uprooted by the thousand years of oppression. So, it is must to know their culture and language to identify them and evaluate them in a proper way". Language is a part of identity and culture of the subaltern. An understanding of the subaltern's codes of communication, as Spivak thought, are important in the task of translation of subaltern culture. Elias's writing, for this reason, can also be compared with Gabriel García Márquez and Mahasweta Devi.

*Chilekothar Sepai* and *Khoabnama* contain colloquial Bangla language which is obviously the language of the subaltern. Elias uses the local Dhakaiya Bangla for his characters Khijir, *Mahajan*, *Jummoner Maa*, but when he brings Chengtu and others in *Chilekothar Sepai* who are from North Bengal, Elias switches from Dhakaiya Bangla to the typical North Bengal dialogue Bangla which easily can be distinguished from the so called middle class official Bangla. *Khoabnama* is extensively written in North Bengal Bangla because the setting of the novel is that part of Bengal. In his novels, settings, characters, and characters' languages are interrelated.

## CONCLUSION

Hasan Al Zayed perfectly states that Elias shares solidarity with the masses albeit his deep skepticism about systems and socio-cultural determinisms (2008). It is true that Elias had a notion and a desire to uproot existing systems of exploitation (2008). So, through his writing he has tried to translate the marginalized people and their lives. *Chilekothar Sepai* and *Khoabnama* are great examples of that. This positioning towards the subalterns is not a notion to represent this group of people as noble and victim rather the true essence of the subaltern life has got importance in Elias's writing. Elias presents those subaltern characters by placing them in a historical moment to show the importance of the urban proletariat or rural peasants in a particular historical event. Though they are effaced from the official history writing, their involvement and contribution cannot be overlooked. That is why Elias has taken the responsibility of translating these oppressed people and their lives through his novels *Khoabnama* and *Chilekothar Sepai* with the intention of counter-narrativization of history. He has also chosen to address local inequalities and oppressions of the subalterns through these two novels.

Elias has tried to capture the socio-economic reality of the subalterns through the characters Khijir, Tamij, *Jummoner Maa* and Fuljan. Though the setting and context of the novel belong to past, does it differ much from the present scenario of Bangladesh? Bangladesh is no more a British colony, not an oppressed part of Pakistan even. 40 years of Independence have been observed. But still do Chengtu, Khijir, Tamij, and Fuljan stand up against their oppressors? Or do their economic and social positions have changed? These questions are obvious while reading Elias. Still the socio-economic position of the subalterns has not been changed. Both *Khoabnama* and *Chilekothar Sepai* have shown the pre-liberation phenomenon of the subaltern life, but after 40 years of Independence, the position of the poor oppressed people have not changed. Yet Alauddin, Khaibar Gazi, Rahmatullah, Shrafatullah Mandal are still in their position with more power. The dream what Tamij saw as an *Adhiar* (landless farm hand) is not fulfilled and Khijir's revolution for an oppressionless society is misled by the present capitalist society where the economical distance between poor and rich is more acute. Capitalism and multinational companies have taken the place of Rahmatullah and Khaibar Gazi or Shrafatullah Mandal. But still we hope that one day Tamij and Khijir's dream will be fulfilled by their descendents Jummon and Shakhina for which Khijir has given his life and Tamij has left his home to an unknown place.

## Works Cited

Ashcroft, Bill, Gareth Griffiths and Helen Tiffin, eds. *Key Concepts in Post-colonial Studies*. London: Routledge, 2004.

Elias, Akhtaruzzaman. *Chilekothar Sepai*. Dhaka: the University Press Limited, 1986.

———. *Khoabnama*. Dhaka: Maowla Brothers, 1996.

———. *Rochona Shomogro, Vol. 3,* Dhaka: Maowla Brothers, 2004.

Elias, Khalikuzzaman. "Khoabnamar Majhi O Chashira." *Akhtaruzzaman Elias Sharokgrontho*. Ed. Shomiron Mojumder. Kolkata: Omritolok Sahitto Porishod, 1997.

Hawthorn, Jeremy. *A Glossary of Contemporary Theory*. London: Arnold, 2000.

Iqbal, Shahid. *Kothashilpi Akhtaruzzaman Elias*. Dhaka: Jatiya Grontho Prokashoni, 1997.

Kamal, Ahmed. "East Bengal at Independence." *History of Bangladesh 1704–1971*. Ed. Sirajul Islam. Dhaka: Asiatic Society Bangladesh, 2007.

Mohammad, Anu. *Elias O Prosner Shokti*. Dhaka: Shrabon Prokashoni, 2009.

Morton, Stephen. *Gayatri Chakrovorty Spivak*. Oxford: Routledge, 2003.

Moniruzzaman, Taluklder. *The Bangladesh Revolution and its Aftermath*. Dhaka: The University Press Limited, 2009.

Maggio, J. "'Can the Subaltern Be Heard?': Political Theory, Translation, Representation, and Gayatri Chakravorty Spivak." *Alternatives* 32.4 (Oct.–Dec. 2007):419–443.

Rushd, Abu. "Akhtaruzzaman Eliaser Khoabnama: Ak Mullayon." *Akhtaruzzaman Elias Fire Dekha Sarajibon*. Ed. Mojibul Haq Kabir and Mahbub Kamran. Dhaka: Magnam Opas, 2000.

Sofa, Ahmed. "Eliasnama: Khoabnama." *Akhtaruzzaman Elias Fire Dekha Sarajibon*. Ed. Mojibul Haq Kabir and Mahbub Kamran. Dhaka: Magnam Opas, 2000.

Spivak, Gayatri C. *In Other Worlds: Essays in Cultural Politics*. New York: Routledge, 1987.

———. "Negotiating the Structures of Violence." *The Post-colonial Critic: Interviews, Strategies, Dialogues*. Ed. Sarah Harasym. New York: Routledge, 1990. 138–151.

———. "Can the Subaltern Speak?". *The Postcolonial Studies Reader*. Ed. Bill Ashcroft, Gareth Griffiths and Helen Tiffin. London: Routledge, 1999. 24–29.

Zayed, Hasan Al. "Late Style as Politics." *Harvest: Jahangirnogor Studies in Literature and Language*. 23 (2008):35–52.

# 7

# Acts of Refuge, Acts of Naming: On Translating Sindhi Identity as 'Minor'

*Soni Wadhwa*

> Migrant communities are representative of a much wider trend towards the minoritization of national societies.
>
> Homi Bhabha

## PARTITION: SINDHI LITERATURE AND HISTORY

"Sindhis hate History," my History teacher once said. And as if that was not enough, she insisted, "Even today". Most of my musings about academics, scholarship, history and literature have been since then indebted to that public statement in a private classroom. Though my mental laziness always spared me the trouble of engaging with the issue explicitly, I always recognized my passion for History since it was introduced to me in my third standard. In fact, my love for History was a matter of pride and I flaunted it as much as I could because others either found it very boring and dull or simply too difficult. I, quite rightly, assumed I was an exception.

My teacher's statement should have made me feel better because she was situating the subject outside a particular community and should have therefore, placed me above my community. But I feel very disoriented now. I can merely try to understand that remark and my memory of History in the context of what "Sindhis" remember of "their" "History". The emphasis on "Sindhis", "their" and "History" is crucial because as categories in Humanities, they have been severely scrutinized. The question of "Sindhis" vis-a-vis memory is extremely difficult to pin down. The past that they have left behind is in no way restricted to their experience alone. Sindhis, as a community, cannot claim any ownership or copyright over remembering what happened. The question of "their" memory is even more heavily nuanced – don't we use the expression "they" for others, and outsiders? Should I be addressing my community as "they"? "History", on the other hand, is no longer seen as the capital "H" with a singular, objective agenda. A sensitive historian would today say that there are many histories, each giving a different perspective. And therefore we come back to the question of memory. After all, wouldn't history draw in a lot upon the memory of the person or the community whose point of view is being considered?

I do not remember any instance of identifying myself as a Sindhi merely because I happen to speak (and not read and write in the so-called "original" Arabic script) Sindhi and my foremothers and forefathers migrated from Sindh (now in Pakistan) to Ulhasnagar (a small town close to Mumbai in India) and began to live here as refugees. So, for me, remembering Partition and therefore Sindh has been a painful task – I am required to remember what I haven't gone through. When Partition happened, lakhs of Sindhis (Sindhi Hindus, to be precise) migrated to different parts of India. They came by sea either to Kathiawar or to Mumbai. Though it's easily said, it means leaving all the property, land, business and several kinds of networks and resources in Sindh. There were many who arrived penniless and they had to begin right from the scratch. The sojourn is not well documented except for some sparse material. However, what makes me understand their condition is a very remarkable poem by Mahesh Nenvani:

### "Khiri Machi"

When my brother brings khiri machi,
We face a dilemma:
At dinner, he talks of Sindhu,
The fertile soil, the farmers…
His eyes fill, he chokes,
The fish bone in his throat.
At night, hand on chest,
He groans, tosses, turns.

Inside, the fish
In the desolate night,
Writhes. (in Makhija et al.)

It is a very remarkable poem which touches upon the idea of homelessness, alienation and memory all at the same time very sensitively. The parallel drawn between the fish and the refugee is a sad similarity and it enhances the concept of the minor with such associations.

In more ways than one, this is what literature does to us – it helps us imagine what others have experienced, and are trying to remember. Remember? Yes, my teacher seemed to hint that Sindhis don't want to remember the past, especially the Partition and therefore, cannot negotiate with that part of Indian History. The capital "H" again. There are innumerable poems, short stories, novels, plays and narratives waiting to be heard, remembered though largely forgotten and locating them once more may help bring potential opportunities of making Sindhi literary traditions visible. We have very easily forgotten that Sindhi writing and culture in general are a great legacy of Persian and Arabic influences.

My exposure to Sindhi literature and history has made me realize a few things. It is very embarrassing to confess that it takes us, Sindhis in an immediate context, so long to realize that there are many stereotypes about the community that can be corrected only if they are noted. Rita Kothari, for instance, points out how Sindhi characters, especially in Bollywood films, hardly go beyond the expressions and dialogues like "*vadi saain*" or "*chariya*". Close approximations of these Sindhi terms are "*arey*" in Hindi. The character played by Dalip Tahir in *Hum Hain Rahi Pyar Ke* is an example of such a category of comic-villains generally identified as Sindhi characters. Remembering alone can help us see that Sindhis are not a community lacking in intellectual and aesthetic achievements. The more we try, Salman Rushdie says, the better we remember. Reminiscing is one creative endeavour towards our past and clarifies a few things for ourselves. Again, one of Mahesh Nenvani's poems very aptly demonstrates what it means to remember:

### "A Home for Everyone"

His legs cut,
India became the crutch.

Lying in camp all day,
He hoped some Samaritan would help.
His appetite lost,
He bought bread *pakoda*, nibbled,
Then decided to clean the room.

Moving up to the roof,
He stopped;
In the corner,
A spider cringed.

"I will not destroy the web," he murmured,
his eyes turning wet.

This article is a contribution to the process of thinking about the construction of identity at large, and the ways in which it is influenced by otherization. It is an attempt to look at some selected voices in Sindhi writing (available in translation) to explore how different Sindhi writers reflect upon their past of the community as a whole. The intention here is also to understand the recurring patterns in the articulation of their feelings about Sindh, and for our immediate purposes, to scrutinize how that in turn provides us with a frame of reference to think about their present notions of integration into Indian state/society.

I submit that the voices discussed are not in any way representative of the Sindhi experience as a whole, if such a thing exists at all. The point, however is to listen to these articulations, identify their positions vis-a-vis the community as they see it and then theorize these positions along the lines of the political implications of their arguments. The recurring patterns identified in some of the poems and stories in thinking about their present are: nostalgia for Sindh, feeling of alienation caused by displacement, the articulation of feeling marginalized because of being deterritorialized and further, locating the self and the other against such a deterritorialization.

## TRANSLATING SINDHI IDENTITY AS SUBALTERN/'MINOR'

In other words, the argument in this article focuses on the recognition of the self vis-a-vis displacement and the gaze of the other, and thereby teases out ways in which the changes in their lived behaviour are reflected upon. One important insight into the aftermath of migration is the translation from being a "major" community in Pakistan (or, undivided India, before Partition) to a "minor" community in India. It should be noted that the claim here is not to suggest that the Sindhi community as a whole is a marginalized community. However, the point here is to discuss possible issues in Sindhi writing that could be linked to the minority status of the language. The argument borrows a lot from this concept of "minority" and attempts to extend it to the "minor" as a metaphor and a literary-political term as used by Gilles Deleuze and Félix Guattari. Deleuze and Guattari are well known to have given new dimensions to the way the expression "minor" is discussed in literary and political sense. "Minor", they argue, is not a matter of numbers, but the quality as seen to be associated with the numbers. The "minor" is, therefore, a sensibility and a tradition that is revolutionary in the sense that it refuses to speak on the lines of the "major" which is the norm.

This article attempts to relate this notion of "minor" to the notion of the "subaltern". The suggestion is that the voice of the refugee is deprived and marginalized. The refugee is an outsider in the rhetoric of the nation and therefore he is not offered any space in the hierarchy of the nation. (The act of offering itself implies a hierarchy.) In the case of the Sindhi refugee and her voice in literature, it is this deprivation that makes a case for her to be understood in terms of the subaltern. The issue of the nation is of particular concern here because the coming in of the refugee does not fit into the political definition of migration/exile from one country to another. India and Pakistan, in other words, were not two different nations so to speak, before Partition. Does the displacement of the refugee need to be measured against the country or land that she has come from? Rita Kothari argues that it were the arrival in India and departure from Pakistan that were the most painful experiences for the Sindhi refugees, rather than the violence in Pakistan. I recognize that an immediate reaction to the suggestion of the subaltern perspective being used to understand the voice of the Sindhi refugee would be that Sindhis are not perceived as a marginalized people and they do not consider themselves to be marginalized. However, my suggestion here is that whether they see themselves to be marginalized or not is not in any case an important criterion for them to be studied in the light of the concept of the subaltern. Secondly, I do not propose that the community in the contemporary set-up is subaltern – it is the refugee in selected (translated) Sindhi writing that can be understood to be subaltern. Thirdly, she is also a subaltern because the Partition has caused a rupture in the cultural sensibility that she could have inherited, had she not been displaced. The loss of the influences of Persian, Arabic and Sufi syncretic traditions on the Sindhi refugee's way of life and her intellectual and aesthetic make-up and writing is remarkable. I also recognize that Sindhis who came to India are primarily Hindus and are therefore a majority, "major" and hence the norm. So that would in fact turn them into the dominant, elite people who from the mainstream marginalize the others, below in the hierarchy. Such a notion about the "major" would take us back to the general way of seeing the dominating category as a homogeneous category. Even if the argument of seeing the community as the "major" holds to be true, it does not in any way disqualify it from being understood as "subaltern". The argument is, of course, open to debate but I also submit that the attempt here is very limited and is only applicable within certain provisionalities.

The attempt is largely to articulate the overlaps across identity and history, along the agency of space – public/private/communitarian – symbolizing diverse pathways of tracing the impact of localities on the ways we perceive ourselves and, choose, at times to be perceived. The intention is to go beyond historical imagination and attempt to outline the mapping of layered identities as grafted on ourselves, or at times deliberately built upon.

The following poem by Krishin Khatwani effectively brings alive the dilemma of the community in the translation after Partition:

> Our youngsters
> When they ask
> Of our sons and daughters
> Who were our elders
> How were they
> Our children
> After thinking a while
> Will answer with heavy hearts
> We don't know from which country our elders came
> Where dropped their tongue
> What they wrote you can't read
> Their songs you can't sing
> Seems neither were they your elders
> Nor are you their young ones. (in *Indian Literature*, 149)

Bhabha says something similar:

> Such fantastic renaming of the subjects of cultural difference do not derive their discursive authority from anterior causes – be it human nature or historical necessity – which, in a secondary move, articulate essential and expressive identities between cultural differences in the contemporary world. The problem is not of an ontological cast, where differences are effects of some more totalizing, transcendent identity to be found in the past or the future. Hybrid hyphenations emphasize the incommensurable elements – the stubborn chunks – as the basis of cultural identifications. (Bhabha, 219)

The very act of negotiating between the two generations about one's origins is quite telling on the processes that have impacted the formation of identity as the next generations see it. Fred Dallmayr says: "…identity [is] the work of an ever-renewed creative praxis, a praxis mediating between convention and invention and between past sedimentations and imagined possible futures" (in Baral and Kar, 14). This helps us address the absences in Sindhi writing in a much better way to scrutinize the simplistic positions upheld by writers who do not go beyond mourning the loss of Sindh. The understanding of strong relationship between identity and narratives becomes a crucial space to engage with the self, the other, and the other constructs like the nation. Dallmayr's position could be seen as an extension of Cave's as he points out more explicitly the connection between both identity and narratives as texts – each a praxis on its own discursive level. His position is also similar to that of Stuart Hall in that he (Hall) addresses the relation of fluid nature of identity and identity as a process and a becoming. It is precisely such a complex understanding of identity as always in motion that seems to be absent in Sindhi writing. And also, to reiterate, it in no way undermines the freedom of expression of Sindhi writing at all, or else the model of "minor" literature that is used to understand Sindhi writing would prove to be contradictory if the latter is dismissed as waste and repetitive.

The essentializing of Sindhi culture does not allow for exploration of that very "creative praxis" in terms of exploring other ways of connecting with society and the other individuals and communities. By submitting to essentializing, such an articulation about the self does not consider other possibilities of being (and becoming, of course) and gives way to chauvinism. Rita Kothari seems to investigate this problem when she analyzes the influence of Hindutva on political affiliations of Sindhis and their religious practices; an instance of which arises in Sindhis' participation in the Godhra carnage (2002) and the 1969 riots in Gujarat:

> While the Sindhis of Gujarat show no desire to accept the Muslims, they in turn remain rejected and marginalized by the mainstream Hindu Gujaratis who think of the Sindhis as 'dirty', 'shrewd' and 'Muslim-like' people. Was the Sindhi hatred for the Muslims a result of this marginalization? .... Were the Sindhis of Gujarat retaliating for their sufferings during Partition and settling old scores, so to speak? Or had living in Gujarat created communal tendencies in them that had hitherto not existed? Was their newly acquired Hindu identity a result of their efforts to shed their sense of stigma? (Kothari, xvii)

Any encounter with the mainstream community (like the Gujarati Hindus) is seen as predominantly pressurizing and universalistic. To quote Dallmayr again:

> In [such a] confrontation, the idea of "universalism" often serves as a camouflage for particular hegemonic ambitions – ambitions which tend to be resisted on the part of non-hegemonic societies or cultures through a retreat into nostalgic (and essentialized) forms of parochialism, communalism, or ethnocentrism. One exit route from this (potentially violent) clash of identities – route favored by some postmodern thinkers – is the strategy of constructivism, a strategy which negates or "deconstructs" all existing identities in favor of contingent fabrication. (in Baral and Kar, 27)

The gesture towards Hindutva and loss of syncretism are merely two instances of growing parochial attitudes of the community towards the self. Also interesting is the other avenue that Dallmayr suggests as a more productive approach towards hegemony and that is the postmodern turn, the recognition of "contingent fabrication" in the process of identity formation, which is absent because of essentialization of Sindhi identity. Further, Chanchala K. Naik elaborates that "the postmodern critiques of subjectivity" see "individual identity (as) a myth and an illusion .... conflict-ridden, often self-deluded fundamentally opaque to themselves, and let alone able to master" (in Baral and Kar, 68). On the contrary, Sindhi identity in the words of the poets discussed above, seems to be a concrete ground for expressing grief over the loss caused by the partition – an act of conscious choice, very legitimate in its concerns, but it does move beyond and locates the self in the recognition as refugee, as somebody leading a "Number Two" life, as the inheritor of the Indus Valley. It is quite difficult to account for a representation of what Sindhis have left behind even in second or third generation poets. As Bhabha notes:

> What is at issue is the performative nature of differential identities: the regulation and negotiation of those spaces that are continually, *contingently*, "opening out", remaking the boundaries, exposing the limits of any claim to a singular or autonomous sign of difference – be it class, gender or race. Such assignations of social differences – where difference is neither One nor the Other but *something else besides, in-between* – find their agency in a form of the "future" where the past is not originary, where the present is not simply transitory. It is, if I may stretch a point, an interstitial future, that emerges in-between the claims of the past and the needs of the present. (Bhabha, 219, italics original)

Moreover, imagining the self in the community across generations involves a dialectic of its own. Naik discusses Hernadi in this context:

> Hernadi argues that memory and imagination – the directedness of belief and desire toward a postulated past or a hypothetical future – affect the individuals who do the remembering or imagining. Mutual awareness that two or more persons share certain memories often leads to reciprocally constitutive impact on the ongoing formation of each separate self. Therefore, the self is historical and is both constituted by and constitutive of a community. (in Baral and Kar, 71)

Such a mutual recognition between the self and the community produces identity literature. Bijay Danta gives an insightful account of the event of writing in a new place, after movement and the conditions which lead to the production of identities, but of "new mythologies" (or "subversive strategies" or "modes of revision") that help the migrant to engage with the new land, the new people, the left-behind departure and the moment of arrival:

> The race for new mythologies then would be able to account for the self subterranean fantasies and quests on the one hand and the more accessible public images of the self, on the other. One of these may refer to the pride of the images one carries from a lost era; the other may refer to the images of pride that one would hope to give to one's grandchildren and their grand children. (in Baral and Kar, 100)

These myths are suggestive of a collective imagined expression of what we are today and a necessary element of psychological continuity – a first step in the process of adaptation and negotiation with the new land.

## POST-PARTITION EXPERIENCE

History and identity lead to the questions of post-Partition experience and look at the primary concerns of the community – on the one hand, there is an emotional description of the difficulties faced in the camp, largely constituting the gaze reminding the self of being refugees and on the other, there is some attempt at identifying the blame for such a condition. The attempt here is to understand the experience as refugee as a 'minor' or 'subaltern' experience. The Sindhi is also a subaltern because her literature and her voice have been relatively marginalized in history. The notion of the subaltern is also used here to critique the attitudes towards Sindhi writing as non-literary because there strongly exist strong standards of recognizing the 'literary' without taking into consideration the literary tradition that Sindhi as a language may have to itself.

A very relevant study in terms of the development of Subaltern Studies and its agenda has been conducted by Gayatri Chakravorty Spivak in her highly celebrated essay, "Can the Subaltern Speak?" One of the main arguments of the essay is that representation, in the sense of "speaking for" is debunked by Western thinkers because they feel that the nature of modernity is (or should be) such that the oppressed should speak for themselves since the intellectuals no longer identify with their condition and would not be able to present their state as effectively and as sensitively as the subalterns would do themselves. Spivak questions the notion that representation is dead and each individual (and thereby perhaps as a signifier of a community) has every specific empowering agency, which with the onset of democracy, gives her the space to speak for herself, to make herself heard (though the argument is that even in the space of the subaltern, it is the man who has been reached out to in the subaltern studies so far). When she says that "[R]epresention has not withered away", she establishes a gesture towards a crucial task of an intellectual to continue to make attempts at making the subalterns heard using diverse strategies. Subaltern history writing is one such method but is rigorously "taxonomic" and "essentialist" (284–285) as she herself puts it. "*Because* "the person who speaks and acts ... is always a multiplicity", no "theorizing intellectual ... [or] party or ... union" can represent those who act and struggle" (*FD*, 206) (282). The argument of freewill and self-representation is easily championed by Gilles Deleuze and Michel Foucault because according to Spivak's understanding of their stand, "... the Other as Subject is inaccessible" to them (282): "According to Foucault and Deleuze (in the First World, under the standardization and regimentation of socialized capital, though they do not seem to recognize this) the oppressed, if given the chance (the problem of representation cannot be bypassed here), and on the way to solidarity through alliance politics (a Marxist thematic is at work here) *can speak and know their conditions*" (283) (emphasis original).

This situation, as it does not apply to the "Third World" situation, with a brilliant illustration in the example of the sati, also applies to the marginalized condition of the Sindhi community and writing. The Subaltern Studies group confronts this question in the context of the project of imperialism and sees it as bringing forth a history coloured by "predominantly elite achievements" (Guha, quoted in Spivak, 284) but they seem to fail to recognize, according to Spivak, that the subaltern subject, "irretrievably heterogeneous" (1442) and their narration of history is seen as nuanced with the "master-slave dialectic" (285). However, the useful contributions made by the Subaltern Studies group is that of identifying the dominant groups at different levels and recognizing that the degree of domination of the same category/ class/element differs from place to place which brings us directly to the question of the major/minor here.

In another essay, "Deconstructing Historiography", Spivak argues that subaltern consciousness is the consciousness of the "collective"

– the community or recognition of the ethnic self. We shall see how it gets reflected in Sindhi writing.

Dipesh Chakrabarty discusses the rise of diverse perspectives in the writing of history especially those of "previously excluded groups" (Chakrabarty, 97), which brings us to the possibility of considering the Sindhi refugee as a subaltern but, as mentioned earlier, the status (not in an enviable sense) of the subaltern has been used to understand the situation of peasants and tribals and therefore, it seems, is hesitant to incorporate Sindhis perceived as (homogenously, stereotypically) wealthy. The 'history from below', as subaltern studies defines itself, is an attempt to become an instance of "good" history which "are supposed to enrich the subject matter of history and make it more representative of society as a whole" (Chakrabarty, 97). And because the Sindhi perspective on history seems to be missing, it has a lot of potential to help build "good histories". To illustrate, we rarely come across Sindhi names in the freedom struggle. Is it that like Partition Studies, historians have very categorically chosen to remain silent about issues like (lack of) violence in Sindh and disturbing arrival in India? Or just that Sindhis just didn't participate in the struggle for independence? Just as history, at least textbook histories, which are a very forceful lesson in the constitution of difference and recognition, remain largely silent about the contribution of North West Frontier Province and East Bengal in the "national" struggle for independence, the Sindhi participation remains a hidden issue. This is not to deny that here is a possibility of non-participation (which is unlikely) but the point is that the reasons for the same should be visibly investigated. The argument here is that because of the reasons stated above, Sindhi perspective is minor or subaltern and Chakrabarty helps us understand what it means to be categorized as minor:

> The problem of minority histories thus leads us to the question of what may be called the "minority" of some particular pasts. Some constructions and experiences of the past stay "minor" in the sense that their very incorporation into historical narratives converts them into pasts "of lesser importance" vis-à-vis dominant understandings of what constitutes fact and evidence (and hence vis-à-vis the underlying principle of rationality) in the practices of professional history. Such "minor" pasts are those experiences of the past that always have to be assigned to an "inferior" or "marginal" position as they are translated into the academic historian's language. (Chakrabarty, 100–1)

Chakrabarty goes on to elaborate:

> Just as the "minor" in literature implies "a critique of narratives of identity" and refuses "to represent the attainment of autonomous subjectivity that is the ultimate aim of the major narrative," the "minor" in my use similarly functions to cast doubt on the "major". (Chakrabarty, 101)

There are various ways of getting access to such a history:

> Some scholars now *perform* the limits of history in various ways: by fictionalizing the past, experimenting to see how films and history might intersect in the new discipline of cultural studies, studying memory rather than just history, playing around with forms of writing, and other similar means. (Chakrabarty, 106)

It would be appropriate here to scrutinize certain voices in poetry as an entry point to understand that subaltern past.

The fragments discussed here show a lot of concern for the construction of the new nation and how they are received within it. The focus seems to be largely on the critique of the nation and the voice of the refugee. The following lines are ideal to begin with:

> Nationhood springs from one's home
> How can I claim ownership in a sublet house? (in Makhija et al.)

The idea here raises complex questions pertaining to nation and nationalism critiquing the "given" nature of feeling of belongingness. It reflects an assertive attempt to resist the given influence of nationalism on identity and a very explicit articulation of distance.

The focus now shifts to resistance:

> You prostitute politics!
>
> You have destroyed the peace of nations.
> Chori! Snatched away our wisdom,
> Set brother against brother,
> Made humanity helpless.
>
> You prostitute,
> Leave Us Alone! (in Makhija et al., 11)

The speaker in the poem seems to address that there is a very potential force that works to decide the condition of the ordinary people and recognizes that force to politics. The political impacts upon the personal. And one way to resist or to voice the dissent is the abuse "prostitute". Another speaker trying to vent out anger in another poem is a woman:

"Congresswallah's necks should be broken,
those men have done us injustice."
Pounding the clothes on the river bank,
Pohu's mother curses.

"They gifted Sind to those jats,
terrible conditions thrust upon us.
Even Jinnah did not care,"
Pohu's mother curses.

"Stripped here, stripped there,
the winds turned upon us."
Sharing her woes with other women,
Pohu's mother curses. (in Makhija et al., 12)

The curse is a direct address to Congress and Jinnah who were known to be the large players in the formation of the two nations. All the stanzas in the poem reflect upon each of the woes inflicted upon the people seen as refugees. The resistance is seen elsewhere too:

Politics, such a curse!

Like stone-age men,
Hiding in snake-ridden,
Cave-like barracks.
A tola of oil, dal,
Two handfuls of flour,
A ghaghar of water;
The whole family
Deprived of ration. (in Makhija et al., 26)

The material conditions that the refugees were forced to face is described in such fragments. The means were inadequate and refer to the extreme condition of the so-called "rehabilitation". The poverty is a constant interference with the mental peace which gets noticeable in the refugee situation. And what the individual says therefore becomes the voice of the collective:

> 'Becoming minor', Abdul JanMohamed and David Lloyd remind us, "is not a question of essence ... but a question of subject position". Such a position articulates 'alternative practices and values that are embedded in the often-damaged, - fragmentary, -hampered, or – occluded work of minorities'; and having been "coerced into a negative, generic subject position, the oppressed individual transforms it into a positive collective one". (Bhabha, 229)

One such voice says:

Drowning in wine, sober I lie.
Pitying my fate, awake I lie.
What is life worth when the soul is caged?
How long can a bird be content when it cannot fly?
I pine to sing song after song, so free,
But right then, the grocer's bill tugs at me! (in Makhija et al., 28)

Many poems reflect upon the financial status of the refugees as a contrast to the comfortable conditions of the past. There is a sense of deep loss in the tone while describing the present:

Walking, walking, the soles fall off;
We need shoes of iron, shoes of steel.
The cobblers surely must thank us!

May God give our government wisdom
To provide footwear in ration too.
With our feet covered, we will bless them. (in Makhija et al., 29)

These lines are very remarkable in their attitude towards bureaucracy, talking about the way the government is unaware of how things operate at the ground level ("below") and how the officials do not have any idea about the needs of the refugees. Perhaps the situation would remain the same for ever:

A victim of politics,
Driven out,
I have taken refuge here.

After so many years,
Still a refugee.
A refugee forever. (in Makhija et al., 39)

The recognition as refugee leads to identity as refugee and the sorrow that follows reflects upon how marginalization has affected the self. The self again is seen through the association with the past and the allegory touching upon the same agony is reflected in metaphors of creatures as minor as a fish:

> This liminality of migrant experience is no less a transitional phenomenon than a translational one; there is no resolution to it because the two conditions are ambivalently enjoined in the 'survival' of migrant life. (Bhabha, 224)

What Bijay Danta says in the context of the new mythographies is particularly interesting here:

> As a subversive historian of the self's other and the other's self, the new mythographer has to be always on the guard. His body is both a celebration of his own boundless self and at the same time a repudiation of the other's bond and bounds, frames that it cannot do without. That he is skeptical of new names and new roles is not surprising. For, these roles and names given to the newly arrived traveler coincide with a moment of ceasing to be, a moment of naming/maiming. This is so as the new name – refugee/immigrant/political asylum seeker/ job seeker/parasite – at once divorces the recipient from his natural/former self, by being bound with a giver of names, a new name. The idea is to use the new location but resist the new role....The history of public rejection in consequence a history of private troubles, subterranean acceptance, and fractured conscience. (in Baral and Kar, 106)

## CONCLUSION

The subaltern, the minor, the refugee and the migrant are some of the important strands to study marginalization. Several studies like *Engaging Cultural Differences* have attempted to understand the phenomena of immigration and events like multiculturalism. A couple of essays in the book helps theorize the concepts of difference and identity. Marcelo

M. Suarez-Orozco, for instance, describes the immigrant situation in the US: "...the most basic rule governing public attitudes about immigration: we love immigrants at a safe historical distance but are much more ambiguous about those joining us in the here and now" (23). He also argues that the assumption of homogeneity leads one to believe in a "relatively uniform 'mainstream'" culture as if there is a single coherent concept of nationality, or culture on the lines of cultural identity. He identifies two spheres of culture – the instrumental and the expressive – the former refers to "...the skills, competencies and social behaviours required to successfully make a living and contribute to society" while the latter refers to "...the realm of values, worldviews, and patterning of interpersonal relations that give meaning, and sustain the sense of self" (13). While the demand for acculturation (from within and without) on the lines of instrumental sphere would invite consensus, insistence on expressive acculturation would invite heated debates and what worsens the situation is that there is no coherent, unified mainstream culture to be accultured to. As Marcelo M. Suarez-Orozco puts in the American context: "The first issue is the question, acculturating to what? American society is no longer (if it ever was) a uniform or coherent system" (35).

Amitav Ghosh talks about the idea of diversity somewhat in the same vein: "It is impossible to be imperfectly Indian....Were it possible to be an imperfect Indian, everybody in India would be. This is not merely because India has failed to develop a national culture. It is not a lack. It is in itself the form of Indian culture. If there is any one pattern in Indian culture in the broadest sense it is simply this: that the culture seems to be constructed around the proliferation of differences (albeit within certain parameters). To be different in a world of differences is irrevocably to belong. Thus anybody anywhere who has even the most tenuous links with India is Indian; potentially a player within the culture" (Ghosh, 78). Austin Sarat narrates the example of Tina Isa, a second generation 16-year old daughter of Palestinian émigrés who killed her for her American ways of living (like dating an African American) which "brought shame and dishonour on the family name". In that context, Sarat attempts to understand the reaction of the (non-migrant) American peoples: "One response...law" (397).

This constitution of difference can help us understand the (mis)recognition of Sindhi refugees (which though strictly speaking is not an immigrant situation any longer in India and we have explored how it is more a matter of internal displacement rather than international issue) as "parasitic" aliens inviting doubts about their ethics and business practices. That leaves us with further questions about history, identity and identification:

> Binary divisions of social space neglect the profound temporal disjunction – the translational time and space – through which minority communities negotiate their collective identifications. For what is at issue in the discourse of minorities is the creation of agency through incommensurable (not simply multiple) positions. Is there a poetics of the "interstitial" community? How does it name itself, author its agency? (Bhabha, 231)

## Works Cited


Bhabha, Homi. "How Newness Enters the World." *The Location of Culture.* London: Routledge, 1994: 212–235.

Chakrabarty, Dipesh. *Provincializing Europe: Postcolonial Thought and Historical Difference.* Princeton: Princeton University Press, 2000.

Danta, Bijay. "The Race for New Mythologies: Travelling Identities in Postnational Discourses." *Identities: Local and Global.* Ed. Kailash C. Baral and Prafulla C. Kar. New Delhi: Pencraft International, 2003.

Ghosh, Amitav. "The Diaspora in Indian Culture." *Public Culture* 2.1 (Fall 1989):73–78.

Baral, Kailash C. and Pratulla C. Kar. *Identities: Local and Global.* New Delhi: Pencraft International, 2003.

Kothari, Rita. *The Burden of Refuge: The Sindhi Hindus of Gujarat* Chennai: Orient Longman, 2007.

Makhija, Anju, and et al., ed. *Freedom and Fissures: An Anthology of Sindhi Partition Poetry.* New Delhi: Sahitya Akademi, 1998.

Sarat, Austin. "The Micropolitics of Identity – Difference: Recognition and Accommodation in Everyday Life." *Engaging Cultural Differences: The Multicultural Challenge in Liberal Democracies.* Ed. Richard Schweder, et al. New York: Russell Sage Foundation, 2002. 396–416.

Spivak, Gayatri Chakravorty. "Subaltern Studies: Deconstructing Historography." *Subaltern Studies Vol. IV: Writings on South Asian History and Society.* New Delhi: Oxford University Press, 1985, 330–363.

Spivak, Gayatri Chakravorty. "Can the Subaltern Speak?" *Marxism and the Interpretation of Culture.* Ed. Cary Nelson and Lawrence Grossberg. Urbana and Chicago: University of Illinois Press, 1988. 271–313.

Suárez-Orozco, Marcelo M. "Everything You Ever Wanted to Know About Assimilation But Were Afraid To Ask." *Engaging Cultural Differences: The Multicultural Challenge in Liberal Democracies.* Ed. Richard Schweder, et al. New York: Russell Sage Foundation, 2002. 19–42.

# Problems of Praxis: Translating Indian Literatures

# 8

# Mediation of 'Meaning' beyond Consumption and Production: Translating Identity in Marginalized Texts

*Hemang Desai*

## INTRODUCTION

For the sake of practical convenience in problematizing the secondary status accorded to translation in academia in particular and in "culture industry", to borrow Adorno's coinage, in general, I would start off by recounting the proceedings of a meeting, which took place in the Department of English of an elite university of Gujarat, with the professedly noble aim of initiating the freshers into literary studies. Being the youngest, I was fidgeting in my position of privilege that had landed me amongst veteran scholars, one of whom was my own university teacher. When it came to deciding a novel to be studied by first year students, I dared devilishly to propose an Indian fiction in English (or in translation which, I remember, I spoke under the breath) at which my esteemed teacher flew into a lion rage screaming "Why not have something English?" and by English, as she later clarified, she meant *Pride* and *Prejudice* and *Tom Jones.* This was when we had just finished celebrating the diamond jubilee of Indian Independence and I couldn't help reflect upon the futility of the discursive spaces like "Indian Literary Studies" or "Indian Literature(s)" that we so passionately and rigorously seek to construct.

To my honourable teacher, as to many others who often fashionably suffer from delusions of decolonization, Indian Literature in English (translation, under the breath) signified a derivative, inferior, secondhand, unaesthetic (coloured?) category which paled into pathetic insignificance when compared with the "original semantic unity" (Venuti, 1992) of the literature created by (dead?) white European males. John Docker wryly attributes this to the ruling anglocentric assumption, in the university teaching of English, consequent upon the total experience of colonialism and neocolonialism, that "standards" can be set only by the study of great English Tradition of "matured cultural history" (Docker, 1978). As a postcolonial nation, we might justifiably implicate the colonial discourse which fixed such self-deprecating blinkers on our literary eye-span that we turned purblind to the rich heterogeneity of indigenous literary-cultural tradition, but as for the relegation of translation to secondary and derivative activity, coming well behind other more valued forms of cultural practice, the centrality of original versus copy binary to the Western, Platonic-Christian metaphysics has to be held responsible. By shedding unsympathetic light on the Romantic-Mimetic assumptions embedded in this traditional approach to translation, Theo Hermans exposes its soft underbelly in unequivocal terms: "If the literary artist is viewed as a uniquely gifted creative genius endowed with profound insight and a mastery of his native language, the work he produces will naturally come to be regarded as exalted, untouchable, inimitable, hallowed" (Hermans, 1985: 7). It should not, then, surprise one that Western theoretical perspectives on translation are woefully fixated on the glorification of the original and the valorization of notions of transparency, equivalence and fluency as positive attributes of translation. In obsequious deference to such essentialist and simplistic theoretical conceptualization of translation, the activity of translation in East as much as in West, despite its exponential proliferation, continues to be invisible, and on that account, undervalued.

## WRITING AS REWRITING

In the middle of such stultifying and suffocating academic-literary climate, more so for the readers than the translators, poststructuralist discourse flowed in like a current of fresh air. Radical and avant-garde perspectives like deconstruction and intertextuality have remarkably problematized the very conceptions of originality and superiority, both of writer and his work, by foregrounding notions of textual openness, heterogeneity and intrinsically derivative nature of all texts, irrespective of the original or the translation. Forwarding a counter-argument to the corpus approach, the non-essentialist approach to translation disclaims the idea of literature as a self-governing, autonomous category and views it as functioning in a more expansive socio-cultural frame, as influencing and being influenced by multifarious socio-politico-economic "signifying practices" maneuvering within that framework. Semiotician Julia Kristeva looks upon any signifying system as already consisting of other modes of cultural signification (Kristeva, 1988). Thus, the formulation that a text is a locus of not only other literary texts but also other modes of signification like myths, fashion, indigenous medicinal systems, food, metaphysical structures, literary genres and devices and other symbolic structures contends that all writing is derivative and thus a form of rewriting.

The discipline of Translation Studies experienced a much-needed paradigm shift around mid-1970s in the seminal theoretical formulations of André Lefevere, Gideon Toury, Theo Hermans and Itamar Even-Zohar. Polysystems theorists, as they were called, viewed literature as a complex and dynamic system and further advocated an approach to literary translation which is descriptive, target-oriented, functional and systematic. They drew the problematic of translation away from the obsessive idea of finding equivalents to a systematic concern with the critical examination of "the norms and constraints that govern the production and reception of translations...in the place and role of translations both within a given literature and in the interaction between literatures" (Hermans, 1985: 10–11). They were interested more in describing the status, function and reception of a translated text in the target culture as well as the power of culture on the decisions that a translator makes than in explicating the process of translation. In a radical formulation, André Lefevere posits that the quest for *the* meaning of/in a text is overambitious at best and futile at worst because meaning(s) is (are) derived under a set of strict controls and definite regulations which, more often than not, seek to adapt a work of art to a specific ideology or to a certain poetics or to both. He extends this problematization of the process of arriving at meaning in a literary work to all those activities which are directly or indirectly involved in generating or imparting meanings like criticism, translation, anthologization, literary historiography, etc. and covers them under an umbrella term "refractions". Refractions, to Lefevere, "are made to influence the way in which readers read a text. As such they are a powerful instrument in ensuring the 'right' reading of works of literature and in perpetuating 'right readings'" (Lefevere, 1984: 89). In other words, refractions rewrite a text to validate, valorize or redefine the value structures of a canon.

These important discursive notions of essential referentiality of literary texts or "interliterariness" and the political motivations behind even random acts of refractions provide interlocking grounds for the investigation of the translation of a marginalized text from a non-canonical, erstwhile colonized language like Gujarati into a globally hegemonic language like English. The qualification "marginalized" here primarily designates a text grounded in marginalized subculture as distinct from mainstream culture, though in the case of Nazir Mansuri whose short fiction will be discussed in this essay, the epithet refers to the non-canonical and thwarted status of the writer and his work as well. My primary contention is that the back-of-beyond and extremely indigenous culture as well as subtly unfamiliar poetics that these texts intertextually and metonymically evoke make them fall out of favour with publishers and even editors who are too scared to transgress the line of Western literary canon even at the risk of self-gagging their subalternity.

## POETICS OF NAZIR MANSURI'S FICTION

Nazir Mansuri's short fiction, though rewarded by Katha Foundation (1997) and Sanskruti Pratisthan (1999), has remained at the threshold of mega-publishing houses whose not-so-manifest credo is to print for Anglo-American readership. The translations of his work have been rejected by a variety of refractors on the grounds of their unreadability and stiffness caused specifically by his rigid insistence on protecting and preserving the quintessential cultural superstructure underpinning his work even in translation.

Nazir's work stands as a seminal milestone in the hoary tradition of Gujarati literature because it brings to light the typical dialect, myths, life-styles and socio-political dimensions of a hitherto-neglected, vibrant sub-culture. Laid against a typical rustic locale, around straggly villages on the sea shore of Diu, India, *Dhal Kachbo* (2002), Nazir's first collection of short stories which can be roughly translated as "*Shielded*

*Tortoise"*, gives an unprecedented insight into the primitivistic and dark life lived by fishermen community in Gujarat. Away from the hustle-bustle of dehumanized urban life, Nazir's plots unfold in back-of-beyond, seaside, gigantic ranches where elements of nature, both meek and ferocious, coexist and fight for survival. Eerie ranches sprawling in hundreds of acres, chock-a-block with palms and indigenous fruit-trees become a theatre of ceaseless struggle for survival amidst cocks and hens, ferocious wolves, birds of prey like sea hawks and kites, tom-cats, human beings and "the nature red in tooth and claw".

The book has unearthed a brave new world before Gujarati readership; a densely-packed primal world where strapping fishermen go out fishing and engage in bloody feud either with gargantuan sharks and whales or with whirling sea itself; where voluptuous fertile women and serfs slave untiringly in ranches, gorge away a lot of food, down vast quantities of liquor and indulge boisterously in carnal desires. Largely untouched by the winds of alleged development, this neolithic world seems to celebrate primal instincts over sophistication, id over superego, and primordiality over civilization. Simultaneously, this world throbs with black magic, talismans, magical threads, sorcerers, witches, ghosts, possessed women, witch-doctors and above all an unpredictable sinister fate. This society has its exclusive cultural superstructure underpinned by largely uninstitutionalized systems of worship, rituals, medicine, lifestyle, beliefs, and behaviour; it projects standards of love, sex, marriage and family constitution that are far too liberal and progressive as compared to those of the ossified, 'civilized' society. For example, in respect of the binary of love and sex, this primitive society privileges the sentiment love over sex which is manifested in the social approval of the kind of relationships which are rejected as unholy, incestuous and abnormal by civilized Indian society. Nazir's characters celebrate quintessential love that transcends the constraints of caste, creed and pseudo-propriety. This world of the subaltern might fly in the face of logic, rationality and prudery, but it is transparent, pure, passionate and miles (and eons) away from dirty, political hypocrisy of the respectable.

## PROBLEMATICS OF TRANSLATING A MARGINALIZED TEXT

Fundamentally, the problem with translation and reception of a literary text stems from issues related to the interpretation of material and social culture (including law, economics, and so forth), history, values, and world view; serious problems with the transference of literary features such as genre, characters, plotting, symbols and literary allusions; as well as the inevitable questions of linguistic interface (Tymoczko, 1995). In general, translators have to grapple with the metonymic aspects of a literary text which unfold in terms of content, generic features, intertextuality and culture at large. These metonymies collectively constitute a literary system in which a text like that of Nazir's is ensconced. If the source and target language systems are related to each other, as for example English and French, the target readership and literary canon will have little problem in comprehending the source text's metonymies in the translation and accommodating the translation into its literary hall of fame respectively.

Thus, a text like Nazir's in English translation becomes opaque to non-native readership because the unusual abundance of cultural-specific signifiers makes the information load of his stories too heavy to execute even a fairly smooth reading, let alone comprehending the intricate web of motifs and symbols running through the narrative. To make the matters even worse for the future of a marginalized text in translation, there is substantial evidence in cognitive science for the human tendency to adapt and assimilate new information to the informatory patterns always-already available in brain (Mitter, 1987). In the face of such self-reflexive doubts about the effective accomplishment of the mission that inspires the taxing activity of translating marginalized text, the now-proverbial task of the translator is flung into a serious, tearing limbo. In such a situation, a translator makes a conscious decision as to choosing the definite norms that would govern his translation strategy. Depending upon the selection of strategic norms, in Gideon Toury's (1980) words, a translator ends up making either an "adequate translation", i.e. one that transmigrates the metonymies of original text as much as possible, or an "acceptable translation" i.e. one that either readily compromises/erases the metonymic specificities of the original in the interest of readability and comprehension or radically supplants them with the metonymies of target culture and literary system to ensure that the translation becomes popular and widely accepted in target readership and literary canon. Needless to say, adequate translations come with a package deal of introductions, glossaries, footnotes, appendices, commentaries and other paratextual devices which serve to decode the metonymies of source text to a considerable extent. It is understandable that not all the information serving metonymic functions in a text from a foreign literary system can be realized in translation. Thus, for effective management of information load, a translator has to be extremely selective in his choice of the aspects of the source text, i.e. linguistic, generic, cultural, historical or ideological that he wishes to valorize or downplay in the target text with a vengeance.

Now, the strategy of selection and omission that a translator of a marginalized text chalks out is largely governed by, what Lefevere calls, a "control factor" which operates from within and outside the literary system of the target language. The dominant poetics of target literary system constitutes the inside factor which "can be said to consist of two components: one is an inventory of literary devices, genres, motifs, prototypical characters and situations, symbols; the other a concept of what the role of literature is, or should be, in the society at large" (Lefevere, 1987: 25). As stringent as the inside regulatory mechanism is the outside control factor of patronage represented by royal court, political/religious institutions and last but not the least the publishers with or without monopoly over the book/magazine publishing trade. These apparently innocuous factors exert enormous political influence over the refractors to undertake refractions in such a manner that they fit perfectly into poetological and ideological frames of the receptor language and society respectively.

## POLITICS OF BOOK PUBLISHING IN THE THIRD WORLD: THE CASE OF NAZIR MANSURI

The insidious power of these inner-outer control factors upon the strategy of translation adopted by a translator is nowhere felt so perceptibly and significantly as in the Third World. Philip Altbach (1975) contextualizes the problematic surrounding the publication of Third World Literature by examining the uneven relationship between Third World nations and industrialized countries who dominate the international intellectual system through their control of the means of knowledge production. He draws on the bleak socio-economics of book publishing in developing countries to aver that issues of economic viability, required technology, low literacy rates, low per capita purchasing power, distribution bottlenecks and market size make it incumbent upon the Third World nations to depend hopelessly upon the developed nations for knowledge production and consumption.

This dependency for cultural production is aggravated by political and trade relationships that the two worlds share. First World export streamlined technology, publication grant, subsidized books and most importantly branches of giant multinational publishing houses to the developing countries. Altbach says, "Commercial arrangements built up over years of colonialism persist in many developing countries. Branches of British and French publishers continue to operate in Third World… The advantages of foreign firms – expertise, the backing of foreign capital and a worldwide distribution network – have made the emergence of indigenous publishers even more difficult…" (Quoted from Ashcroft, 1995: 410). Such a complex web of economic and intellectual relationships and traditions reaffirms and deepens the pattern of uneven, imperial relationship existing between the colonized and the colonizer.

Though much of what Altbach says holds true even today, in the period of more than three decades following Altbach's analysis, things have changed substantially, if not radically. With globalization, India has accomplished considerable feats in the domains of infrastructure, literacy rates, technology and even market size. The *Cambridge Encyclopedia of the English Language* confirms that 5 per cent of the total Indian population speaks fluent English. However, in spite of these improved material conditions, the production of books reflecting the needs and concerns of the indigenous authors and readership has not automatically come about primarily because the unaltered and reactionary psychological conditions. Not only do the subsidiaries of British and French publishers dictate terms about who and how to publish/translate, a whole new breed of metropolitan, neocolonial centers of power pose a considerable psychological barrier to valorization of native cultures and literary tradition through translation. In the post-global marketplace, publishing budgets of even the neoliberal native publishers are governed by authors, famous and canonical, by Western standards, as well as by the power of the absent "center". This center is largely constituted by "university hierarchy (the god-professor); by the system of recruitment of staff (appointing people, English, American or Australian, whose primary teaching interests are expected to lie in English literature); and by the use of tenure to enforce anglocentric stability and continuity" (Docker, quoted from Ashcroft, 1995: 444). Docker's definition of the literary "transcendental signified" acutely overlaps with Lefevere's identification of the control mechanism within the literary system represented by critics, reviewers, teachers of literature, translators and other rewriters who adapt literary texts to the poetics and the ideology of their time. It is unfortunate that irrespective of space and time Lefevere's expansive category of refractors shrinks quite often into a singular undifferentiated university hierarchy which undertakes criticism, anthologization and translation of literature apart from teaching it. This putative center of Third World queerly subscribes to the post-World War II, anti-ideological Western view that great (Anglo-American) literature delineates universal human feelings and dilemmas, while the inferior literatures of the colonized cultures are morbidly strident and "too simply concerned with the local and temporary, the political and national..." (444). Third World subscribers to such a metropolitan view of literature owes obsequious allegiance to dynamic Western critical tools and apply them to literatures produced in postcolonial societies in order to otherize them. Thus, at a time when the post-colonial literatures were dexterously examining history, national, ethnic and communitarian identities, various ideologies and traditions, the West beat an alarmed retreat in the form of Fredric Jameson's theory of national allegory. Jameson's theory is grounded in the hypothesis that capitalistic cultural production is determined by a radical split between the private and the public realms and that the delineation of private realm of lived experience is always culturally superior to the political dynamics of the Third World. He says, "Even those which are seemingly private and invested with a properly libidinal dynamic – necessarily project a political dimension in the form of national allegory" (Jameson, 1986: 65). Jameson's theory is parochial at best and colonial at worst because most of the First World critics, like Jameson himself, base their aesthetic pronouncements on works mediated by establishments linked to the First World, often handpicked for their allegorical, political content, for these works are not marketed as fictions, but as fictions of India, Africa, Brazil and the like (Palakeel, 1996). In reality, much of the Third World literature that transmigrates into First World languages is selected just for its political, ethnographic and anthropological character rather than for any intrinsic literary merit. Thus what has remained static in the shifting dynamics of colonial and postcolonial relations between the East and the West is the idea of "western fantasies" of Third World literature. While the Orientalist translators necessarily exoticized it, the postcolonial First World academia allegorized it and the motivation behind both these exercises remains proverbially political. Naturally, the post-Holocaust "cultural cringe" of Western literary academia that penetrated the critical values of neocolonial power-centers serves as a stick to beat translator's mode of refraction into conformity or catastrophe.

## BLIND MAN'S BUFF: THE QUEST FOR IDENTITY

The image of a talented, blindfolded postcolonial writer hunting desperately for a publisher, apart from its huge comic value, is particularly catchy because the writer gropes to catch hold of someone in a place where there is nobody at all and the fault lies with none but the writer who is scared stiff of opening his eyes. Concomitantly, untying the blindfold enables the writer-translator to realize and assert the quintessential identity of the culture he foregrounds through the text. The reason behind the rejection of the translations of a Third World marginalized text, like that of Nazir, by publishers and academia is twofold in nature. First, Nazir doesn't feed, even remotely, the allegorical fantasies of the Anglo-American academia-literati. In fact, the primitive society and bizarre subculture that unfold in Nazir's work are unlikely to find analogues in surrounding communities and locality of Gujarat, let alone their national counterparts. Paradoxically, as the writer scratches beneath the primitive skin of his characters, the reader confronts a masterful delineation of concerns and topos which are typically modernist and even post-modernist in essence. The theme of love and its corollaries like sex, loneliness, anxiety, pining and death become a vital connecting link between "the vulture" and "the culture" in Nazir's stories. Almost all the stories in *Dhal Kachho* are built around the human hunger for intense love and the overwhelming need for emotional anchor in life, the absence of which results in searing pangs of alienation, emptiness and inner void. Issues, which are considered social and literary taboos in Gujarat and India, like roots of sexuality, measure of development and alternation of sexual orientation, homosexual, lesbian and allegedly incestuous relations, intercaste and crosscreed associations, etc. receive a candid, psychoanalytical articulation in Nazir's stories. What makes Nazir's exploration remarkable is the fact that sex and sexuality are undergirded by the singular sentiment of love; love is the only precondition of sex; it doesn't need to achieve approval certificates from institutions of marriage, caste, religion and respectability. Moreover, Nazir's work exceptionally examines the existentialism of sexuality, i.e. it proffers moving narratives of the feelings of angst, anguish, exuberance, aspirations, trepidations and frustrations as experienced by people pitted against love, death and erratic fate. Nazir seems to reject the theory that existential angst, loneliness and emptiness are exclusively urban or metropolitan concerns; people located on the opposite extreme experience them with greater intensity and force in all probability. Thus Jameson's theoretical musings encounter a perfect foil in Nazir's work.

Secondly, Nazir's adamantcy about preserving the essentially (sub)cultural texture of his work and rooted metonymies even in translation flies sharply in the face of the post-war "cultural cringe" of the West. No doubt, in the absence of metatranslation, Nazir's world would surely tickle the exotic fantasies of the Western readership, but that's not usually the way a committed artist would have his work transmitted. Being exceptionally meticulous about the craft and aesthetics of the genre of short fiction, Nazir gives immense importance to literary-stylistic aspects like imagery, symbolism, paragraph sequences and the overall structure of his stories. As a part of his multi-pronged narrative technique, he often gives vivid and, at times longish, descriptions of the natural surroundings which, far from being aesthetic for its scenic elegance, evokes a distinct sense of the uncanny and the sinister throughout the story. The mystery, thus enlivened in atmosphere, becomes instrumental in reflecting the mystery surrounding the fate, intentions, motivations and emotions of his characters. Though mythopoetic in nature, his stories are extremely realistic in their descriptive style with layers and layers of mythical, historical, and existential meanings. Rich and significant employment of dialect and noteworthy use of myths and archetypes, a complex semantic network of symbols and motifs and dense, lively descriptions, novel lexis and syntax emanating from this strange subculture weave together an intricate network of meanings and significations which often sound alien and bizarre even to mainstream Gujarati literati, let alone Anglo-American readership.

## AGENCY OF A TRANSLATOR

The processes of patronage and control by which colonial and neo-colonial powerbases continue to intervene in selecting, licensing, publishing and distributing the text of the post-colonial world and the degree to which the inscriptive practices, choice of form, subject matter, genre, etc., is also subject to such control have received far less attention that they deserve (Ashcorft, Griffiths, et al., 1995). The agency of the translator of a marginalized text is seriously undermined by these sociological, psychological and political dimensions of post-colonial textual studies. The capitalistic, consumerist factors, both local and global, compel the translator to toe the baseline expectations of the target readership by homogenizing the poetological, ideological and cultural differences that the source text so prominently manifests. Impelled by vested mercenary interests or otherwise, the absent center plays the colonizers' first cousin using translation as a significant technology for homogenization, subordination, otherization and oblique domination. In her seminal book *Siting Translation* (1995), Tejaswini Niranjana draws on Benjamin, Derrida, and de Man to identify the contexts of representation and power in intercultural transfer. She upholds, "In a post-colonial context the problematic of *translation* becomes a significant site for raising questions of representation, power, and historicity. The context is one of contesting and contested stories attempting to account for, to recount, the asymmetry and inequality of relations between peoples, races, languages" (1). Niranjana's claim that the postcolonial theory and translation can "reinvent oppositional cultures in nonessentializing ways" (46) is compatible with the poststructuralist call for the celebration of heterogeneity. Thus, the postcolonial translator should conscientiously tune his/her translatorial efforts to paradigmatic rather than syntagmatic level so that political tendencies of homogenizing and continuity can be resisted and a discursive space for the assertion of socio-cultural identities can be constructed. Critical of the communicative model of translation, Niranjana emphasizes that just as one can't aspire for accuracy in translation, a complete denial of historicity and referentiality is impossible. The challenge of post-colonial translation lies not so much in doing a balancing act between the heavy demands made by the source and the target cultures as in promoting the political model over poetical or epistemological one. Unlike the literary-cultural transaction through languages between two European countries like France and England, the nature of transaction between an Indian regional language like Gujarati and the last yet unbelievably powerful vestige of colonial past, i.e. English is inarguably underwritten by politics and subtext of power. The political agenda of postcolonial translation is to articulate a discourse wherein differences are not only rewritten and recognized but valorized.

## CONCLUSION

Thus, a postcolonial translator negotiating a marginalized text such as that of Nazir Mansuri has to be alert to the fact that witting or unwitting subscription to aesthetic or consumerist assumptions as to the production/control of the meaning of a marginalized/subculture literary text not only seriously undermines the socio-cultural identity and values of a given community being depicted in it but also becomes instrumental in erasing the already endangered heterogeneity of literary traditions that are indispensable for the survival of human civilization.

## WORKS CITED

Altbach, Philip G. "Literary Colonialism: Books in the Third World." *Harvard Educational Review* 15. 2 (May, 1975):226–236.

Ashcroft, Bill, Gareth Griffiths and Helen Tiffin, eds. *The Post-colonial Studies Reader*. London and New York: Routledge, 1995.

Docker, John. "The Neocolonial Assumption in University Teaching of English." *South Pacific Images*. Ed. Chris Tiffin. St. Lucia, Queensland: SPACLALS, 1978:26–31.

Hermans, Theo, "Translation Studies and a New Paradigm." *The Manipulation of Literature: Studies in Literary Translation*. New York: St. Martin's Press, 1985. 7–15.

Jameson, Fredric. "Third-World Literature in the Era of Multinational Capitalism." *Social Text* 15 (1986):65–88.

Kristeva, Julia. "The Revolution in Poetic Language." *The Theory of Criticism: From Plato to the Present*. Ed. Raman Selden. Harlow: Longman, 1988. 417–418.

Lefevere, André. "'Beyond Interpretation' or the Business of (Re)writing." *Comparative Literature Studies* 24.1 (1987):17–39.

———. "That Structure in the Dialect of Men Interpreted." *Comparative Criticism* 6 (1984):87–100.

Mansuri, Nazir. *Dhal Kachbo.* Ahmedabad: R R Sheth Prakashan, 2002.

Mitter, Partha. "Can We Ever Understand Alien Cultures?" *Comparative Criticism* 9 (1987):3–34.

Niranjana, Tejaswini. *Siting Translation History, Post-Structuralism, and the Colonial Context.* Hyderabad: Orient Longman, 1995.

Palakeel, Thomas. "Third World Short Story as National Allegory." *Journal of Modern Literature* XX.I (1996):97–102.

Toury, Gideon. *In Search of a Theory of Translation.* Tel Aviv: Porter Institute for Poetics and Semiotics, 1980.

Tymoczko, Maria. "The Metonymics of Translating Marginalized Texts." *Comparative Literature* 47.1 (1995):11–24.

Venuti, Lawrence. *Rethinking Translation – Discourse, Subjectivity, Ideology.* London and New York: Routledge, 1992.

# 9

# Translating Culture and 'Cultural Translation' in Jayant Khatri's Gujarati Short Stories

*Manoj Chhaya*

"*We are a world evolving in translation*".

G.J.V. Prasad, 2005

## TRANSLATION, CULTURE, LANGUAGE

In an anonymous quote, languages are compared to a patient suffering from haemophilia, in need of constant transfusion for survival. In the wake of globalization and multiculturalism, it is hard to think of a language wholly independent of influences from other languages. The overpowering presence of English in addition to plurality of voices, languages and cultures, as it has often been remarked, problematizes the translation in/from/among Indian languages. Although, as Kothari (2006: 1) notes, the word "translation" has leaped out of the conventional boundaries of its meaning (cf. Trivedi 2005), the act of translating remains to be an exercise practical and empirical in nature, and hence the discipline of Translation Studies is increasingly using "thinking aloud protocols" in the last two decades. Translating creative texts reveals diverse aspects of equivalence between/among languages and thus throws light on their relationships too. Dorothy Kenny interestingly suggests that "a careful study of collocational patterns in translated text can shed light on cultural forces at play in the literary market place and vice versa" (1998: 519).

## TRANSLATION AND GUJARATI LITERATURE

With the acceptance of English as one of Indian languages, it is an interesting area to examine the influence of English on Indian languages and, more importantly, of Indian languages on English. Translated literature forms a chunk in almost all Indian languages. "Regional" literatures (or as G.N. Devy calls them – Bhasa literatures) share a two-fold relationship with the source language of translation. Translated literature is already a part of the source culture and language. After translation, it also members itself in the target literary body. Translations into Gujarati are a case in point. The body of literature translated into Gujarati is vast and it is possible to find Molière, Flaubert and Tolstoy to Frost and Eliot. Popular bestsellers like Dale Carnegie, Richard Bach and J.K. Rowling are available too. Close at home, translations ranging from Tagore to Abdul Kalam are available in Gujarati. On the other hand translations *from* Gujarati are comparatively few. As Kothari (2006: 73) reminds us, the best-known literary creation in Gujarati, *Saraswatichandra* too is unavailable so far in English translation. Similarly, in a publication like *Indian Literature*, the number of short fiction translated from Gujarati is disappointing compared to those from other Indian languages. Of late, however, the scene is under a change. The unequal relationship makes one take up the question of choosing a text for translation. While in some cases it may be a political or commissioned choice, liberal choice is governed by a high degree of respect for the source text. Kothari (2006: 74) surmises "...whenever a language or culture has been perceived as being rich and dominant, and a repository of ideas, aesthetics and poetics, there has been a rush to translate from it into other 'receptor' languages and cultures."

Lack of translations from Gujarati has often created misunderstandings about Gujarati literature, as also has led to its underestimation. If lack of translation is the only reason, it is desirable that salient works are examined in translation. Theoretical frameworks in Translation Studies cannot be applied to a literary body without substantial examples. Ramakrishnan (2006) maintains:

> The political boundaries of linguistic states in India do not coincide with their cultural boundaries due to the complex history of social and cultural formations in India. This has meant that the translational discourses of the Indian subcontinent have been rendered unintelligible in our institutional climate of debates and dialogues.

In order to evolve a poetics of translation for Gujarati, the present article tries to analyse selected short stories of Jayant Khatri, a twentieth century writer in Gujarati. The reasons for choosing Khatri are many.

## JAYANT KHATRI: CONTRIBUTIONS TO GUJARATI SHORT STORY

Jayant Khatri was a doctor by profession, born and brought up in Kachchh. He was exposed to the struggles and tragedies of the downtrodden since an early age. Owing to the medical profession of his father (and later his own), he knew the pains and miseries of human body. In 1923, when he went to Mumbai with his elder brother, he had an insider's view at the lives of the mill-labourers. His sympathy for the lower classes found an expression first in sketches and ink-paintings, marked by the same vividness of observation and mastery of expression that one finds in his stories. His life in Mumbai nourished his skills. It was in Mumbai that he read influential thinkers like Freud, Marx and Engels. Khatri did not write voluminously. In his life-span of fifty-nine years he wrote for almost twenty-five years. However, the output is only fifty-two short-stories, an unfinished novel, a one-act play (*Mangal Pandey*), and a monologue (*Hatya*). Although his lectures, articles, and letters are numerous, his literary fame is as a short-story writer. An obvious question that arises out of these details is about the reasons for his great fame despite limited output. When Khatri started writing, there were established names like "Dwiref" and Dhumketu in Gujarati short-story. Khatri accepted the heritage of these two writers and paved a way ahead, with his modernist tendency. He is now unanimously accepted as the pioneer of modernism in Gujarati short fiction and is often compared to Suresh Joshi and Chandrakant Bakshi. Khatri focused more on the form of the stories rather than on their content. Although he wrote intuitively, his writings show remarkable consciousness about the process of writing.

Khatri's writing cannot strictly be located between definite dates. But his creative period is generally estimated from 1940 to 1967.

There are three published collections of his short stories: *Foran* ("Droplets", 1944), *Vehtaan Zarnaan* ("Flowing Streams", 1952) and *Kharaa Bapor* ("High Noon", 1968). These collections contain forty-one stories. Out of the total of his fifty-two stories, the rest are unpublished. Khatri's writings show double sensibility. His stories like *Ame Buddhimaano* ("We Intellectuals"), *Yaad ane Hun* ("Reminiscence and I"), *Anandnu Maut* ("Ecstasy and Agony"), *Avaaj Ajvaalan* ("Sound, Light"), *Ardho Divas* ("Half Day"), *Cybil,* and *Dead End* are built upon his urban experience. On the other hand, *Kalo Maalam* ("Black Malam") and *Gangi ane Ame Badhaan* ("Gangi and We All") are woven around the people who are deeply attached to sea. *Khichdi, Nathuni Aswasthtaa* ("The Discomfort of Nathu"), *Mohammad,* and *Krishnajanm* ("The Birth of Krishna") focus on the downtrodden characters in rural Kachchh and Gujarat. Being an affirmed communist, Khatri had always identified himself with the wretched.

Khatri is known for his directness, vivid imagery, sharp description, and mastery in using symbolism. Kachchh was very dear to Khatri but he does not blindly magnify it. The stories like *Khara Bapor*, *Dhaad* ("The Outlaw") and *Maatino Ghado* ("The Mud-Pot") closely describe the life of this land. The cognitive theory of metaphor can best be illustrated in Khatri's stories. Khatri also tried to wrap the general theory of relativity in one of his stories *Tej, Gati ane Dhvani* ("Light, Speed, Sound"). With an increasing consciousness about the trends of modern and postmodern writings among Gujarati critics and authors, Khatri is now unanimously considered to be an experimental and innovative master who added a new dimension to Gujarati short stories.

## KHATRI AS POSTCOLONIAL CULTURAL TRANSLATOR

Khatri is often identified with Kachchh, native for him and setting for many of his stories. However, he chose Gujarati over Kachchhi as the medium of his writing. The apparent reason for his choice might be his maverick attitude and his wide exposure in Mumbai, but one cannot fail to consider a possibility of Khatri "translating" – knowingly or unknowingly – Kachchhi culture in Gujarati. Kachchhi and Gujarati share a dialectical relationship as languages. Kachchh for years has been a region that either could not or did not assimilate with the "mainstream" Gujarati culture. Given the differences of geography, culture and lifestyle, the isolation could be justified to some extent. These facts lead one to believe that Khatri could not have served the purpose of narrating Kachchh had he not used Gujarati. Thus Khatri becomes a case in point for the "cultural translation" noted by Trivedi (2005), quoting the cases of Rushdie, Lahiri and Kureshi. This "new" sense of translation can be traced in Khatri almost half a century ago in a different context. However, the sense of "loss" felt in the postcolonial "cultural translators" is remarkably absent in Khatri's writings. Translating Khatri in English, then, becomes a second translation. The postcolonial view on "cultural translation" finds relevance in the act of translating Khatri into English too. The English translation, as Ketkar (2006) observes with reference to his translation from Marathi, saves the translator from the binary opposition of identities (Khatri too escaped the binary identities by writing in Gujarati and proclaiming his roots in Kachchh.) Ramakrishnan (2006) aptly comments on the relationship between translation and identities: "Translations...are deeply implicated in the history of social and political formations as well as in narratives of identity."

However, Khatri offers a rich narrative and linguistic experience to those lamenting the turn towards "cultural translation". Analysis of any translated text depends largely on the linguistic aspects of the text because the process of interlanguage translation is essentially a linguistic act. Any language, in turn, is rooted in the culture where it is spoken and expresses cultural attributes and properties. The dichotomy of language-culture relationship is not easy to solve. The dichotomy problematizes the process of translation, as the question that arises while translating a text is if the text should change according to the receptor context or it should retain its identity as a member of SL. The dichotomy and lack of exact equivalence cannot of course stand in defence of untranslatability because the translator has the responsibility of finding a solution to the most daunting of problems.

Examining Khatri's writings in translation lead us to certain general issues specific to Gujarati – English translation. Nida (1975) identified several categories responsible for the changes taking place in translation: (1) word classes (2) grammatical categories (3) arrangement of words (4) hierarchy of semantic constituents (5) areas of meaning and amount of information (6) endocentric and exocentric structures and (7) relationship of linguistic form to semantic functions. These categories can broadly be accommodated under three heads: lexis, grammar and cultural associations. Lexical equivalence is basic to any translation. In case of absence of equivalent terms in the target language, one has to think of ways to fulfil the function of equivalence. While translating Khatri, the problems are not so much with "word classes" but certain groups of words need special attention for two reasons: either they do not have the exact equivalent in English or the equivalent does not convey the meaning of the original. Such "non-transferable" words are actually rooted in the source culture, and as a referent they refer to an object which may either be "alien" to the target culture, or may not have the same function in the TL system as that of the source object. Thus while there is a deferral of meaning in translation on the one hand, there is astounding equivalence too on the other, as Jakobson (1959) pointed out.

Kristeva's well-known conception of a text as a composition of diverse modes of cultural signification (like myths, fashion, indigenous medicinal system, musical system, festivals, food, metaphysical structure, rituals and religious practices, superstitions in addition to common textual structures) justifies the challenge posed while translating Khatri. Gujarati kinship terms like *bapaa, maasiba, bha, derani-jethani* carry with them a specific sense of distinct relationship. When translated, they might lose the sense and affect the unity of the translated text. In Khatri's *Khichdi*, protagonist Lakhdi calls her father *bapaa*, which has an endearing sense and rustic colour. A challenge for the translator is to reconstruct this sense and colour in translation. Lakhdi's father calls her "Lakhi" while all other characters and the narrator call her Lakhdi. It seems that the character is originally named Lakshmi. The special address by her father hints at the entwined relationship the father and the daughter share. Unless clarified, such changes in addressing terms might create misunderstanding for an English reader. The word *maasibaa* in *Yaad... ane Hun* simply means "aunt" in English. But the English word is used for many relations while the Gujarati term is restricted to address a sister of the mother. The suffix *–baa* makes the term an honorific form of address, which is not possible in English translation. Moreover, in Indian cultures, a maternal aunt is supposed to be closer to children. (In some of the practices, she even substitutes mother). Thus the relationship between the narrator and his aunt gets clear only with some explanation. *Vaansli* ("The Flute") has several incidents where many characters address the same person according to their own relationship with him. In such addresses, the name of the character remains the same but the relationship suffixes change. When Peeru goes to meet his friend Godhu, he is addressed by the members of Godhu's family in a variety of ways (Peeru*kaka*, Peeru*bhai*, Peeru *fakir* and so on). These forms become the equivalents of the name and need alternative ways to convey the distinct sense of address. (Sarla Jagmohan (1982) has translated *Vinodkaka* as "Uncle Vinod") In *Kalo Maalam*, Osu addresses his elder brother, an expert sailor, as *bhaa*. The term is typical to Kachchhi culture and means not only "brother" but is a general honorific term. In other cases words like *Saheb* and *Sheth* connote the socio-cultural hegemonic relationship that is instrumental in the sexual exploitation of Lakhdi (*Khichdi)* and Ranal (*Maatino Ghado)*.

Mangrove trees are a part of the Kachchhi locality. The trees are locally known as *cher*. In *Dhaad*, Ghela addresses mangrove trees as *cheriyaan*. This diminutive form of address shows the affinity and affection the character feels with the surroundings. Ghela's pet words for the trees show his identification with nature. In the colloquial way of addressing names like Ghela and Bhima get changed to Ghelo and Bhimo. Thus the same name ends with different endings. It is better in translation to unify the name throughout a text. In some instances, Bhima is colloquially called *Bhimo Oont,* literally meaning 'Bhima, the camel'. While translating I have resorted to periphrasis.

Khatri's stories reveal interesting issues at the level of grammatical categories too. As an experimental writer and a modernist, Khatri dexterously used dislocation of syntax to project the mental states of his characters. Two of the stories – *Khichdi* and *Yaad...ane Hun* – are particularly important from the point of view of translating tense and time. *Khichdi* typically uses routine past different from the accepted forms of past tense in English. It is while translating that one realizes the distinction in the usage of tense and time. It seems that Khatri is using a common oral story-telling technique. *Khichdi* uses two types of past tense. In the initial part of the story, the writer describes the routine activities and a long stretch of life in a rut in routine past. In oral story-telling, this would not seem unnatural. After the middle of the story Khatri describes the story in simple past, perhaps to announce the turning point when Lakhdi fails to earn her daily wages. In English translation one can either use "used to" construction or can turn the construction with "would". Interestingly, equivalence is not a mechanical concept and spreads across categories. The sense of routine past in the initial sentences is conveyed with the combination of the simple past verb form with adverbs like "every day". This can be an example of what Catford (1965) called "Level Shifts" (where the meaning conveyed by grammar in SL is conveyed by lexis in TL).

The case of *Yaad...ane Hun* uses present tense to describe even the past experiences of the narrator. The story uses almost a stream-of-consciousness structure for narration. The narrator comes back to his hometown after seven years. Riding on the stride of memories and observing the gap of seven years, he remembers a chain of events. To give a probe into the narrator's mind, Khatri uses long descriptions in present tense. In Gujarati, the present tense does not have strict variations as it has in English. The spoken variety of Gujarati does not distinguish strongly between simple present tense and present continuous tense. Therefore, it is for the translator to judiciously choose the apt variety of tense. Khatri also uses constructions to suggest "immediacy" or a sudden occurrence with help of an auxiliary verb – *padvu*. Such constructions carry the immediacy of unconscious and instinctive actions that call for periphrasis by using adjectives and adverbs in translation.

The cultural nuances in *Khichdi, Maatino Ghado* and *Yaad... ane Hun* demand cultural familiarization on the part of translators and readers. The title *Maatino Ghado* draws from the traditional Indian analogy comparing a maiden girl with a fragile earthen pot. In the same story Ranal's denial to go with her parents is meaningful only in the light of the customary sense of dedication a girl develops after marriage. The narrator's comment associating Ranal's sexual encounter with "a little water" would be a forced justification if one fails to understand some subtle signs suggesting scarcity of water in the setting of the story. Lakhdi's occupation in *Khichdi* is fetching and delivering water in households. The occupation may not be easy to visualize unless one understands the setting of the stories - the rural Gujarat 40 years ago when there were no water-taps. "Lakhdi" seems the colloquial form of the name Lakshmi. Culturally, the name signifies wealth but Khatri perhaps chose the name ironically to build up a contrast between Lakhdi's "rich" name and the wretched life she leads. In *Yaad...ane Hun* Gulab is introduced as "a singer and a prostitute". While an Indian reader reading in English would easily understand the tradition of "singer-prostitutes" who were accomplished artists and dancers, for a foreign reader the description calls for additional details. The challenge for a translator is to translate apparently inexplicable things without making them explicable in familiar terms and at the same time without alienating them.

## CONCLUSION

As short story is a European form domesticated in Gujarati, translating Khatri's short stories is in some ways a "reverse-translation" in terms of the form. Translating Khatri's short stories thus gives an opportunity to examine the transformation of the form too. The maze of lexical, grammatical and cultural issues taken as examples in the foregoing text reminds us of Benjamin's comment declaring any attempt to establish one-to-one relationship between translation and the original futile. He takes up an analogy of cognitive process to illustrate this point:

> To grasp the genuine relationship between an original and a translation requires an investigation analogous to the argumentation by which a critique of cognition would have to prove the impossibility of an image theory. There it is a matter of showing that in cognition there could be no objectivity, not even a claim to it, if it dealt with images of reality; here it can be demonstrated that no translation would be possible if in its ultimate essence it strove for likeness to the original. (Benjamin, 1999: 73)

Translating Khatri makes one realize that translation of creative texts bear a distinct identity and tend to turn hybrid.

## WORKS CITED

Benjamin, Walter. "The Task of the Translator." *Illuminations.* Ed. Hannah Arendt. Trans. Harry Zohn. London: Pimlico, 1999. 70–82.

Catford, J.C. *A Linguistic Theory of Translation: An Essay in Applied Linguistics.* London: Oxford University Press, 1965.

Jagmohan, Sarla, ed. *Gujarati Short Stories,* New Delhi: Vikas Publishing House, 1982.

Jakobson, Roman. "On the Linguistic Aspects of Translation." *On Translation*. Ed. Reuben Brower. Cambridge and Massachusetts: Harvard University Press, 1959. 232–239.

Kenny, Dorothy. "Creatures of Habit? What Translators Usually Do with Words." *The Corpus Based Approach, Meta* 43.4 (1998). 515–23.

Ketkar, Sachin. "Translation of Bhakti Poetry into English: A Case Study of Narsinh Mehta." *Translation Today*. 3.1–2 (2006) <http://www.anukriti.net/tt5/jhome.asp>.

Khatri, Jayant. *The Outlaw and other Stories*. Trans. Uma Randeria and Rohini Patel. Gandhinagar: Gujarat Sahitya Academy, 2004.

Kothari, Rita. *Translating India*. New Delhi: Foundation Books, 2006.

Nida, Eugene A. *Language Structure and Translation*. California: Stanford University Press, 1975.

Prasad, G.J.V., Interview with Pratiksha Thanki, *Baroda Times*, 18$^{th}$ April, 2005.

Ramakrishnan, E.V. "Mapping Indian Traditions in Translation: Concepts, Categories and Contestations." *Translation Today*. 3.1–2 (2006) <http://www.anukriti.net/tt5/jhome.asp>.

Trivedi, Harish. "Translating Culture vs. Cultural Translation." *91$^{st}$ Meridian* (May 2005). <http://iwp.uiowa.edu/91st/vol4_n1/>.

# 10

# Problems of (Cultural) Translation: Translating Gujarati Poetry

*Asha Makhecha*

## TRANSLATION: HISTORICAL PERSPECTIVE

> "Translation is the wandering existence of a text in a perpetual exile."
>
> J.H. Miller

While Translation Studies is a recent development as a discipline, translation is as old as language and literature. The history of translation focuses on the theory of translation, or on the practice of translation, or on both theory and practice of translation. Focusing on the history of translation is both necessary and inevitable because of the continuous developments occurring within the discipline of Translation Studies. As a discipline emerging in 1970s, Translation Studies analyses needs, methods or strategies with regard to translation. The nature of language and sociolinguistic issues create a large variety of problems in translation. New conceptual means provided by scholars working from a variety of theoretical perspectives have made it possible to produce the history of translation. The history of theory of translation raises questions such as: (a) What do translators have to say about their art? (b) How do translators have been evaluated at different periods? (c) What kinds of recommendations have been made by translators? (d) How is the discourse of translation related to other discourses of the same period? On the other hand, the history of practice of translation deals with questions like: (a) What has been translated? (b) By whom has the text been translated? (c) Under what circumstances has the text been translated? (d) In what social or political context has the text been translated?

Translation scholars since ages have been investigating answers to these questions. As a result, adequate models have been formulated, highlighting specific genres in combination with spatial and temporal restrictions. The attempt is made here in this article to present a brief overview of poetry translation first in the Western tradition and then in the Indian tradition elaborately, and to raise the problems of translation of regional Indian poetry into English, specifically the cultural nuances richly embedded in Indian poetry. Through an illustration of sociocultural and linguistic issues involved in translation of postcolonial poetry into English, translation is broadly understood in the essay as a creative act or a creative process.

## Poetry Translation: The Western Tradition

Though there is enormous literature on theory, practice and history of translation in the Western tradition, George Steiner's *After Babel* which divides the history of translation into four periods would be helpful in grasping the history and problematics of translating poetry in the Western tradition. They are: (a) Primary Statement and Technical Innovation (46 BC – 1813): The first period extends from Cicero's famous percept not to translate *verbum pro verbo* (in *Libellus de optimo genere oratorum*, 46 BC) and Horace's reiteration of it (in *Ars Poetica*, 26 BC) to Hölderdin's commentary on his translations from Sophocles (1804). It ends with Alexander Frazer Tytler's *Essay on the Principles of Translation* (1792) and with Friedrich Schleiermacher's essay "The Different Methods of Translating" (1813). (b) Theory and Hermeneutic Inquiry (1813–1946): This second period extends from Friedrich Schleiermacher's essay to Valery Larbaud's *Sous l'invocation de Saint Jérome* (1946). (c) Automatic/Machine Translation (1940–1960): The third period extends from the invention of machine translation to a reversion to hermeneutic approach with the discovery of Walter Benjamin's paper "Die Aufgabe des Übersetzers"(1923) and with the influence of Heidegger and Gadamar. (d) Reversion to Metaphysics (1960 onwards): The fourth period extends from the reversion to metaphysical approach to the present time.

Translation is considered as an invention of the Romans who lacked creativity and therefore Roman translators like Cicero, Horace and Longinus translated Greek classics and commented on the art of translation. In his study of English versions of St. Birgitta's *Revelations*, Domenico Pezzini (2008) investigates devotional writing, a very specific genre that is produced at crossroads of literature and sacred writing in the Middle Ages. One of the most revolutionary events in the history of English style has been the authorized translation of the *Bible* by King James. The recovery of the original spirit of Christianity was thus sought by Protestant England through an act of translation. It is well known that Chaucer was translating the style of Boccaccio into English when he created his *Canterbury Tales*. Chaucer was acknowledged from the beginning as a translator of note.

Translation in the fifteenth century broke new ground due to a greater professionalism which characterized literary production in the fifteenth century and this growing professionalism paved the way for Caxton's printing press. Virgil's *Aeneid*, Book II and IV translated by Henry Howard, Earl of Surrey (1517–1547), the greatest of the pre-Elizabethan poetic translators along with Thomas Wyatt (1503–1542) offers a major literary source. Translation was regarded as a supreme art during the Renaissance. Apart from important Renaissance translators like Hornby, North Florio and Holland, George Chapman, in his "Epistle to the Readers" of translation of Homer's *Illiad*, observed that the translator should avoid word for word translation and try to recreate the tone and spirit of source language text in target language text, i.e. bring about transmigration.

Translation contributed greatly to the development of major literary forms in the seventeenth and eighteenth centuries. Sir John Denham, Abraham Cowley, John Dryden, Alexander Pope and Dr. Samuel Johnson were major translators of the period. Denham considered translation of "poesie into poesie" difficult as there are chances of loss of spirit in poetry, and therefore advised translators of poetry to recreate a text by adding a new spirit into translation. This period produced the translation strategy of taking liberty required by fluency for rendering foreign poetry and prose. One of the best examples of this is Abraham Cowley's *Pindarique Odes* (1656) which came to rank among the most widely circulated of translations. The age also introduced theories of translation. The English translators were theorizing the aesthetic autonomy of the translated text. John Dryden's *Preface to Translation of Homer's Iliad* (1680) is one of the greatest examples of this kind which opposed the libertine translation practiced by Cowley and identified three kinds of translation: metaphrase (word for word translation), imitation (extravagant translation), and paraphrase (between metaphrase and imitation). According to Dryden, a translator must be a poet if he/she is to translate poetry.

Goethe, Schlegel and Schleiermacher were important practitioners and theorists of translation in the nineteenth century, especially the later two who expounded the hermeneutic approach to translation. Later in the century, the Victorian translator H.W. Longfellow through his translation of Dante's *Divina Commedia* demonstrated that the tone and spirit – the very essence of original poem – can be retained in translation. The Pre-Raphaelite poet Dante Gabriel Rossetti, in his preface to translation of Early Italian Poets viewed that "The only true motive for putting poetry into a fresh language must be to endow a fresh nation, as far as possible, with one more possession of beauty". Edward Fitzgerald's translation of *Rubaiyyat of Omar Khayyam* produced during the same period is considered a landmark in history of translation for the poetic transfusion of poetic spirit from Persian to English and the representation of ideas and images of the original in a new form. After 1960, valuable contributions in terms of practising translation of poetry and formulating principles underlying this practice were made by poets like Ted Hughes, W. Elizabeth Bishop and Ezra Pound. Finally, James Holmes's practice and theory of translation produced in a bunch of essays *Translated: Papers on Literary Translation and Translation Studies* is noteworthy in recounting history of translation of poetry. Refuting the idea that in order to translate poetry one must be a poet, Holmes argues: "In order to create a verbal object of the metapoetic kind, one must perform some (but not all) of functions of a critic, some (but not all) of functions of a poet, and some functions not normally required of either critic or poet. Like the critic, the metapoet will strive to comprehend as thoroughly as possible the many features of the original poem, against the setting of the poet's other writings, the literary traditions of the source culture, and the expressive means of the source language. Like the poet, he will strive to exploit his own creative powers, the literary traditions of the target culture, and the expressive means of the target language in order to produce a verbal object that to all appearances is nothing more nor less than a poem" (Holmes, 11). The metapoet links these two activities – the poetic and the critical – by his/her own activity of organizing and resolving a confrontation between (i) the norms and conventions of one linguistic system, literary tradition, and poetic sensibility embodied in the original poem, and (ii) the norms and conventions of another linguistic system, literary tradition, and poetic sensibility of the metapoem to be created. This activity involves the process of making appropriate decisions. The metapoet's capacity to create a new verbal object i.e. translated poem is determined by these three factors.

## Poetry Translation: The Indian Tradition

Several problems arise when attempting to deal with the earlier tradition of translation in India. The evidence is extremely patchy, partly because of a predominantly oral tradition and partly because of the destruction of innumerable texts by climatic conditions. The Indian sub-continent is marked by a plurality of languages and cultures in one space, providing a unique mosaic of verbal communications, which has withstood the test of time over centuries. Languages belonging to different families show parallel trends of development during a long history and characterize the nation as a single composite region. Almost 70 per cent of the population, mainly in the Northern half, speak Indo-European languages such as Hindi, Punjabi, Gujarati, Marathi, Bengali and Nepali, derived directly from Sanskrit; another 20 per cent mainly in the South speak Dravidian languages, namely, Tamil, Telugu, Kannada and Malayalam; the rest speak Austro-Asiatic languages, Tibeto-Burman languages and Dardic languages. The main non-indigenous language, English, is used alongside their mother tongue by most educated people.

The first need for inter-language communication in the country probably arose through trade during 2500–1500 BC. This is primarily due to the Aryans, who settled in Indus area in the later part of the second millennium BC. They spoke Sanskrit, an Indo-European language, and brought with them a wealth of poetry which they subsequently collected together under the name *Rigveda* or "Hymns of wisdom"; another group of Aryans moved into Persia at around the same time and their sacred book, the *Avesta*, reflects a very similar culture to that of the *Rigveda*. The Aryans regarded themselves as superior to the indigenous people and tried to preserve their cultural and linguistic purity. Only they were allowed to learn and use the Rigvedic hymns. Even after the advent of writing and development of vernacular languages, the Vedic texts were considered so sacred that only commentaries written in Sanskrit had been found until late medieval times, and certainly no translations until Western scholars gained access to them in the 19th century.

In the middle of the 3rd century BC, the Indian emperor, Asoka followed an ideology of non-violence and universal compassion, which was reflected in Buddhism. His pillar inscriptions written in local languages must have required some translation-type activities. Indian Buddhist scholars travelled to China in the 1st century AD and were responsible for some of the earliest translations of Buddhist texts into Chinese. Ashvaghosha's poem *Buddhacarita*, the "life of Buddha", represents the earliest surviving classical Sanskrit poetry.

The Hindu Epics, two of the most important source texts were consolidated during c.100-1000. The *Mahabharata* (300 BC to AD 300) tells the story of a major war, probably representing the Aryans's eastward expansion along the Ganges valley. The *Ramayana* (200 BC to AD. 200) is about the abduction of Prince Rama's wife Sita by the king of Lanka, Ravana, and her subsequent rescue, probably echoing the Aryans's southward movement. It is difficult to tell in which language a text was originally written; it has been suggested that the extant Sanskrit versions may have been translated from original *Prakrit* versions.

In the case of Jainism and Buddhism, the texts were written in Sanskrit but later the trend was reversed and translation mainly proceeded from Sanskrit into other languages. For example, the Bhakti religious movement not only composed original material in vernacular languages, but also translated many devotional poems, as well as the Epics and *Puranas* into Dravidian languages. As Devy writes, "The whole *Bhakti* movement of poetry in India had the desire of "translating" the spirituality from Sanskrit to the languages of the people." (Devy, 49) With regard to Dravidian languages tradition speaks of three *sangams*, "competitive poetic assemblies" at Madurai. No texts survive from the first, the Tamil grammar *Tolkappiyam* is supposedly a product of the second, and the eight anthologies of Sangam poetry (over 2000 poems) are from the third. Sanskrit works, such as those of Kalidasa and the Epics, were adapted to Telugu and made available to popular audiences. Similarly, Kannada and Marathi texts were adaptations of Sanskrit originals.

The University of Nalanda in the north-east of India was particularly renowned for training translators from the fourth century onwards. The texts were translated from Sanskrit into Chinese and vice versa. From tenth century onwards, under Islamic Sultanate, Sanskrit competed to a certain extent with vernacular languages as Muslim poets began to write in Hindi and in other local languages. In the 14th century AD, although the regional languages were diverging and flourishing, the population of the subcontinent was beginning to share a considerable degree of cultural homogeneity. Religion was a major spur to translation. During the time of Mughal Empire, much of the literature was translated from Sanskrit into Urdu, Turki, Persian, and Arabic. The *Upnishads* had about 50 of them translated from Sanskrit into Persian by 1657. Sanskrit *Puranas* have been found in Persian translations. Persian also gave rise to Urdu, which influenced both Hindustani, the vernacular language of the North, and Hindi.

The first phase of Indian literature in English translation (ILET) covers a wide range – from N.B. Halhead's *A Code of Gentoo Laws, or, Ordinations of the Pundits, from a Persian Translation, made from the Original, written in the Shanscrit Lnaguage* (1776) to the series of translations by various Oriental scholars edited by Friedrich Max Müller in 50 volumes of *The Sacred Books of the East* (1879–1910). Books written on all the subjects in Sanskrit or in Persian were attempted in this phase. The colonial Oriental scholars did not touch the books written in modern Indian languages as the main interest in these translations was of the nature of comparative studies of philology and culture.

As a result of the colonial project of translations, the significant phase engaged the Indian translators in the same kind of work that the Orientalist scholars had done in the past. After a century of Halhead's *Gentoo Laws*, Sri Ramakrishna Gopal Bhandarkar's critical edition of Bhavbhuti's *Malti Madhav* (1876) appeared. The interest in philology continued in this phase but the liberal translations were also visible. Many of the forgotten works of the Indian scholars were edited and translated into English before printing them. It is largely these translations that make the works of Panini, Bhartrihari, Bharata, Abhinavgupta Vishwanath and others available today. All these translations were made for the Indologists and for Indian students.

Sri Aurobindo is the greatest figure in the third phase. The phase begins with his essays on translating Vyasa, Valmiki, and Kalidasa. The third phase ends with the autobiography of Gandhiji, translated by Mahadevbhai Desai. All the translations during this phase were aimed at Indian audience. Sri Aurobindo took great interest in Indian life and literature. He had to discover the heritage of India literally. As he learnt Sanskrit and Bengali, among other Indian languages, he started translating into English. Translation was a casual activity for Sri Aurobindo initially, but later on, it became a preoccupation with him. His early translations were those of the passages from the *Ramayana* and the *Mahabharata*. His love for Sanskrit poetry and Kalidasa is well-known. Evidently, Sri Aurobindo proposed to translate the whole of Kalidasa and write a full length study on the great poet. He considered the translation important to give the real picture of the greatness of Kalidasa's poetry. His essay "On Translating Kalidasa" contains not only examples and justification of his translation but also propounds a generalized theory of translation. All his writings on this subject belong to the decade of 1890s. He also translated the 28 hymns to Agni, and that can be considered as a major contribution to Vedic literature.

Very often the original words are transliterated in translation under the excuse of the absence of the equivalent terms in the TL. But Sri Aurobindo was not in favour of this practice. His observation in support of his argument is noteworthy. He observes a fallacy common among the SL community. The people who know the SL imagine that the words of their language convey the same grandeur to the readers of the TL too. They tend to believe that no equivalent in the TL can convey the sense of the word in question. While the latter contention is true, it is for the translator to produce an equivalent effect. Considering the gap between the cultures involved in translation, Sri Aurobindo noticed that the words fail to carry their meaning when the gap between the cultures is too large (as between Sanskrit and English). The present practice of retaining more and more original words by transliterating them has contextual reasons. When Sri Aurobindo translated, it was the time of colonial rule and the audience for translation was largely foreigners.

During British Empire, the need for translations of Indian texts was recognized early on by the British East India Company administrators. Indian scholars were initially reluctant to teach Sanskrit to the Europeans but European academics sponsored the establishment of learned societies, such as the Royal Asiatic Society, the Pali Text Society, and so on, and continued the production of translations of Sanskrit and Pali texts. The Independence Movement also encouraged linguistic activity in local languages and in English as well as translation between them. Rabindranath Tagore translated his own work from Bengali into English and was rewarded the Nobel Prize for Literature in 1913. Most Bengali works imbued with patriotism were translated in English and regional languages during this phase.

In the modern era, the translated works, mostly via English translations, are found in a great number which include Vedic texts, the Hindu Epics, Puranas and Upnishads, and classical Sanskrit drama; English poetry by Keats and Tennyson; Shakespeare's plays and poems; Bengali poems, plays and novels; Hindi and Urdu poetry; the Gospels and other Christian texts; American literature; Cervantes, Tolstoy, Ibsen. More recently, many Indian scholars have engaged themselves with the theoretical concerns of the discipline. Among such pioneers are Sujit Mukherjee, A.K. Ramanujan, Dilip Chitre, Bhalchandra Nemade and Ganesh Devy. Sujit Mukherjee's pioneer and influential book *Translation as Discovery* (1981) considered translations in the twentieth century and made initial attempts to formulate theory of translation in India. According to Mukherjee, translation necessitates close reading; and therefore it is the most useful methodology in training the reader of literary texts: "A literary text habitually uses words the total effect of which is greater than the sum of what the words may individually add up to. Discovery of this totality is the real joy that literature has to offer, and translation is one of these modes of discovery" (141).

Rita Kothari has contributed considerably in the theory, particularly with her book *Translating India: The Cultural Politics of English* (2003) deliberating on the politics of English in translations in India. Her observation regarding the use of English in the present time is that English is the language of the new generation. Translation, for Kothari, becomes a daily act in the language of the cosmopolitan youth. The use of English in e-mails and short messages has changed the linguistic conventions and has given a new shape to translation activity. Although many would find this argument in favour of code switching rather than in favour of translation, it has a great support from the lifestyle.

## Tradition of Translation in Gujarati Literature

Translation is a natural activity in a multilingual society like India possessing its "translating consciousness". It emerges as a confluence of human social instinct and cultural impulse. Indian literary traditions, as Ganesh Devy views, are essentially traditions of translation wherein the writer is tested his "capacity to transform, to translate, to restate, to revitalize the original". The Gujarati literary tradition has benefited considerably from its translation activity interwoven in this larger Indian tradition. Translations from Oriental languages like Sanskrit and

Persian were made into Gujarati. The translation of Sanskrit works of Kalidasa, Bhavbhuti and Bhasa were attempted by Navalram, Dhruv, Tribhuvan Gauri Shankar Vyas, Nanalal, Balshankar, etc. which raised issues of translation of poetry. A great amount of translated literature from several Indian languages, particularly from Hindi and Bengali, is available in Gujarati language. Almost all literary works of Bankim Chandra Chattopadhyay, Rabindranath Tagore, and Sharat Chandra Chattopadhyay are accessible in Gujarati. In this regard, translations from Bengali done by Mahadev Desai, Narhari Parikh, Nagindas Parekh, Jayanti Acharya, Jugatram Dave, Suresh Joshi, Niranjan Bhagat, Shrikant Trivedi, Ramnik Meghani, Bholabhai Patel, Anil Mehta, Jashwant Dave, Suresh Dalal and Jagdish Joshi are noteworthy. Likewise, Navnit Madrasi has translated around sixty books directly from South Indian languages. Comparatively translations from Marathi into Gujarati like *Gyaneshwari*, *Geeta Rahasya*, *Shyam ni Maa*, *Vyas Parva*, *Yugant*, *Thank you Mr. Glad* and the whole of V.S. Khandekar are also available. Umashankar Joshi donated the total sum of the award, *Bhartiya Gyanpeeth* to publish a series of poems written by seven modern Marathi poets under Gangotri Trust.

During post-independence period, literary journals have made a remarkable contribution in this direction. Magazines like *Sanskriti*, *Manisha*, *Kshitij*, *Etad*, *Setu*, *Kaumudi*, *Prasthan*, *Rekha* and *Vi-Vidyanagar* ought to be mentioned in this regard. The contribution of *Gujarat Vidyapeeth* and *Navjeevan Prakashan Mandir* is equally important. The literary figures like Rasiklal Parikh, Maganbhai P. Desai, Sundaram and Umashankar Joshi have contributed to the translations of literary texts and to the discourse of translation. Joshi viewed translation of poetry as more problematic than that of prose because even minor change of word from source to target language will affect the metre and rhyme in poetry wherein best words are pruned and arranged in best order: "The problem of translating poetry, in brief, is that of not going away too far in *bhashantar*, in changing language, and of creating an independent work with illumination of originality in a new language" (Joshi, 35). Similarly, Mulshankar M. Bhatt and Ramanlal Soni have provided translations of children's literature. Gujarat Granth Nirman Board, Gujarati Sahitya Parishad, and Gujarat Sahitya Academy have supported this activity. Hence, Gujarati language and literature have benefited considerably from translations of world literature. As Rita Kothari writes, "Translation from Indian as well as European languages has been an integral part of the literary and cultural life of Gujarat. Literary styles in Gujarati owe a great deal to translations made available in Gujarati...In contrast, very little from Gujarati literature has made inroads into other languages, particularly English, perhaps because English poses its own set of problems and has its own dynamics" (Kothari, 73).

## ILLUSTRATION: THE PROCESS OF TRANSLATION

> "The translator adds a new spirit which gives life and energy to the words."
>
> Sir John Denham

The process of translation is very well equated to the process of transmigration of soul, the Indian traditional concept of *Parakaya Pravesha* (entering of the soul into another body). There is no synonymity between two languages or indeed within a single one. Translation attempts a task of making two unique verbal entities coincide. A language is not only a clear medium through which experience is communicated but is something inseparable from the experience it communicates. Every language is a unique way of looking out of man's non-differentiated prison of existence. J.C. Catford (1965) observes, "The language we speak forces us to select and group elements of our experience of the world in ways it dictates. It provides a kind of grid, or series of grids, through which we see the world."

In fact, translation as an act of interpretation involves a creative approach to the literary text. The concept that each translator interprets the text is obvious by the fact that no two translations of the same text are identical. The socio-cultural, semantic and stylistic aspects of a literary piece of work can effectively be translated by interpretative techniques like substitution and condensation (as will be illustrated through translation of a Gujarati poem written by Harish Meenashru[1] in the following pages of the article). This view seems to be more useful for a comprehensive analysis of the process of translation.

1. This poem has been taken from *Samipe*, a Gujarati literary magazine, September, 2005.

*Pankhi malo bandhe chhe*
*Kalpavriksha ni bakholman.*
*Aa pankhine visheshan to chhe nahin*
*Etle ek athwa ekaki –*
*Evun khataripoorvak to kem kahevay?*

*Fate chhe agharan abh*
*To vijali tarat zabuki sandhe chhe*
*Ne fafadata pankhihridayne vale chhe sav saheli shata*
*Pan avun kahine*
*Bahu bahu to rachi shakay*
*Saral sukh dukhnan sandigdh kalpan, – ethi shun?*

*Peli moti parovava jevi gharelu aa vat nathi.*
*Ahin to vijalina zabkare, game tyare,*
*Malaman nanakado dav lagvano bho chhe.*
*Ne badhun bhasam thai gaya pachhi,*
*Vali pachhun dhagali rakhmanthi navu pankhi pankho fafadave*
*Etli dantkathani amanya pan aa vanman*
*Kon rakhe chhe? – Ne rakhni dhagaline bhalaman karyathi ye sho fayado?*

*Vanman pankhioni naatman rivaj chhe*
*Etle bandhe chhe malo. Kalpavrikshni bakholman. Nachhutake.*
*Baki inda mukashe, sevashe ne sambhalashe ghargrihasthi*
*Evo bharoso to koine padato nathi, aa akhyanman*

*Ratne bahane tadhubol aakash bhinshatun rahe chhe andhakarman otprot bhashane,*
*Pankhino svar chirava mathe chhe potana aandhala aakarne,-*
*Umang ke aajiji*
*Aarat ke orata*
*Avajnan evan nam padava aa vanman koi rokatu nathi.*
*Pankhine ankhathi mathata avajna koi pras malato nathi. Haji vali.*

*Aakhi rat*
*Parabhav pamelu kalpavriksh pankhiman kheravatu rahe chhe kharkhar tharthar pandada aakhi rat*
*Ne ajachak pankhi to bas oodatu rahe chhe thadiyana andhakarman.*
*Aakhi raat. Farfar farfar*

*Marag famfosatu, aakhi rat, sarsar sarsar oode oode akhi rat.*
*Ne chhekchhevate*
*Chapp daine chain le chhe zeenu amathu beej ne pho fate chhe*

*Bhasha bhunsai gai pachhi, kagal to thik, kagalano anasar pan bachyo nathi:*
*Have aa shunyane shunya kahevani mari to jigar nathi.*

## The Bird-Being

A bird is building a nest
Into the hollow of a *Kalpavriksha*[2].
This bird does not have any adjective
So sole or solitary –
How can one say confidently?

The heavy skies are tearing
Lightning flashing at once stitches
And the fluttering heart of a bird
Finally finds a very easy ease.
But by saying so
At the most one can create only ambiguous images
Of simple pain and pleasure, – so what?

This is not the household matter of stringing pearls.
Here in the flash of lightning, at any moment
Lurks the fear of an eruption of a small fire in the nest.
And having burnt everything into ashes
Once again, for a new bird to flap its wings from the heap of ashes
Who shows that much reverence for a legend in the forest?
And what's the use even of recommending the heap of ashes?

In the forest there is a custom in the community of birds
So it builds. A nest. In the hollow of a *Kalpavriksha*. Willy nilly.
Otherwise no one believes in this *Akhyan*[3]
That it would lay eggs, hatch them and raise a family

---

2. *Kalpavriksha* – a legendry tree that can fulfill the wishes of an individual.
3. *Akhyan* – a form of narrative poetry retelling stories from Indian scriptures.

In the guise of the night
The chilled sky keeps on embarrassing
Language engrossed in darkness,
Bird's voice strives to tear
One's own blind form, –
Ardour or entreaty
Aspiration or ambition
Nobody tarries in this forest to offer such names to the sound
Nobody finds any rhyme of sound striving to transcend the bird.
So far.

Althru the night
The vanquished *Kalpavriksha* keeps shedding leaves into the bird, althru the night.
And undemanding bird simply keeps on flying into the darkness of the trunk, althru the night.
Groping for the pathway, althru the night, whizzing deep down, althru the night.
And at last
It quickly picks up a tiny seed and there breaks the dawn.

Language – having wiped out
Let alone the paper
Not even its trace is left.
Now –
I dare not call this void a void.

## Lexis

*The Bird-Being* encapsulates the urge of sublimation, flight into higher realms of Being. Here the bird symbolizes the existence with mystic destiny of taking a new form from its own ashes. In this section, at times the poet is trying to decipher the realities by reinterpretation of myths with modern sensibility. The other poems in this anthology *Pankhipadarth* do also have this kind of lexical challenges as translation involves the transfer of "meaning" contained in one set of language signs into another set of language signs through competent use of dictionary in order to overcome lexical encounters.

In fact, in the process of translation something is lost and something is gained. Although gaining is a new perspective of reality, translation is an affair of compromise. Since every language has its geniuses, finding out the equivalents for the TL words/terms in the SL from the TL creates lexical problems. And many a time it happens that a translator finds more than one equivalent for a single SL term as he/she is looking for 'a meaning' and not 'the meaning'. This becomes more problematic as he/she has to choose one out of many. And the wrong choice is always dangerous. Translation is a process of approximation. Or it is rather a process of making decisions or precisely speaking, it is a process of making right decisions at right places and at right times. And while making decisions a translator must not confine himself/herself to a well but he/she has to think of an ocean.

Line no. 2 *kalpavriksha ni bakhol ma...*

*Kalpavriksha*, in the source language, is a mythical tree in the Hindu religion, which is believed to grace all desires. Thus, it does not have any lexical equivalent in the target language.

Line no. 22 *...aa akhyan ma...*

Here is a word *akhyan* which is one of the literary forms of the SL. It does not find its equivalent in the TL. Thus, it is an untranslatable term whose lexicalization does not serve to ignore its identity as foreign entity because this word has a unique connotation.

Line no. 38 *have aa shunya ne shunya kahevani mari to jigar nathi...*

In the case of a word with a wider range of SL meanings the problems increase. In the above mentioned line the term *shunya*, literally means *zero*. But the suggestive meaning is *shunyavakash*, i.e. *void*. The suggestive meaning mainly depends on the peculiar expression of the word in the text with a particular motive, its shades of meaning and particular social context.

## Socio-Cultural Issues

As Jury Lotman views, "No language can exist unless it is steeped in the context of culture; and no culture can exist which does not have at its centre, the structure of natural language" (Quoted in Bassnett, 22). The translator becomes a cultural and linguistic mediator, who needs to know specific cultural concepts reflected in both languages: SL and TL. Every language is bound to a particular culture with its own specific concepts, which are revealed in its linguistic ways of expressing things. Differences between cultures are not located exclusively at the lexical level, but at the level of culture-specific practices, popular beliefs, myths, omens, superstitions and rituals.

Line no. 12 *peli moti parovava jevi gharelu aa vat nathi...*

This has reference to a mythological tale where a female saint, named *Gangasati* is asking her daughter-in-law and disciple *Panbai* to utilize the present time and to perform the task assigned, otherwise there will be darkness all of a sudden and the things will remain incomplete. Now the translated version of this is, "*this is not the household matter of stringing pearls*" which actually does not convey the myth behind.

The translator of a literary text is not only concerned with establishing equivalence of natural language but of artistic procedures also. And those procedures cannot be considered in isolation, but must be located within the specific cultural-temporal context within which they are utilized. A poem is perceived as an artifact of a particular cultural system, and the only faithful translation can be to give it a similar function in the target cultural system.

## Music

Gujarati is a language that depends on sound to make meaning. Many of its descriptive words are highly onomatopoeic and thus almost impossible to render in English. In *Bird-Being II*, the sounds like *khar khar, thar thar, sar sar*, and *far far* describe different actions of the Bird and since they are highly onomatopoeic, they are impossible to be translated. And most Indian languages, including Gujarati, use repetitive sounds either to intensify their meaning or to indicate the boringly or annoyingly repetitive aspect of the action. The beauty of such compositions lies in the meticulous word music elicited by means of assonance, alliteration, consonance, internal and end rhymes and repetition. W.H. Auden rightly points out that the sounds of words, their rhythmical relations and all meanings which depend upon sounds, such as rhymes and puns, are untranslatable.

## Semantics

A poetry translator also faces problems on the semantic level. He/she may not always understand the nuances of the source language. It is not easy to express the local sentiment into a foreign language. There are certain words which carry different meanings when the contexts vary. While translating words into the TL, one has to be very careful regarding their semantic aspects.

Line no. 38 *have aa shunyane shunya*
*kahevani mari to jigar nathi...*

Here the term 'shunya' does not mean *zero*, it means *void*. Translations celebrate the plurality of meanings inherent in the original.

In poem "Orange-II"
Line no. 13 *narangi bhasha ni kahevat*
*banavatan batris lakshano hatan...*

Here the phrase *batris lakshano* literally means *thirty two features* but if it is translated literally, it may create confusion or misunderstanding in the minds of the native speakers of the TL because referring the culture of the SL, the phrase indicates "all features".

## Grammar

If the problems related to stylistics and semantics are vexing, the grammar of the language poses no less a dilemma to the translator. There is a world of a difference in the syntactical organization between the Gujarati language and the English Language, for example English language sentences have a rigorous SVO word order except in the passive voice. But Gujarati has more inflections by the agency of which the sentence patterns freely vary from SOV to OSV. Due to this flexibility of the word order and greater possibility for inflections, the Gujarati sentence structure becomes assimilative in nature.

In "The Bird-Being",
Line no. 7 *to vijali tarat zabooki sandhe chhe...*

In Gujarati a verb is inflected according to the gender of the subject especially in the past tense, even when the subject is as genderless as the first person. The English verbs are gender-neutral in nature. In this line the verb *zabuki,* i.e. "flash" indicates that the subject *vijali,* i.e. "lightening" is a form of feminine gender. But the same thing is not conveyed through its translation.

Line no. 8 *ne fafdata pankhi hriday ne...*

Line no. 11 *saral sukhdukh na...*

In these two lines there are terms like *pankhihriday* and *sukhdukh.* These are compound words in the SL, but during the process of translation when they are transformed into phrases as in the TL, they are not found as compound words.

In general the grammatical modifications can be made the more readily, since many grammatical changes are dictated by the obligatory structures of the target language. The translating of poetry obviously involves more adjustments than prose, for rhythmic forms differ far more radically in form, and hence in aesthetic appeal. Moreover, Harish Meenashru's poems are culturally loaded texts full of Sanskrit/Urdu terminology. Hence the search for equivalents poses several problems. It is a challenge to capture the rhyme, rhythm and tonal quality of the poem. Most of the poems suffer at the phonological and lexical levels. A poet so ungovernable is not only difficult to translate but also difficult to understand. His genius is indeed elevated and unconfined. Adam Tankarvi observes that Harish Meenashru is a difficult poet to translate into English. Apart from the subtleties of tone, sound and voice, his poems are full of word-play, conversational phrases, allusions and newly-coined ex-dictionary words. Much of it is lost in translation. However, what remains is also worth presenting to the English audience.

## CONCLUSION

"Each text is unique, yet at the same time it is the translation of another text. No text can be completely original because language itself, in its very essence, is already a translation – first from the nonverbal world, and then, because each sign and each phrase is a translation of another sign, another phrase" (Paz, 154). However, this argument by Octavio Paz can be turned around without losing any of its validity: all texts are original because every translation, upto a certain point, is an invention and as such it constitutes a unique text – a re-creation. As Derrida says, every original work is the translation; every translation is an original work. An understanding of the history and the practice of translation has revealed the following insights:

1. Each language represents a separate reality.
2. An Indian poem translated into English ought to read like an English poem but must not cease to be an Indian poem.
3. The problem of equivalence involves the utilization and perception of the object in a given context.
4. Language is the heart within the body of culture. A surgeon, operating on the heart cannot neglect the body that surrounds it.
5. No translation is culturally neutral.
6. There can naturally be nothing like an "absolute" translation.
7. Translation is a creative art. A translator has to be as skillful, crafty and creative as the writer is.
8. The main purpose of translation of a creative work is to produce a replicated creative work in the TL, which can give aesthetic satiation to the reader.
9. Sir John Denham wrote, "The translator adds a new spirit which gives life and energy to the words."
10. Translation is certainly a re-creative if not creative process.

## Works Cited

Baker, Mona and Gabriela Saldanha, ed. *Routledge Encyclopedia of Translation Studies.* London: Routledge, 1998.

Bassnett, Susan. *Translation Studies.* London: Routledge, 2002.

Catford, J.C. *A Linguistic Theory of Translation.* London: Oxford UP, 1965.

Dave, R.A. *Religion and Poetry.* Vallabh Vidyanagar: Sardar Patel University Press, 1986.

Derrida, J. "Living On". *Deconstruction and Criticism.* Trans. James Hulbert. New York: Continuum, 1979. 62–142.

Devy, G.N. "Translation Theory: An Indian Perspective." *Translation from Periphery to Centrestage*. Ed. Tutun Mukherjee. New Delhi: Prestige Books, 1998.

Elliott, Julia, ed. *The Oxford Compendium of English*. New Delhi: Oxford University Press. 2001.

France, Peter. *The Oxford Guide to Literature in English*. New York: Oxford University Press, 2000.

Gopinathan, G. and S. Kandaswamy. *The Problems of Translation*. Allahabad: Lok Bharti Prakashan, 1993.

Holmes, James, Translated: *Papers on Literary Translation and Translation Studies*. Amsterdam: Rodopi, 1988.

Joshi, Umashankar. "Problems of Translating Poetry". Trans. A.K. Singh. *Studies in Translation*. Ed. Mohit K. Ray. New Delhi: Atlantic Publishers, 2008. 33–44.

Kothari, Rita. *Translating India: The Cultural Politics of English*. New Delhi: Foundation Books, 2006.

Mathews, J. "Third Thoughts on Translating Poetry". *On Translation*. Ed. R. Brower. Cambridge: Harvard University Press, 1959. 67–77.

Meenashru, Harish. *A Tree with Thousand Wings*. Ed. and Trans. Piyush Joshi. Vallabh Vidyanagar: Lajja Communications, 2008.

Muller, F. *The Sacred Books of the East*. Trans. Orientalist Scholars. New Delhi: Oxford UP, 1879–1910.

Mukherjee, Sujit. *Translation as Discovery and Other Essays*. New Delhi: Allied Publishers, 1981.

Nida, Eugene A. and Charles R. Taber. *The Theory and Practice of Translation*. Leiden: Brill, 2003.

Nida, Eugene A. *Language Structure and Translation*. Stanford: Stanford University Press, 1975.

Paz, Octavio. "Translation: Literature and Letters." *Theories of Translation: An Anthology of Essays from Dryden to Derrida*. Ed. Rainer Schulte and John Biguenet. Chicago: The University of Chicaso Press, 1992:152–162.

Pezzini, Domenico. *The Translation of Religious Texts in the Middle Ages*. Bern: Peter Lang AG, 2008.

Schulte, Rainer and John Biguenet, eds. *Theories of Translation: An Anthology of Essays from Dryden to Derrida*. Chicago, USA: The Universoty of Chicago Press, 1992.

Shinhji, Bhagvat, ed. *Bhagvadgomandal*. Rajkot: Praveen Prakashan, 1944.

Steiner, George. *After Babel: Aspects of Language and Communication*. New York: Oxford UP, 1998.

Talgeri, Pramod, and Satyabhusana Verma. *Literature in Translation: From Cultural Transfer to Metonymic Displacement*. Mumbai: Popular Prakashan, 1998.

Ziya Us Salam. "Translation Today: A Fruitful Dialogue", Literary Review, *The Hindu*, May 4, 2008. <http://www.hindu.com/lr/2008/05/04/stories/2008050450030100.htm>

# Contributors

**Aroma Kharsiing** is Assistant Professor at the School of English Literary Studies, The English and Foreign Languages University, Lucknow. She has done research on post-apartheid South African White literature and contributed to books such as *J.M. Coetzee: Critical Perspectives* (2008).

**Asha Makhecha** is Assistant Professor at the Department of English and Communication Skills, C.Z. Patel College of Business and Management, Vallabh Vidyanagar, Gujarat. She is a translator and has been doing research in the field of Translation Studies.

**Hemang Desai** teaches at the Department of English, N.V. Patel College of Pure and Applied Sciences, Vallabh Vidyanagar, Gujarat. He has edited and translated post-global and postmodern Marathi poetry into Gujarati in *Anuvidhan* (2010) and selected Gujarati short-stories by Sundaram into English in *Thirsty Fish and Other Stories* (forthcoming). Apart from publishing translations of works by Arun Kolatkar, Dalpat Chauhan, Nazir Mansuri, etc., he has written articles on translation studies in journals like *Indian Literature* and *Dialogue*. Presently he is working on translation of contemporary Gujarati poetry into English.

**Manish Solanki** is Assistant Professor at the Department of English, Sardar Patel University, Vallabh Vidyanagar, Gujarat. He is currently working on postcolonial and diasporic literatures.

**Manoj Chhaya** teaches English at F.G. Polytechnic in Adipur, Kachchh, Gujarat. His dissertation was in the area of Translation Studies and he has published articles on the subject in several journals. He has recently received a fellowship from USIEF to visit University of Pennsylvania, USA.

**Nazia Sultana** is a Research scholar at the East West University, Dhaka, Bangladesh.

**Piyush Raval** teaches at the Department of English, Sardar Patel University, Vallabh Vidyanagar, Gujarat. He has carried out a research project 'Negotiating Identities: Globalisation, Culture, History'. He is the recipient of a translation fellowship from the Centre for Contemporary Theory, Baroda, and has published translations of excerpts from Gujarati Dalit autobiographies into English in *An Anthology of Gujarati Dalit Literature* (2011).

**Sachin Ketkar** teaches at the Department of English, The M.S. University of Baroda, Vadodara, Gujarat. He recently published the book *(Trans)Migrating Words: Refractions on Indian Translation Studies* (2010), edited and translated *Live Update: An Anthology of Recent Marathi Poetry* (2005) and published a volume of his Marathi poems *Bhintishivaicya Khidkitun Dokavtana* (2004).

**Soni Wadhwa** is a research scholar at the Department of English, University of Mumbai, Mumbai. She has worked on Sindhi diaspora and published articles in journals like *Journal of Contemporary Thought*. Presently she is engaged in a research work on migration.

**Stephanos Stephanides** is Professor at the Department of English Studies, University of Cyprus, Nicosia, Cyprus. A poet and a translator, he has co-authored books like *Beyond the Floating Islands* (2002) and *Translating Kali's Feast: the Goddess in Indo-Caribbean Ritual and Fiction* (2000), co-edited *Cultures of Memory/Memories of Culture* (2007) and published a translation *Niki Marangon: Selections from the Divan* (2001).

# Index